Criminal Justice in Colonial America, 1606–1660

Criminal Justice in Colonial America, 1606-1660

Bradley Chapin

The University of Georgia Press
Athens

Designed by Sandra Strother Hudson

Set in 11 on 13 Janson

The paper in this book meets the guidelines for
permanence and durability of the Committee on
Production Guidelines for Book Longevity of the Council
on Library Resources.

Printed in the United States of America

Library of Congress Cataloging in Publication Data
Chapin, Bradley.
Criminal justice in colonial America, 1606–1660.
Bibliography: p.
Includes index.
1. Criminal justice, Administration of—United States—
History. I. Title.
KF9223.C53   345.73'05   82-2753
ISBN 0-8203-0624-X   347.3055   AACR2

TO MARGARET KIMBALL

No man ought to be wiser than the law.

SIR EDWARD COKE
Preface to *First Institute*

Contents

Tables

Acknowledgments

Though these acknowledgments are brief, I am indebted to the institutions and individuals who offered advice or aid in the preparation of this book. The College of Humanities of The Ohio State University permitted me to arrange my teaching schedules to allow several substantial periods of time for research and writing. The Dean of the College, Diether H. Haenicke, subsidized some of the mechanical work of preparing the manuscript. Two editors at the University of Georgia Press were most supportive. Iris Tillman Hill gave the manuscript its first editorial reading, and Charles East showed faith in it through an extended period of revision. Two of the readers for the press did their jobs thoroughly and perceptively. Their suggestions led to significant revisions. David T. Konig offered valuable advice about the method of estimating the population of New England counties. I am also indebted to N. E. H. Hull and Peter Hoffer, each of whom read the entire manuscript, Professor Hoffer more than one draft. Their suggestions were helpful in many ways but were especially so in the preparation and presentation of the statistical materials. I thank Sandra Strother Hudson for choosing the woodcuts that appear on the title pages. By evoking the times, they illuminate the text. My thanks to Margaret Kimball are not pro forma. She made preliminary searches of thousands of pages and caused me to rewrite many opaque passages.

B.C.

Criminal Justice in Colonial America, 1606–1660

Chapter One

Substantive Criminal Law

Seven jurisdictions were established in colonial America before 1660: Virginia, Plymouth, Massachusetts Bay, Maryland, Rhode Island, Connecticut, and New Haven. Of necessity each colony created a system of criminal justice. A numerous and varied cast of characters, lawmakers and lawbreakers, made the records of those systems, among them John Winthrop, squire, governor, judge; Web Abbey, sometime servant, deviant hermit; Roger Ludlow, lawmaker, magistrate, deputy governor; Goody Knapp, housewife, witch; John Lewger, rector, attorney general, councillor; John Dandy, miller, blacksmith, murderer; Samuel Gorton, protagonist of English law, legislator, judge; Nepaupuck, Indian brave, murderer; George Yeardley, adventurer, planter, councillor, governor; and George Spencer, farmhand, buggerer.

All of these persons except Nepaupuck were English. The England they had left was perceived as disorderly, immoral, and crime-ridden. As participants or observers they had seen there an archaic, inefficient, and capricious judicial system attempting unsuccessfully to stem a tide of vice and crime. They shared the common knowledge that the criminal law of England was infamous.

As the first wave of English people crossed the Atlantic, a vigorous and sustained criticism illuminated the deficiencies and excesses of English criminal law. Its bifurcated and obscure body lay amid a jumble of statutes and precedents. Expressed largely in bastard languages, law Latin and French, much of it was written in cryptographic court hand. In sharp contrast, the process of bringing persons to judgment by this law was highly visible along a line of jurisdiction stretching down from the Kings Bench and Star Chamber, through the assize, quarter session, borough court, and leet. Assize and quarter session carried the bulk of the burden of criminal law enforcement. Court days were part carnival, part horror show. At the assize, judges spread the hangman's noose wide and wrote wholesale lessons in retribution. Capricious forms of mitigation made trials a deadly game of dice. A notorious felon might save his life by reading a verse; a drifter might die for stealing a sheep. In another direction were different traps, the church courts, set to catch men and women lured into acts perceived to be immoral. The archdeacon embraced the business that misbehavior brought into his court because it was profitable. Intruding into private lives, the archdeacons were often abusive and corrupt.

The men responsible for establishing the jurisdictions in the colonies must have believed that they could create better systems of social control than the ones they left behind. The fact that they had left England indicates that they must have been receptive to new options in establishing a system of criminal law. The documents that empowered them set no precise limits to their authority as legislators and judges. The laws they were to make were to be reasonably consistent with and not repugnant to English law. Three thousand miles of open ocean and a government at home with troubles of its own guaranteed that there would be no sustained, strict scrutiny of consistency or repugnancy. Four of the seven new jurisdictions had no enabling documents other than those voluntarily created by the people. Surely the founders of those communities had options. The first American lawmakers would have the freedom of chancellors and the power of judges.

The English experience made clear what areas needed reform: the law must be reduced and clarified by positive statement or unmistakable precedent; a more rational relationship between crime and the method and incidence of punishment must be found; the structure, jurisdiction, and procedure of the courts must be simplified; public peace and morality must be guaranteed by public, rather than private or parochial, justice.

Law Sources

The arriving colonists could draw from their experience a variety of materials from which to fashion criminal law. Because they were Englishmen, they were not likely to jettison the parent law and launch a wholly new experiment. In fact, the largest part of the

TABLE 1.1.   SOURCES OF THE SUBSTANTIVE CRIMINAL LAW
(in percentages)

	English	Indigenous	Biblical
Rhode Island	86.2	12.9	0.9
Virginia	81.1	18.9	–
Plymouth	59.0	36.7	4.3
Maryland	54.6	43.6	1.8
Massachusetts	41.2	20.0	38.8
Connecticut	38.8	21.2	40.0
New Haven	34.8	22.4	42.8
Percent of total	56.5	25.1	18.4

new law would be taken from the old. During the decades of the
first migration, English law was subjected to searching scrutiny.
The demand for reform, essentially a demand for a simpler, more
rational, and more humane law, would inform the makers of colonial law. In four of the five jurisdictions where radical Protestant-
ism was to prevail, the Bible furnished obvious and transcendent
precedents for criminal law.

The parent English law provided 57 percent of the total body of
substantive criminal law in the seven colonial jurisdictions established before 1660. Eighteen percent of the law derived from the
Bible. The remaining 25 percent has been labeled "indigenous."
This last category is somewhat amorphous. It was not law designed
to meet "frontier" conditions; rather, its primary sources were two
movements that were seeking to modify English criminal law in the
late sixteenth and early seventeenth centuries. One movement took
the form of a persistent series of attempts to remove from the
church courts jurisdiction over several types of personal misconduct. Another and broader based movement sought a general
reform of English criminal law.[1] Table 1.1 shows the relative percentages of English, indigenous, and biblical law as found in the
American jurisdictions in 1660.[2]

The English character of early American law is not surprising,
but reasons for the relative preference for the parent law are clearer
for some colonies than for others. English law probably predomi-
nated in the Chesapeake colonies because officials there remained
responsible to authority in England and because it served their conservative social purposes.[3] The distribution of preferences sub-
sumed under "indigenous" seems to indicate that the movements

for law reform and public control of conduct had considerable impact on judges and legislators in all colonies. The degree to which the three Puritan colonies infused their law with Old Testament precepts sets them apart.

A simple division between the New England colonies and those of the Chesapeake is misleading. Viewed statistically, the criminal law of Rhode Island and Plymouth seems more akin to that of Maryland and Virginia than to the law of their Puritan neighbors. Special factors appear to have been at work in the shaping of Rhode Island and Plymouth law. The preamble to the Plymouth code of 1658 declared that its authors "had an eye principally" on "the Ancient platforme of God's lawe."[4] Thus it is strange to find that no item of this code or the compilation of 1636 is based in explicit Mosaic precedent, nor is any expressed in biblical language. Because Plymouth lacked formal authorization to create a government, William Bradford showed concern from the beginning as to whether it had the right to punish criminals.[5] The publication of written law that deviated sharply from English law might have attracted the attention of English officials, and this was best avoided. Another reason for the dearth of explicitly biblically based law may have been that God's earthly agents were not so immanent in Plymouth as they were in the Puritan colonies. Pilgrim piety was more earthy and primitive. The written record of the Plymouth legal experience leaves the impression of a practical set of rules that stated the consensus among pious, pragmatic men. They were content if their law reflected "the Ancient platforme" by achieving "morall equitie."[6]

The Rhode Island code, with its 86 percent preference for English law, contrasts starkly with the Puritan codes by rejecting the model of Israel. Though next to nothing is known about the authorship of the code, it seems probable that the founders of the colony played a large part in shaping it. Roger Williams said that the code had been written on the island, and this would suggest that William Coddington and Thomas Hutchinson were among its authors. Though there is no evidence that Williams or Samuel Gorton, the other founders of Rhode Island, had any part in writing the code, it is consonant with their ideas. All rejected the idea that Old Testament law should be a model. The code is taken primarily from Michael Dalton's standard English manual for justices of the peace.

TABLE 1.2. LAW SOURCES: CRIMES
AGAINST THE PERSON, 1660
(percentages)

	English	Indigenous	Biblical
Capital			
Murder	100	–	–
Manslaughter	73.3	6.7	20.0
Rape	68.6	17.1	14.3
Witchcraft	72.9	5.7	21.4
Noncapital			
Assault	85.7	10.0	4.3
Defamation	85.7	10.0	4.3

Gorton had insisted that all dependent corporations must use English law.[7] Williams rejected the Israelite state and Mosaic law as miraculous occurrences having no explicit relevance for later polities, so he was left with no ready alternative to English law. The bizarre organization of the code, its one clear non-English aspect, is consistent with Williams' typology, which was unusual because it rejected the Old Testament as a series of antecedent examples for New Testament persons and institutions. The code's organization, hitherto unexplained, is extrapolated from two verses in Paul's first epistle to Timothy. Following that text, the major heads of the code became "Touching Murdering of Fathers and Mothers," "Touching Whoremongers," and "Touching Men-Stealers." Christ, not Moses, recommended valid principles of law to other nations. As a surrogate of Jesus Christ, Paul carried the principles of law to the Gentiles.[8]

The practical effect of preference for different sources of substantive criminal law is best illustrated by analysis of treatment of types of crime in the colonial law. In frequency of occurrence and colonists' perceptions, the major categories of crime in America before 1660 were (1) those against the person, (2) those against property, (3) those involving sexual acts, and (4) those that were perceived as socially harmful misconducts.

In law concerning crimes against the person, the colonists heavily favored the English law (Tables 1.2–1.5 show the sources of law in the seven jurisdictions). This preponderance makes possible a pervasive generalization about early American law: the traditional English law would be followed if it was perceived to be rational and just. The new environment did not stimulate change for its own sake.

A second major generalization is anticipated. Where the colonies deviated from the English law of crimes against persons, they moved largely in the direction of leniency. They did so by giving judges alternatives to the death penalty. For example, Maryland, Massachusetts, and New Haven left judges with optional punishments for rape. Maryland did not demand the death penalty for a witchcraft conviction. Though Massachusetts and New Haven seemed to move in the direction of a law more harsh than the English model by following the biblical rule, which appeared to require the death penalty for manslaughter, no one hanged for this crime. In fact, in every colony, the only crimes that mandated the death penalty were murder and treason.[9]

The small deviation from English practice in regard to assault and defamation derives from provisions of the New Haven and Rhode Island codes. Among the Anglo-American jurisdictions they alone chose not only to give a positive definition of these acts, but to make them clearly criminal under the rubric of disturbing the peace. Overall, the colonial acceptance of English practice in regard to assault and defamation shows that no great change occurred in the temperament of English men and women when they emigrated. Quick to give and quick to resent offense, they expected and got civil remedies and criminal penalties in colonial courts.

Although the colonial law of crimes against persons remained basically English law, the colonial law of crimes against property was largely indigenous, as indicated in Table 1.3. The colonial legislators and judges made their sharpest practical departure from English law in dealing with various types of theft. Thus they cleansed the law of what was then perceived to be its greatest inhumanity and ended the need for the complex devices that had been used in England to mitigate the severity of the law of larceny and theft. The Englishness of colonial law under the rubrics burglary and robbery is accounted for by the fact that colonial lawmakers tended to use English concepts and terms when describing these crimes. The great indigenous reform was the virtual abolition of the death penalty for crimes against property. The colonists replaced the hangman's noose with a variety of penalties:

TABLE 1.3.　LAW SOURCES: CRIMES AGAINST PROPERTY, 1660
(percentages)

	English	Indigenous	Biblical
Burglary	44.0	56.0	–
Robbery	44.0	56.0	–
Larceny	2.9	52.8	44.3

branding, whipping, terms in a house of correction, and multiple restitution.[10] In part, the Puritan colonies followed the Bible in effecting this reform. It seems highly likely that the colonies responded to the demands of the English advocates of law reform. That movement spread across the spectrum of English politics and society, and the emigrating Englishman must have been aware of its demands. Law reform had as its least common denominator the demand that penalties for crimes against property be made more rational and humane.

The question remains why this reform, unrealized in England, could be effected in America. The mazelike intricacies of English law made piecemeal reform difficult. Reformers there, ranging from statesmen such as Francis Bacon and Matthew Hale to radical Levellers and Fifth Monarchy men, could not agree on an agenda of reform. Factional politics and constitutional crises took precedence over reform.[11] In contrast, colonial judges and legislators could respond pragmatically to social problems and install more realistic law. In part they could do so because they were not constrained by a class of professional lawyers.[12] Another answer to the question is that life must have been perceived as more valuable in the colonies. As a matter of policy it must have seemed that no great harm was done if the hangman thinned the horde of vagrant Englishmen. In the colonies, the need for labor urged the use of penalties that might bring redemption.

Seventeenth-century Englishmen regarded any sexual act performed outside the marriage bed as a mixture of sin and crime. The distributions in Table 1.4 reflect several tendencies. The pronounced shift away from English sources in the categories of adultery and fornication/bastardy were in part the result of the failure to establish church courts. The colonists imposed harsher penalties than those provided by English ecclesiastical law. The other relevant

TABLE 1.4.   LAW SOURCES: CRIMES INVOLVING SEXUAL ACTS, 1660
(percentages)

	English	Indigenous	Biblical
Buggery/Sodomy	70.0	8.6	21.4
Adultery	21.4	35.7	42.9
Fornication/Bastardy	28.6	50.0	21.4

factor is that the Puritan colonies followed whichever law source provided the most stringent rule in cases of sexual misconduct.

Recognized in both England and America as abominable sin, indeed *clamantia peccata*, crying sins, buggery and sodomy had been statutory felonies since the time of Henry VIII. Colonial legislators and judges would have agreed with Sir Edward Coke that these were crimes against God and nature.[13] The Bible strongly supported the English texts. Though the language of all the New England codes made the detestable nature of these crimes clear, New Haven went beyond ordinary Puritan statutory rhetoric to preach a sermon on "Sodomiticall filthinesse." The code provided the death penalty for all forms of anal intercourse, "carnall knowledge of another vessel then God in nature hath appointed to become one flesh." Male masturbation in the presence of others, an act "which tends to the sin of Sodomy, if it be not one kind of it," was to be punished at discretion, which extended to the death penalty "if the mind of God revealed in his word require it."[14]

In England, adultery was within the jurisdiction of the ecclesiastical courts. Though the Bible demanded death for the act, the church courts imposed much milder penalties. This huge discrepancy created one of the grievances that radical Protestants held against the ecclesiastical court system. In 1650, the first Parliament of the Protectorate made adultery a capital crime.[15] That adultery should be treated as a serious crime was not exclusively a Puritan conviction. In his instructions to the royal council of Virginia in 1606, James I sharply reduced the number of capital crimes, but he recommended death for adultery.[16] Regardless, Virginia courts followed ordinary English ways, treating adultery as a minor offense to be dealt with by the parish vestry or county court. A statute of 1645 ordered churchwardens to present adulterers to the county courts along with fornicators and whores. In 1658, Virginia be-

latedly and only very partially followed the parliamentary example
by giving the county courts power to impose minor fines on convicted adulterers. Maryland left the punishment of adulterers to the
discretion of the county courts.

The extreme difference between English practice and biblical
mandates relative to adultery caused anguish in New England. As
early as 1631, the Massachusetts assistants raised adultery to the
capital level by court order. The General Court later abrogated and
then reaffirmed the order. The first Massachusetts code, the Body
of Liberties of 1641, placed adultery unequivocally among the capital crimes.[17] Connecticut and New Haven followed the example.
The discrepancy between English law, the Bible, and their consciences bothered legislators in Plymouth and Rhode Island. The
Rhode Island code made it clear that its authors despised the act
"whereby men do turn aside from the naturall use of their own
wives and do burn in their lusts for strange flesh." Nevertheless,
English practice stood in force, but "with this memento, that the
Most High will judge them."[18] The Plymouth code also showed
ambivalence. Its authors first placed adultery in a category with
fornication and provided discretionary punishment. The word
"adultery" was then crossed out and placed under the rubric of capital offenses, where, last in the list, the text reads equivocally,
"Adultery to be punished."[19]

The court records bear witness that seventeenth-century men
and women led very active sex lives, by no means confined to the
marriage bed. In England, the main responsibility for punishing
fornicators lay with the church courts, though the justices of the
peace might also be concerned. Dalton lists fornication as one of
the acts for which a justice might take surety for good behavior.
The real concern of the government was with bastard children who
might become charges against the parish. The justices tried to find
the putative father, but failing that, sent mother and child to the
house of correction for a year.[20]

Following the English model, the first Virginia House of Burgesses charged the ministers and churchwardens with seeking out
"all ungodly disorders," among them "suspicions of whordoms, dis-
honest company[,] Keeping with weomen and such like."[21] The
minister might admonish, suspend from church and finally, with
the approval of the governor, excommunicate an offender. A later

Virginia statute dealt with the persistent problem of bastards born to servant girls. As a preventive measure, men caught fornicating with female servants paid five hundred pounds of tobacco to the parish or suffered a whipping. In the event of a birth, the father paid fifteen hundred pounds of tobacco to the woman's master or served him for one year. Maryland left the punishment of fornicators to the discretion of the justices. Rhode Island followed the law that "the Wisdome of the State of England have or shall appoint."[22] In 1642, Connecticut defined its capital laws. Immediately following came the plaintive note that "frequent experience gives in sad evidence of several other ways of uncleanes and lasivious caridges practised among us."[23] They left the punishment to the judge's discretion, as did Massachusetts and Plymouth originally. Plymouth later made distinctions about the timing of copulation. If the act occurred before contract to marry, the couple paid a fine of £10 or were whipped and imprisoned up to three days. Copulation after contract, but before marriage, brought a fine of £5. Later the Connecticut and Massachusetts codes set it out that fornication "shall be punished either by enjoyning to Marriage, or Fine, or corporall punishment, or all or any of these."[24] In the Puritan colonies, fornicators also faced church discipline.[25]

In attitudes toward illicit sexual acts, the Chesapeake colonies again mirrored the parent law. If such acts were threatening to marriage and the family, they were perceived as moral problems to be solved in the family, neighborhood, or church. The primary concern was practical. Pregnancy reduced the efficiency of servant women, and bastards had to be supported. Though the same practical considerations existed in New England, they were incidental to the moral issue. Such acts put individual salvation in jeopardy, menaced the integrity of the family, compromised the purity of the church, and tempted God to bring down wrathful retribution on a sinful society. Except Rhode Island, the New England colonies threw the full weight of the disciplinary apparatus of church and state against illicit sex.

The record shows that attempts to control behavior by statute were by no means unique to the Puritan colonies of New England. In virtually every session of Parliament during the reigns of Elizabeth I and the first two Stuarts, members debated personal conduct laws. During the period when the first colonies were being

TABLE 1.5. LAW SOURCES: MISCONDUCT, 1660
(percentages)

	English	Indigenous	Biblical
Drunkenness	94.3	5.7	–
Cursing	100.0	–	–
Lying	–	25.0	75.0
Idleness	50.0	50.0	–
Apparel	–	100.0	–
Sabbath Violation	100.0	–	–

settled, Parliament enacted laws against drunkenness, cursing, idleness, and Sabbath violations.[26] Table 1.5 shows that to a large degree laws regulating personal conduct in the colonies reflected English law.

Though the principle that the law should control conduct won general acceptance, the impulse in that direction often came from Puritans, who saw these misconducts as sins to be purged from society by a moral reformation. The control of most of these acts had been the business of the church courts. The movement to bring them within the jurisdiction of the public courts showed a general conviction, emphasized by Puritans, that ecclesiastical justice was corrupt and lax.[27]

Beyond the moral issue, there were very practical social and economic reasons why these acts should have been suppressed. Drunkenness and idleness contributed to endemic disorder.[28] High reasons of state urged legislators to force everyone to attend the services of the established church, and Sunday afternoon revels could produce riotous behavior. Profane language produced altercations and assaults. Drunkenness had bad economic effects. Excessive consumption of beer wasted grain; the drunkard's habit kept him from his work.

The Chesapeake colonies put laws on their books to repress drunkenness, cursing, and Sabbath violations. That they did not go as far as the Puritan colonies in regulating behavior probably showed agreement with the sentiment expressed by a member of Parliament: "Every evil in a state is not to be met with in a law."[29] Puritan legislators and judges obviously disagreed. Installed in New England as an unrestrained majority, they legislated morals. They brought over every English conduct-regulating statute, added lying to the calendar, and in Massachusetts and Connecticut temporarily revived the Elizabethan statutes against excessive apparel, which forbade most persons from wearing certain styles, fine fabrics, and ornaments of precious metal.

English law was the model for colonial law in the area of offenses against trade and justice. The distribution of sources for these heads of law are set out in Appendix Table A. English law had regulated the quality and price of goods from early times. It had also attempted to eliminate speculators by providing penalties for attempts to forestall, regrate, or engross goods at or destined for the market.[30] Colonial lawmakers wrote an erratic record under the heading of offenses against trade. Most established standards of quality. Others attempted to exclude the speculator from the market temporarily. Some legislated a general concept of "just price." This scattered legislation clearly had its roots primarily (78 percent) in English law.

The English system of justice rested on implicit assumptions: courts and juries acted without fear or favor; the truth was found by the testimony of men under oath; cases tried real issues; the record was true and inviolate. Contempt, embracery, perjury, barratry, champerty, and forgery compromised these assumptions.[31] All of these acts would be punished in the colonies, but, as in England, statutory definition was scattered and not comprehensive. Colonial practice, when visible, so far mirrored English practice that its source has been estimated to have been 87 percent English.

The bulk of the criminal law shows that geographic region made only a small difference in the source of law chosen in the colonies, English law predominating everywhere in crimes against persons, trade, and justice; indigenous law in crimes against property and misconducts; the Bible or ecclesiastical precedents having considerable impact on definitions of sexual offenses everywhere. Certain crimes, however, called forth very different law in different colonies. In this class of offenses were the great crime of treason and its lesser cousin, sedition. The English law of treason was based in an ancient statute that had been extended by judicial interpretation. The definition of acts of lese majesty that menaced the sovereign ought not to have been tampered with by subsidiary corporations, but several colonies did. Virginia, anxious to express its loyalty to the Stuarts, made it treason to doubt Charles II's right to the throne. Maryland, Plymouth, and Rhode Island acknowledged that the English law of treason operated within their jurisdictions but created a dual allegiance by elevating to the capital level attempts to betray their own governments. The codes of the three Puritan colonies failed to affirm the allegiance owed to the king. They emphasized their sense of autonomy by providing the death penalty for the treacherous betrayal of their commonwealths. Protection of a colonial plantation from betrayal could not have had roots in English law; therefore, the sources of these laws are described, under the title "sedition," as 86 percent indigenous and 14 percent biblical. The colony-by-colony distributions are given in Appendix Table A.

In their zeal for literal biblicism, the three Puritan colonies departed from the parent law by making capital crimes of apostasy, blasphemy, man stealing, and incorrigible disobedience to parents. Though acts of apostacy and blasphemy might have come to trial in English church courts, the source of these code provisions was so obviously biblical that a quotient of 100 percent in that category has been assigned. With the possible exception of blasphemy,[32] the absence of prosecutions makes these Puritan laws appear to have been mere hortatory rhetoric.

Modes of Expressing the Substantive Law

Following the model of the parent state, the colonies defined the nature of criminal acts and prescribed punishments by two methods: judicial usage and positively stated legislative law. The colonists brought with them the operating principle of the common law that law should arise out of evolving experience as interpreted by the judges. By 1660 the seven colonies expressed an average of 24 percent of their substantive criminal law by judicial usage. The degree of commitment to the common law principle varied widely among the jurisdictions (see Table 1.6).

Virginia and Maryland left such a large part of the responsibility for defining criminal law to their judges because the power of governments in the Chesapeake colonies was derivative. In Virginia, ultimate authority rested first in a company located at London and then with the king. In Maryland, power lay with the lord proprietor of the Calvert family. The commissions to the governors placed

TABLE 1.6. CRIMINAL LAW
DEFINED BY JUDICIAL USAGE, 1660
(percentages)

Virginia	64.6
Maryland	49.1
Plymouth	35.2
Massachusetts	7.6
Connecticut	8.0
Rhode Island	4.8
New Haven	0.0

responsibility for maintaining law and order squarely on them and their councils. In Virginia, the royal commissions ordered governors to "Direct and Govern Correct and punish our Subjects" and to do so "according to the Lawes and Statutes of this our Realm of England."[33] The possibility of local legislative activity in the area of criminal law was thus largely removed at the outset. Virginia's commitment to judicially defined law becomes even more emphatic and rises to nearly 90 percent of the corpus when the statutory output of one assembly is deducted. Under the surveillance of the English Commonwealth, the session of 1658 established legislative penalties for adultery, fornication, cursing, drunkenness, and profaning the Sabbath. The remaining minuscule body of criminal legislation consisted of temporary laws. Though the governors of Maryland operated under somewhat different rules from their Virginia neighbors, they approximated the Virginia method of defining criminal law. By the charter, law was to be made by the proprietor with the "assent" of an elected assembly. In regard to the criminal law, the charter provided that no penalty could reach life or loss of a member unless it was based in an act of the assembly.[34]

These Maryland charter provisions created great confusion in the province and added a second reason for the absence of statutes. Calvert insisted that only he could make the law; the assembly demanded the initiative. For long periods this conflict left the statute book blank, and the governor and council made and administered the criminal law at their discretion. In 1642, the proprietor and the governor approved some skeletal statutes that technically met the charter mandate relative to capital crimes. These laws required the death penalty for treason, betrayal of the proprietor, and murder. They provided optional punishments for a dozen other traditional felonies that were merely named in the statute. In effect, the assembly had left felony law to be defined by judicial usage.[35]

Executive control of the entire judicial process by the Chesapeake magistrates also stemmed from their concept of society. The Calverts attempted to resurrect medieval agrarian society. The Virginians wished to reproduce the contemporary English agrarian society. Wealth was obviously in land, and it could be unlocked only if a subservient labor force could be located on the land. Indentured servants made up a large part of the population in both colonies, and many of them came from unstable parts of English society. If these laboring people were to be kept under control, it was wise to give the judges independence and discretion. The crime of larceny furnishes an explicit example. Economically it made no sense to hang great numbers of the "lesser men." It was sound policy to let them fear that they might be hanged. Judgments of death for theft came down in Maryland and Virginia, but they were very much the exception to the usual sentences of whipping. A criminal law defined by judges operated *in terrorem* among the laboring people.[36]

Table 1.7 shows that New Englanders experienced long periods of discretionary justice before giving positive statement to the substantive criminal law through the enactment of codes.[37] In the New England settlements, an average of sixteen years passed between the organization of governments and the promulgation of criminal codes. The durability of discretionary justice in New England may be explained in part by the fact that whereas the governors of Virginia and Maryland were responsible to an external authority in England, the elected leaders of the New England colonies (except Rhode Island) bore a much weightier responsibility to the ultimate authority, God. He had set out the basic law in the Pentateuch for these New World Zions. Both the Bible and John Calvin made the magistrate the agent for the enforcement of God's law. In the final chapter of the *Institutes*, Calvin elevated the magistrates, placing their bench alongside His seat. The magistrates were God's "deputies," "a living law."[38] Such authoritative texts legitimized discretionary justice in New England.

New England judges argued that discretionary justice was superior to positive, prescriptive law. Discretionary or "arbitrary" justice was a major political issue in Massachusetts during the 1630s and 1640s.[39] The deputies in the General Court argued that a crimi-

TABLE 1.7.   JUDICIAL USAGE IN NEW ENGLAND

	Founded	Code	Years of Judicial Usage
Plymouth	1620	1636	16
Massachusetts	1629	1648	19
Connecticut	1635	1650	15
Rhode Island	1636	1647	11
New Haven	1638	1656	18

nal justice system was arbitrary unless it was based in legislation that defined criminal acts precisely and prescribed penalties. John Winthrop set out the explicit defense of discretionary justice in "A Discourse on Arbitrary Government" (1644). He denied that the rule of the magistrates had been arbitrary. They had applied the most fundamental law, God's law, and where that law was silent they had exercised discretion. The result was just because the magistrates were "Gods upon earthe." The burden of the "Discourse" was its attack on prescript penalties. Legislatures dealt speculatively with future acts; judges dealt with concrete causes before them. Only a judge could know whether a specific penalty would cause pain, the very purpose of punishment. A fixed fine that would be of no concern to a rich man could destroy a poor one. Circumstances altered cases, making discretion essential. A youth of honorable reputation might tell a harmless lie. He ought not to suffer the same punishment as "an olde notorious lyer" who had lied maliciously. If the penalty was fixed, "any Schoolboye might pronounce it: and then what need of any speciall wisdome, learninge, Courage, zeale or faithfulnesse in a Judge?"[40]

Without elaborate justification, the governor and assistants in Plymouth and New Haven administered the criminal justice systems at their discretion for an extended period of time. They were small communities with a core population sharing an apparent consensus about law and order. By regularly reelecting the governors and assistants the settlers implicitly approved magisterial justice. There is some evidence that the founders of Connecticut left Massachusetts in part because of discontent with its system of justice. Yet, the people of Connecticut lived with a very similar system for fifteen years. Elected by a wider constituency than the Massachusetts magistrates, the Connecticut judges enjoyed the respect of their community. In 1642, the Connecticut General Court set out the capital laws of the jurisdiction. Having done so the members noted "sad evidence" of many other crimes. Because such offenses varied with circumstances, it was not deemed wise to control them with "particular and expresse lawes." Rather, the deputies confirmed the power of the magistrates to impose "severe and sharpe punishment" because they "approve of what hath bine alreddy done." The people of Connecticut chose to be judged by magistrates guided by God's law.[41]

Before 1660, the prevailing mode of defining criminal law in the colonies shifted from judicial usage to legislative prescription. This shift occurred for three reasons: first, discretionary justice generated opposition; second, demographic factors seemed to recommend more precise law; third, political conditions in England created a favorable climate for the change. The pressure for positive law was felt first and most directly in New England. By 1660, the New England colonies had defined almost 90 percent of their substantive criminal law by legislative enactment.

Discretionary justice generated overt hostility in Massachusetts. During the 1630s, the magistrates there set a tone of severity. With no statutory authorization, the Court of Assistants tried and condemned persons for manslaughter, larceny, contempt, assault, battery, scandalous speech, drunkenness, adultery, running away from service and disobeying masters, fornication, cursing, idleness, seditious words, attempted rape, "light behavior," murder, bigamy, and heresy. Punishments ranged from hanging to admonition.[42]

If the ordinary people caught up in the judicial system complained, there is no record except for an occasional defiant utterance.[43] The magistrates also imposed penalties on extraordinary persons who deviated from the rigorous orthodoxy of church and state. With summary process and severe punishment, the magistrates filled up a catalog of arbitrary actions. Among the condemned were Thomas Morton, Philip Ratcliffe, Samuel Gorton, John Underhill, Roger Williams, John Wheelwright, William Coddington, William and Anne Hutchinson, Samuel Maverick, and Robert Child. The magistrates prejudged these cases and conducted inquisitions rather than trials.[44] The defendants were articulate, and some raised the issue of arbitrary justice in the colony and in England. Winthrop noted complaints about arbitrary justice as early as 1635; the people, he believed, wanted a body of law "in resemblance to a Magna Carta."[45]

Arbitrary criminal justice was one cause of the explosive expansion of New England during the 1630s. Coddington, Gorton, and the Hutchinsons surely would have agreed with Roger Williams's comment to Winthrop that "the face of Magistracie" had not been appealing to the people of Rhode Island.[46] In 1654, the people of Providence counted among their blessings that "we have long drunck of the cup of as great liberties as any people that we can heare of under the whole Heaven." They had not been "consumed with over-zealous fire of the (so called) Godly and Christian magistrates."[47]

From Connecticut, Thomas Hooker also voiced discontent with the criminal justice system of Massachusetts. In one sermon he took his text from Exodus and expanded on the warning to Moses that he had taken too much on himself as lawgiver and judge: "Thou art not able to perform it thyself alone."[48] In a letter to Hooker, Winthrop had observed that it was unsafe to refer legal matters to the people because "the best is always the least, and of that best part the wiser part is always the lesser." Responding, Hooker asked "what rule the Judge must have to judge by?" Answering, Hooker wrote that if in

> the matter which is referred to the judge the sentence should lye in his breast, or be left to his discretion according to which [way] he should goe: I am afrayd it is a course which wants both safety and warrant: I must confesse I ever looked at it as a way which leads directly to tyranny, and so to confusion, and must playnly professe: If it was in my liberty, I should choose neither to live nor leave my posterity under such a government.[49]

Demographic changes also led to codification in New England. The original settlers of Plymouth, Massachusetts, Connecticut, and New Haven had largely shared common religious views. They aimed at establishing spiritual communities in which the administration of justice would be a means of maintaining the integrity of their experiments. Both the Bible and Calvin said that they could, indeed ought, to leave the disciplinary function to the magistrates. The 1630s brought a tide of immigration that contained many non-sanctified persons. The rapid expansion of the population also led to the establishment of new towns, thus creating the further problems for law enforcement of distance and diversity. William Bradford noted the problems of rapid growth and dispersal of the population: "The country became pestered with many unworthy persons." Whether or not this characterization of the immigrants is fair, unquestionably people "scattered all over the Bay."[50] So long as the communities had remained compact and homogeneous the law could be made obvious within the framework of magisterial rulings. The need to control a larger, more diverse, and scattered population urged the publication of explicit law.

Finally, the movement toward codification in New England was closely connected to English political developments. The New England colonies had been free to publish codes from the beginning if they chose to take the risk. The risk arose from the attitude of the English government to their lawmaking efforts. Here they faced a dilemma, damned in England if they codified, damned at home if they did not. The Puritan magistrates knew that much of their criminal law, sex crime and larceny for example, could not meet the charter-mandated requirement of consistency with English law. In 1633, Charles I appointed William Laud to be chairman of the Commission on Foreign Plantations in an attempt to extend the king's policy of prerogative government to America. Colonial publication of a nonconforming criminal code would have facilitated Laud's attack on them. Charles's prerogative attempts failed in America for the same reason that they failed in England: he lost control. Presbyterian domination of Parliament for the first years after 1643 made the situation no more secure. The apparent signal to New England came in 1647, when the Independents gained control of Parliament. People who had been dealt with harshly in Massachusetts asked the parliamentary Commission to Control Plantation Affairs, headed by the earl of Warwick, to hear their appeals and extend English law to America. Warwick refused the request and declared "our tenderness of your just privileges, and of preserving entire the authority and jurisdiction of the several governments in New England."[51] Massachusetts then moved quickly to shape the Laws and Liberties, and Connecticut and New Haven followed her example.

The factors that produced the New England codes also operated in the Chesapeake colonies to some degree. They had a similar demographic experience, an expanding and dispersing population, and their legislation was affected by English politics. The misconduct statutes passed during the 1640s and 1650s were responses to the political victories of the English radical Protestants. In Maryland, the struggle between the assembly and proprietor over the issue of legislative initiative can be seen as evidence of a dislike of executive control of the law. Regardless of these apparent similarities, the Chesapeake colonies produced neither codes nor comprehensive statutes. By 1660, Virginia had defined only 35.6 percent and Maryland 50.9 percent of the criminal law by statute. The Maryland criminal laws of 1642 merely listed felonies, therefore the 50.9 percent proportion of positive law there is inflated.

Why did judicial usage survive to such a large degree along the Chesapeake? One reason is that the men who controlled the local political process remained responsible to authority in England. A second is that governors, legislators, and judges largely shared the same economic and social aims. As long as a discretionary system controlled access to land and the people who worked on it, there was no compelling reason to make a positive statement of law. A third reason was that, unlike the lawmakers of New England, the Chesapeake magistrates were controlling a largely illiterate people. Exemplary justice served their purposes better than didactic positive law. Finally, the Chesapeake magistrates had no ideological base upon which to construct positive law. In contrast, Plymouth and the three Puritan colonies had the model of Moses and the Israelite state.

The move toward positive law laid several basic principles at the foundation of American legal experience. People were to have a known law to live by. The movement to code and statute showed an instinctive thrust toward a separation of powers and an insistence on indigenous, legislative definition of crime and punishment.

Statutory Procedural Law

Though the procedural criminal law is the subject of the next chapter, it is appropriate to note that colonial legislators did make these matters a part of the positive law. The procedural rights of Englishmen accused of crime were buried in the common law. Whether they exercised any right, other than trial by jury, was left largely to the discretion of the judge. In contrast, one of the most advanced features of the New England codes was their concern for "Liberties," the procedural rights of those accused of crime. The codes provided specific guarantees.

The two Plymouth codes had least to say on this head, though jury trial was guaranteed. The other codes began with a close precis of the thirty-ninth chapter of Magna Carta. The Rhode Island code stated "That no person, in this Colonie, shall be taken or imprisoned, or be disseized of his Lands or Liberties, or be Exiled, or any otherwise molested or destroyed, but by the Lawfull judgment of his Peeres, or by some known law."[52] The Massachusetts, Connecticut, and New Haven recitals of the great text omitted the judgment of peers from the formula and added the standard of "the word of God" where the public law was defective.[53] The codes contained many specific guarantees: bail, grand and petty juries, right to challenge jurors, speedy trial with equal justice, multiple witnesses in capital cases, no cruel or unusual punishments, no double jeopardy, appeal. They also made a major reform of the consequences of judgment by abolishing corruption of the blood in all cases and forfeiture in most cases.

Form and Substance

The English origins of colonial criminal law as it had evolved by 1660 are unmistakable. The colonists had not "received" the law; they had carried it with them. Differences between the law of the new communities and the parent law mostly reflected the demands for change being made by the English advocates of law reform. To a lesser degree, the Puritan colonies brought in biblically based changes that, with a few exceptions, were largely constructive. Though the changes made in the colonial jurisdictions were not inventions and make up only a short list, they seem remarkable when compared to the English record of the same period. In England, the criminal law exhibited tenacious resistance to change in the face of a persistent, diverse demand for reform. In America, it began to yield to rational and humane impulses.

An obvious difference between English and early American law was form. Colonial legislators reduced the intricate mass of the common and statutory law to brief written statements. Abandoning Latin and law French, they stated the law in English. In the process, they avoided the "loquacity and prolixity," "the noise and strife," of the language of the parent law.[54] Though the reduction and clarification of a body of law is a substantial achievement, the colonial restatement was not merely formal. In recasting the law, the provincial legislators laid at the base of American law the core principle that the people must have a known law to live by.

The main substantive reform being demanded in England was a reduction of the list of crimes carrying the death penalty, a hope that went unrealized there. Colonial legislators achieved this reform by drastically reducing the number of felonies. Most important, they abandoned the death penalty as a punishment for any form of theft. A society that values life over property is more humane than one that prefers property. Moral and material considerations raised the value of life on the scale of colonial justice. The Puritan saw persons as God's creatures and would not destroy them without His mandate. The Chesapeake planter equated wealth with labor. A man or woman dead on the gallows would hoe no more tobacco.

Because early American criminal law was stated clearly and preferred life to property, it remains as evidence of the intent to create a society on the foundation of rational and humane concepts.

Chapter Two

Judicial Proceedings

Interpretation of criminal procedure in early seventeenth-century America is complicated by the condition of both the criminal law of the time and the surviving records. English texts and manuals available to colonial legislators and judges were very erratic, sometimes covering in great detail procedures that had fallen into disuse or that were relatively unimportant. Yet, matters central to the process—for example, the actual conduct of a jury trial—are barely considered. Thus, the colonists had no authoritative English text to guide them in procedural matters. Criminal procedure was changing in the first half of the century; for example, rules relative to criminal evidence had been virtually nonexistent but were beginning to emerge. A final problem for the historian is the state of the court records, parts of which are missing in all jurisdictions. The surviving records show an obvious difference of opinion among court clerks as to what constituted an adequate record.

Preventing Crimes

Though a main purpose of a judicial system is to punish crime, remnants of an ancient system designed to prevent crime remained very much alive in seventeenth-century England. The system of frankpledge had bound all freemen as sureties for the behavior of their neighbors. What had survived was a method of binding specific individuals because their behavior made it appear likely that they might commit a crime. The restraint took the form of a recognizance, a debt acknowledged to be due to the crown if certain conditions were not met. Usually the person with presumed criminal tendencies needed to find one or two men to be his sureties. Recognizances were of two kinds, for the peace and for good behavior. Judges normally demanded recognizance for the peace to end a threat of violence. A constable might ask that persons be bound, or an individual might "swear the peace" against another at whose hands he feared violence. The recognizance for good behavior had more general application. In its modern form it ran back to a statute of 1495 that permitted it to be demanded of those "that be not of good fame." The bond for good behavior had a broad sweep and could reach any suspicious person. Judges used it extensively in cases of moral offenses. A bond, either for the peace or good behavior, usually demanded that the person appear at a later court where it could be determined whether or not its conditions had been met. Failure to meet the conditions of the bond caused the recognizance to be forfeited to the king.[1]

Conditions in the colonies encouraged the use of the recognizance system. Since the communities were small it readily became apparent whether or not a person was meeting the conditions of the bond. In such communities, this formal system of warning and watch was effective. The records of courts of all levels of competence in all jurisdictions are studded with these most commonly used judicial devices. Judges demanded security for the peace at the request of persons who went "in bodily feare" of their lives. The condition might be both general and specific: "keep the peace to King & people & especiall towards Sannert Butler."[2] Judges demanded bonds for good behavior from a wide variety of persons not of good fame: William Lewis, a Catholic, for attacking Protestant books and ministers;[3] John White, not to be alone with Bull's wife; Oliver Weeks, "a common swearer;"[4] others for an "attempt to unclenes with a married woman," for "light carriage," for "sinfull attempt."[5] Joan Andrews, bonded as "an infamous scould & a breaker of the peace," forfeited it for calling Goody Mendum an "Indian Hoare."[6] Everywhere, drunks entered bonds to stay sober. The recognizance bond system made colonial judges active agents in preventing violence and immorality. The system seems to have worked for the records of forfeited bonds are rare.[7]

Summary Proceedings

In the least complex and most common judicial hearing, the summary proceeding, the judge or judges imposed a penalty without indictment or trial. The English law of summary proceeding had two lines of development: contempts of courts or their process and misdemeanors created by statute that gave one or more justices of the peace the power to punish offenders. Though for a long time courts proceeded against contempts by indictment, they had apparently for an equally long time dealt with them by attachment. By this procedure the offending individual was restrained and imprisoned until he could "make" his fine with the judges, the process implying a negotiation rather than a penalty. Both Star Chamber and later Kings Bench could punish summarily contempts committed in any court.[8] By the mid-sixteenth century, over thirty statutes empowered justices of the peace to impose penalties after examination of witnesses and the accused. Though most of these laws dealt with offenses against economic regulations, others empowered the justices to deal summarily with gamblers, poachers, vagabonds, and violators of sumptuary law.[9] The tendency was for Parliament to increase the number of acts that permitted summary punishment. In 1619, Dalton listed most, but by no means all, offenses that justices out of sessions could hear and determine on "view, confession, or examination and proofe," and this "without any Indictment found or preferred."[10] The control of alehouses and tippling, church attendance, and unruly servants had been added to the list. Dalton emphasized that summary proceedings were limited to those cases authorized by statute. Citing William Lambarde, he reminded the justice that he was "*lex loquens*," and he should "containe himselfe within the lists of the law and [should] not use his discretion but only where both the law permitteth, and the present case requireth."[11]

In the colonial jurisdictions, the justices and judges probably proceeded summarily in a great many cases, though the evidence is somewhat confusing, as will be apparent. Certainly they punished contempts summarily by imposing a wide variety of punishments. Massachusetts, Connecticut, and Rhode Island defined contempts by statute, a reform then being advocated in England.[12] Contempts ranged from intemperate words and failure to obey court orders to offenses verging on sedition. It was unwise to call Governor Winthrop "a lawyer's clerke" or Magistrate Ludlow "a just as[s]"; equally unwise to say that at the Virginia General Court "poore men could hardly get any rights" or to describe orders of the governor of Plymouth as "stincking commissary warrants."[13] Punishments for verbal contempts and disobedience to officers and orders included humble public submission, binding to good behavior, whipping, and fines that were often stiff.[14] Aggravated contempts came near to sedition. Rhode Island described all contempts as "a kind of Rebellion."[15] A Massachusetts General Court order of 1637 saw contempts as the cause of "great disorders growing in this common welth" and authorized punishments as severe as banishment.[16] In Virginia, the General Assembly levied the enormous fine of ten thousand pounds of tobacco for a contempt of the governor and government.[17]

Colonial justices also punished "offences of a smale nature"[18] summarily. Certainly they did so for a wide range of infractions during the early period of discretionary justice. In many instances the record is so bare that it would be natural to conclude that most proceedings were summary, but this would probably be a wrong conclusion. In all jurisdictions except New Haven, in most cases the accused could choose whether to be tried by the court or a jury. In small communities the facts of malfeasance would usually have been clear enough, and a jury trial cost money. Most persons chose to be tried by the court although here and there men demanded trials in cases involving minor charges.[19] In most courts there was a grand or presentment jury whose findings in small offenses amounted to a conviction. Such proceedings were not really summary.

Colonial summary proceedings developed roughly along the lines of the English model and sometimes mirrored it. The original instructions to the royal council for Virginia authorized the punishment of "all manner of excesse" at discretion. Such proceedings were to be "done summarily, and verbally without writing" except that the judgment and sentence were to be recorded.[20] The English formula for authorizing a justice to proceed summarily was that he could do so on his own view, the confession of the accused, or the testimony of one or two witnesses. The statute most frequently and accurately copied was the law regulating taverns and drunkenness.[21] Without necessarily using the "view, confession, or witness" formula, colonial statutes provided for summary proceedings in some petty larcenies, abuse of tobacco, idleness, vagrancy, excessive apparel, swearing, lying, Sabbath breaking, and gambling.[22]

The purpose of arrest is to bring a suspected offender before a judge for examination. The English process usually began with the justice of the peace. On complaint, he might issue a summons. That failing, or if more sufficient cause had been shown, the justice issued a warrant to the sheriff or constable. The warrant needed to be specific and set out the name of the person, time, and place of the action, and the cause for which it was issued. A justice, sheriff, constable, or coroner could arrest without a warrant on his own view or on suspicion of felony.[23] When a felony actually had been committed, any person might raise the hue and cry. The constable and all able-bodied men pursued the hue and cry, beginning with the men of the village and, if necessary, of neighboring towns to hunt and pursue the suspected felon.[24]

As in England, colonial law limited the arresting powers of the peace officers. The constable might arrest and confine minor offenders if he had actually seen the infraction, or arrest others and bring them before a judge.[25] A Massachusetts case indicated the limits of a constable's discretion. The Boston constable broke up a drunken brawl, but several offenders eluded him. Without a warrant he arrested two men after the fight subsided, one of them at home. The judge commented that he had exceeded his authority. "The constable may restrain, and, if need be, imprison in the stocks such as he sees disturbing the peace, but, when the affray is ended and the parties departed and in quiet, it is the office of the magistrate to make inquiry and to punish it."[26] Scattered evidence shows that most appearances and arrests resulted from proper warrants and summons. The judges of the Virginia General Court apparently issued general warrants in the early years, but, in 1625 noting "inconveniences" "too long to relate," ordered that none be granted.[27] The Rhode Island code, requiring specific warrants, stated the principle relative to search that by extension applies to arrests: "for a man's house is to himselfe, his family and goods, as a castle."[28] The Massachusetts codes assumed that appearance would be by summons or warrant.[29] Several colonies authorized the hue and cry by statute, and it doubtless would have been used as a common law practice,[30] but examples of use are scarce.

Commitment or Bail

After arrest, the English justice of the peace made the critical decision whether to commit the suspect to jail or let him to bail. Two statutes of the reign of Philip and Mary regulated the procedure of bail
and commitment.[31] The bail statute required that two justices, one
of the quorum, were needed to grant bail. The justices were to examine the accused and those who had brought him before them and cer-
tify the examination to the next assize. The commitment statute
required the justice to take the written examination of the suspected
felon and those who brought him. He was to bind the "bringers" and
any other witnesses to appear at the next gaol delivery. The statute did
not require that any of these examinations be upon oath. Subsequently, the manual writers debated whether or not justices should
take these examinations on oath. The examination of the accused was
without oath because of the basic common law assumption that a
man's guilt was not "to be wrung out of himselfe." The depositions of
the "bringers" and witnesses might or might not be taken upon oath.
In any event, they would not be regarded as evidence admissible in
court unless the deponent was incapacitated.[32]

The decision whether to bail or commit was certainly not casual.
The law assumed a right to bail, and if the justice improperly with-
held it he was liable to suit. Yet, if he granted bail when he ought
not to have, he could be fined. The one clear rule was that a suspected traitor or murderer could not be bailed. Beyond that rule
was an intricate maze of statutes regulating bail. The First Statute
of Westminster (1275) removed bail in twelve categories and provided for it in six others. Dalton listed over 150 acts for which bail
had been taken away by statute. If the examination established
sufficient suspicion or if bail had been removed by statute, the
justice by *mittimis* committed the accused to the custody of the
jailer.[33]

Every colony recognized bail as a basic right. The complex English rules of eligibility for bail were reduced to the simple one that
all persons had a right to bail except those accused of a capital
crime.[34] Circumstances dictated that most offenders be bailed. Jails,
if they existed at all, were inadequate and the maintenance of pris-
oners expensive. Besides, the bailed man would be under the con-

stant scrutiny of his neighbors, making flight difficult. If he did flee to another community he would be suspect immediately as a stranger.

Methods of Prosecution

In England, crime could be prosecuted by presentment, indictment, information, or the finding of an inquisition of office. Though "presentment" was a generic word it usually referred either to an accusation made by a grand jury on the jurors' own initiative and from their own knowledge or to the charges made by the chief pledges in a leet court. In late Tudor and early Stuart times, grand juries appear to have been reluctant to make presentments. Conscientious justices pressed them to do their duty and present lawbreakers.[35] Officers of the courts fashioned indictments and submitted them to the grand juries. A highly formal document, the indictment needed to be exact, including identification of the accused by name, status or occupation, and place of residence; the time and place of the offense; a description of things involved (for example, weapons used, items stolen); and "the manner of fact," that is, a description of the crime. In certain common law crimes, precise word formulas were required and in statutory crimes the key words of the act had to be reproduced exactly. Though the indictment was in Latin, it was read to the prisoner in English. The jury determined whether or not the charge was plausible, and to aid it could hear witnesses for the prosecution, but not for the defense. Regardless of the size of the jury (usually twenty-three), twelve of its members had to find the accusation true. If they did, they returned the bill with the endorsement, *billa vera* (a true bill). Failing to find the bill true, they endorsed it *ignoramus* (We have no knowledge of it; we ignore it).[36] Many trespasses or misdemeanors could be prosecuted on an information (sometimes called presentment) of an officer of the king, a justice of the peace, constable, or the attorney general, or by a private person. It was Lambarde's opinion that spoken suggestions or written informations by a private person were "but of the force to stirre up the Justices to recommend the cause" to the grand jury.[37] Another mode of prosecution was by inquisition of office, commonly an inquiry into a suspicious death by a coroner's jury. A finding that the death was casual (accidental) or from natural causes ended the matter. The inquest might also have found the dead person to be a *felo de se*, a suicide. A finding of anything other than casual death or suicide would be tested in a trial by jury.[38]

The colonies used all of the English modes of prosecution, though often in somewhat variant form. Grand juries functioned in all colonies. In Maryland and Virginia, as in England, the sheriff returned the jurors. The New England towns chose the jurors, and in some jurisdictions jurors served for a one-year term. Such jurors were "sworn presenters," individually responsible for observing the activities of fellow townsmen. A typical colonial grand jury had twelve to sixteen members. New England law explicitly required the grand jury to make presentment of "any misdemeanours" or "breaches of such wholsome laws." Those grand juries were yet another agency in the comprehensive system of watching behavior.[39]

Formal indictments in the colonies were largely limited to capital crimes. As was true of all other instruments, colonial indictments were drawn in English rather than Latin. Colonial indictments met basic standards of exactness in regard to the essential elements of culpability: the person described had committed a specific illegal act with malicious or criminal intent. New England indictments usually met the standards by using simple language without concern for the English phrase formulas. In Virginia and Maryland, the language of some indictments resemble the English models more closely. Before 1660, no colonial indictment in the cases reviewed was quashed for technical insufficiency.[40]

Most colonial prosecutions began with a presentment. In New England, the words presentment and indictment were used interchangeably. Massachusetts prosecutions for capital crimes often began with the declaration: "We the Grand Jury for the Commonwealth of Massachusetts upon our oathes doe present. . . ."[41] In the Plymouth General and Assistants Courts and in county courts everywhere, the business of a session usually began with the jury presentments of trespasses and misdemeanors. The constables and private persons also made presentments. Whether made by juries or individuals, such presentments often amounted to convictions although in many instances it is impossible to determine what, if any, penalty was imposed. The frequency of presentment and its equation with conviction strongly suggest English leet and borough court models.[42] Only the Maryland Provincial Court used formal, written informations, probably because the Calverts maintained an attorney general in the colony.[43]

All colonies used the inquest, and it seems safe to state that no suspicious death went unexamined. Though most colonies established the office of coroner, inquests could be initiated by other officers. The Massachusetts codes ordered an assistant or constable to summon a jury of twelve to inquire into "any sodain, untimely or unatural death."[44] When one man killed another by accident, the finding would often be that it was by "God's visitation" or "by the providence of God."[45] Because of the heinousness of infanticide, inquests examined infant deaths.[46] Juries looked into casual death and awarded deodands, a gift to God of the object causing death, in one case a tree that had fallen on a man and in another a canoe because it had failed "to make way in a storm."[47] In a Virginia case involving a hanging, a coroner's inquest found suicide. This finding was based on the testimony of four persons who discovered the body, and the chain by which the boy hanged was awarded as a deodand.[48] If inquests found suspicion of homicide, the accused stood trial before a petty jury.

Process, Arraignment, and Plea

Procedure between the time of finding an indictment and the beginning of trial furnishes an excellent example of simplification of the law by the colonists. English procedure was laid over and intertwined with complex ancient rules. After indictment, the English justice issued process to bring the accused in for trial.[49] Lambarde described process in a relatively straightforward manner. In crimes less serious than felony, the justice issued a *venire facias ad respondendum*, a summons to appear. If the wanted person did not respond, the justice issued a *distringas* (a distraint of goods and chattels) to compel appearance. *Distringas* failing, the judge then issued *capias alias* and then *capias pluries* (another multipurpose writ, *capias* meant "that you take," in this case, the body) and finally the *exigent* (a peremptory demand by the sheriff made in court for the body of the person). In felony, original process was *capias*, which would be issued three times before the *exigent*. The *exigent* began the process of outlawry, that is, the condemnation of a fugitive without trial. If he failed to come in after a proclamation or "exaction" at a series of court sessions, the judgment of outlawry passed. The consequences of outlawry in lesser crimes was forfeiture of goods and chattels. An outlawed traitor or felon was convicted and anyone could kill him without penalty.[50]

Colonists left the technical apparatus of process behind in England. Judges largely avoided the intricacies of process by issuing a summons or arrest warrant. In fact, suspects were normally either in custody or bound by recognizance to appear, thus making process unnecessary. Process was less formal, as indicated in a Massachusetts General Court order that anyone who did not appear to answer for a crime after being "summoned" three times would be in contempt.[51] It was under the heading "Summons" that the Laws and Liberties mandated simple procedures: "No *Summons*, Pleading, Judgement or any kinde of proceedings in Court or course of justice shall be abated, arrested or reversed on any kinde of circumstantial errors or mistakes, if the person and the Cause be rightly understood and intended by the Court."[52] When it became clear to a colonial court that a suspect had fled, he might in fact be outlawed. In Maine, the General Court at Saco pursued John Bonithon to an outlawry. Apparently, exact English forms were not used. The record says that Bonithon had "been summoned divers times" and that "the law hath had its due proceedings to an outlawry."[53]

In English procedure, the step that followed successful process was either traverse or arraignment. A person accused of a minor crime who responded voluntarily to process might traverse the indictment. By so doing he literally put himself "on the other side" and challenged the chief matter of the indictment. If the sheriff had to bring the suspect in, he was then arraigned on the indictment (arraign meant to put in place, in this instance, put before the jury). The effect of traverse and arraignment was apparently the same, to proceed formally to trial, so the distinction seems useless. The colonists apparently thought so. The word "arraignment" rarely appears in the records. There are examples of persons who had been presented for minor offenses making a traverse, but clearly the alternative in such cases would not have been arraignment. In fact, the colonial traverse seems to have been a privilege extended by the court to stop the verdict implicit in a leet form presentment and allow the issue thus created to be tried by jury.[54]

In an English court, a person faced with an indictment had several options: remain silent; confess; make a plea denying the jurisdiction of the court in the case; demur to the indictment, denying that the act alleged was a species of the crime charged; make one of four special pleas in bar; or plead the general issue, not guilty.

If upon arraignment the accused English felon refused to enter a plea or responded indirectly, he was said to stand mute. The law subjected such a prisoner to the *peine fort et dure*, a process by which weights were added to the body until the prisoner either answered or died. The only conceivable reason that a person would suffer such an excruciating death was that he escaped judgment and thereby avoided the forfeiture of property which guilt for felony entailed. English procedure had not left the *peine* behind as a medieval relic. Persons suffered it fairly often in the time of James I, but during the reign of Charles I and the Commonwealth its use declined very rapidly.[55] The obviously humane action if a person stood mute or entered an erratic plea was to proceed as if he had entered a plea of not guilty. Though Governor Winthrop once threatened a clearly deranged woman who would not or could not enter a plea to a charge of infanticide with the *peine*, there is no evidence that it was ever applied in any colony.[56] In the Massachusetts cases in which religious dissidents would not enter a plea, the court proceeded to trial.

The colonial jurisdictions threw the special pleas in bar onto the growing waste heap of common law debris. By such a plea, an accused Englishman tried to arrest the proceedings by stopping or "barring" the indictment. The special pleas were *auterfois acquit*, *auterfois convict*, and *auterfois attaint*, which pled previous acquittal, conviction, or attainder. The remaining special plea was pardon. Surely this was a complicated way to bar double jeopardy. Massachusetts accomplished the same thing by the simple statement that no person would be twice tried for the same crime.[57]

It was doubtless true that the common subject in England or America would not have been aware of the more sophisticated pleas. But some were aware of them. At his trial before the General Court for alleged abuse of his authority, Winthrop noted that he might have demurred to the charge because what he had done was no crime at all. In Maryland, Giles Brent demurred to an indictment that charged him with failing to carry out his duties in a military campaign. He said that he could not know what the crime was, or even whether the action was civil or criminal.[58]

In Massachusetts, several persons made what amounted to a plea to the jurisdiction of the court with overtones of an informal demurrer. Such pleas either denied the validity of Massachusetts law or the competence of the court to hear the case. Benjamin Sawcer, an English soldier, asked to be tried by court-martial for his blasphemy.[59] Robert Child and his associates challenged the right of the General Court to try them. The vehement denial of jurisdiction by the Quakers was rooted in their religious radicalism rather than in legalisms. One of them, William Ledra, made an impassioned denial of jurisdiction:

> he sayd in open Court, he owed no Subjection to the wicked Laws of this Jurisdiction, sayd he would not owne this Governour to be his Judge . . . your Magistrates . . . I owne them no more Subjection than Daniell to Nebuchadnazar . . . I know your Ministers are deluders & yourselves Murderers and If ever I turn to Such Murderers as you are let all this Company Say I have turned from the God, which is the Salvation of his People & this I will seale with my blood.[60]

None of these pleas against the court's jurisdiction had any effect.

The common law was prejudiced against confessions and demanded that they be made in open court. In American jurisdictions, this easy route to judgment was largely a New England phenomenon. Though Puritans believed that confession needed to be made in open court, they pressed suspects to confess up to the last moment before execution. In capital cases, confession conferred real meaning on the words: "May God have mercy on your soul." The proceedings against George Spencer for bestiality in New Haven illustrate the dilemma that Puritan magistrates might face. The sow that Spencer had allegedly impregnated bore a deformed, one-eyed pig. Because Spencer also had one eye, magistrates saw God working in his mysterious ways to create irrefutable evidence. But a confession would clinch both the moral and legal sides of the case. Before the trial they pressured him to confess, doubtless believing that he would repeat his statement in court. One of the magistrates reminded him of the scriptural text: "He thatt hideth his sin shall not prosper, but he that confesseth and forsaketh his sins shall finde mercie." Spencer confessed, clearly misunderstanding the magistrate's use of the word "mercy." The judge was thinking of the next world, Spencer of this one. Before the trial, Spencer confessed the act eleven separate times and permitted a paper asking for mercy to be put up in church. At his trial, he refused to confess, apparently on the advice of a man who had told him that without it he could not be convicted. Faced with the many persons to whom he had confessed, he admitted that their testimony was true but denied having had intercourse with the sow. The court found him guilty because the "everlasting equity" of the Bible demanded the verdict. Obviously disturbed by his recalcitrance, the magistrates put sentencing over to the next General Court. Exhorted at the second session to confess and "give glory to God," Spencer said "he would leave itt to God." At the gallows, with the rope around his neck, they continued to demand a confession and he apparently conceded that the sentence had been righteous. But that was not enough. Before letting him fall they

> desired [him] to express somthing what apprehensions he had of the haynousnes of his sin, as against God, and whatt impressions of sorrow were wrought in him for itt, and what desires of pardon and mercie in Jesus Christ[.] [H]e could not, though much pressed, be drawne to speake a word . . . and in this frame for ought could be discerned . . . he ended his course here, God opening his mouth before his death, to give him the glory of his rightousnes, to the full satisfaction of all then present, butt in other respects leaving him a terrible example of divine justice and wrath.[61]

For lesser crimes a confession with contrition often brought reduced penalties.[62] Nathaniel Eaton, a Harvard teacher, badly beat a student. Though there were several witnesses, Eaton justified himself. The magistrates called in the elders for consultation. After this Eaton went into open court and made "a serious (seeming) confession." Having fined him and barred him from teaching, the court expected him "to have given glory to God" for the court's clemency, but he failed to do it.[63] In pardoning John Dand, who confessed because "God had bene pleased to bow his spirit," the Massachusetts

General Court did so "to manifest the Courts ready inclination to show all due incuragement to delinquents to confess their errors."[64]

All of these alternative means of answering an accusation were seldom used. As in England, the common, virtually inevitable plea of the colonist in the dock was that of the general issue, "not guilty." The accused put themselves on their country and went to trial before a jury of their peers.

Trial by Jury

In English practice, after the issue had been joined by the suspect's plea, the sheriff returned the jury panel. Jurors needed a freehold of 40 shillings and had to be residents of the vicinage, that is, the county in which the crime had been committed. When the issue to be tried was a matter of life or death, the accused could challenge jurors peremptorily, without showing cause. The common law permitted thirty-five such challenges, one short of three full juries, but a statute of 1305 limited peremptory challenges to twenty.[65] He could also challenge for cause, especially if the proposed juror had been one of the indictors or lacked freehold qualifications. The crown prosecutor could also challenge, but only for cause.[66] The trial consisted largely of a presentation of the case by the prosecution. In felony cases, the accused did not have counsel unless some point of law came into doubt. Evidence consisted of the depositions and the testimonies of witnesses called for the crown to prove the crime. Witnesses for the defense (usually character witnesses) were not under oath. If the accused testified in his own behalf, he did so without oath. When the jurors withdrew, they were given neither food nor fire until they reached a verdict. They normally returned a general verdict, either guilty or not guilty. If the jury was uncertain about points of law, it might return a special verdict, meaning that the jury, having stated whatever it had found to be true, left the judgment to the court.[67]

Colonial legislators and judges had little specific written guidance concerning trial by jury. Regardless, colonial trial practice resembled English procedure. One of the first laws passed in America was the Plymouth order requiring that the trial of "all Criminall facts" would be by jury.[68] When men wished to publicize the goodness of life in America or to defend native judicial practice, they cited the example of the general availability of juries.[69] Certainly all trials of life and death were by jury, and apparently a defendant could have a jury in almost any kind of case if he asked and paid for it.[70] On one occasion in Maryland, none of the councillors appeared at a session of the Provincial Court. The governor announced that under such circumstances all of the cases would be tried by jury.[71] The New Haven jurisdiction provided the one glaring exception to the general availability of juries. Those Puritans were so committed to the Mosaic model that they entrusted the entire trial process to the judges.

Colonial jurors were required to meet the same qualifications as their English counterparts.[72] The jury consisted of twelve men, although the Massachusetts commission to William Pynchon authorized him to use juries of six in the sparsely populated settlement at Springfield.[73] In an unconventional Maryland case, two Indians accused of murder were convicted by a trial jury of twenty-four.[74] The accused could challenge jurors, though Massachusetts admitted no peremptory challenges by requiring that challenges be "just and reasonable."[75] In no case did the accused have counsel. The few references to defendants having attorneys probably were only for civil cases and in most cases meant power of attorney rather than counsel.[76]

The requirements for criminal procedure set out in the Rhode Island code fairly represent the procedure used everywhere:

> In the first place, the Recorder shall present, and if there be time read over the bills of indictment; and if, in case they have been examined or presented by an inquest before, then shall he pass them over; if not, then shall the President sett apart the honest and lawfull men prepared for that purpose, by a solemn engagement, faithfully to enquire touching the bills, and soe shall send them forth with the same.
>
> [The court then heard the civil cases.] . . . then may the Court proceed to deale with such as are bound by recognizance eyther to release them or to continue their Bonds, according as there is just cause, and may read over the Indictments that have been enquired into before, and are now presented true bills, or that were committed to the inquest in the beginning of the Court and are returned true bills. [The court then received the verdicts in the civil causes.]
>
> . . . then let the Recorder call to the Sarjant to bring forth the Prisoners. Before each prisoner lett his indictment be read, and he de-

manded what he saieth to the indictment, whether guilty or not. If
he answer guilty, his confession shall be recorded. If he saith not
guilty, then let him be demanded if he will be tryed by God and the
country, to wit, his countrymen. If he consents, the President shall
call forth the twelve men before him, wish him to look upon them,
and ask if he have anything against them; if not, then he shall charge
them upon the former perill, to deale faithfully and truly in the matter; it being a matter of consequence and moment, and to proceed to
determine according to the light of their consciences, upon the evidence given in, and if any be found Guilty of death, to be reprieved
to the next Court. And thus having issued all matters depending, the
President with the assistants and counsellors shall give forth writs
unto the Generall Sarjant for the severall executions, and so break up
the Court for that time and sitting.[77]

All of this was very straightforward except for the crucial words
"determine," which clearly refers to the verdict, and "upon the evidence given in." English rules of evidence in criminal cases had
been virtually nonexistent and were only slowly emerging in the
late sixteenth and early seventeenth centuries. In part, the confusion about evidence can be found in the origins of juries. The jurors
of the Norman inquests were witnesses as were the jurors in trials
by ordeal. The dialogue in Sir John Fortescue's *De Laudibus Legum Angliae* shows the confusion. The prince asks the chancellor
whether the English law was contrary to the law of God, which
required "two or three witnesses." His mentor responds that "the
law of England never decides a cause only by witnesses when it can
be decided by a jury of twelve men." In another place Fortescue
argued that justice would be done to the accused because the jurors,
his "neighbours," know him.[78] Certainly by 1600 this concept had
become a fiction and the petty jury had become triers of facts presented to them. The question remained what witnesses could offer
what facts to be tried? The Marian commital statute, with its requirement that the justices of the peace take examinations, forced
the justices to find answers to the question, and a law of evidence
gradually began to emerge. Rules began to be developed as to who
was competent to be a witness, the number of witnesses necessary
to convict, and the quality or force of facts as evidence. As to the
competency of witnesses, the civil side of the law provided a rule.

The evidence of parties to a suit was inadmissible. Applied on the criminal side, this meant that the accused and the immediate family could not testify.

Whatever can be said about the rules of evidence in the colonial jurisdictions is based on the capital cases, primarily the homicides. With few exceptions they were the only cases where depositions were preserved. These records show that the accused did not testify. In fact, even their unsworn examinations are rarely in the record. Two exceptions occurred in John Dandy's second murder trial.[79] His examination before two commissioners is on the record, but probably was not used at the trial. The commissioners also examined his wife, Anne. Most of what she said showed her obvious concern with her hot-tempered husband. She had advised him to sell or give away Henry Gouge, the servant who caused so much aggravation. That much of her deposition might have helped her husband. The rest of it could only harm him and must have resulted from questioning. She told how on a previous occasion she had taken out two pieces of Gouge's skull after her husband had struck him with an ax. Gouge's body had been found in a creek, and she said that she did not believe that he had drowned. Because her testimony was taken under oath in open court, the prosecution probably regarded her as its witness. Another example was the entry at the trial of an examination of William Reade, a fourteen-year-old boy accused in Virginia of felonious killing. The examination was not under oath.[80] But these were exceptions. The general rule barred self-incrimination and negative evidence by relatives.

Whether or not the rule against sworn evidence by the accused is seen as an exclusion on the ground of unreliability or as a guarantee against self-incrimination, it should not be concluded that the defendant was silent at his trial. Trials, especially English state trials, usually consisted of sharp exchanges between the defendant and the prosecuting attorney and the judges. Such verbal battles also occurred in the Massachusetts trials of the Antinomians, Quakers, and others whose religious views seemed to menace the commonwealth.

In England, even if the examinations of witnesses were taken under oath, they were not used as evidence at the trial. The depositions served as memorandums for the judges who conducted the trial. This meant that English trials remained oral trials.[81] The same practice seems to have been followed in the colonial trials. The main difference was that virtually all colonial examinations were taken on oath. One reason for this may have been that all serious crimes in the colonies were tried before a central court. Thus, if a witness was unavoidably detained the sworn deposition could be used as evidence. The records are not full enough to prove absolutely the oral tradition, but there is no reason to think that American trials proceeded for the most part on the evidence of written depositions. Again the second Dandy murder trial is helpful. After the jury was impaneled, the record reads:

> Proclamation was made that all [who] could give in any Evidence in the behalf of his highness the Lord Protector of England &c: against the prisoner at the barr Should Come in and appeare before the Court upon forfeiture of their Recullisanance [recognizance] and they Should be heard; for the prisoner Stood upon his Deliverance.
>
> Upon which Proclamation the Wittnesses did appeare, and being Called by their Names were Sworne and did deliver themselves their Oathes in the Court to the Jury, and before the face of the prisoner who having all Lawfull Libertie and time to make his defence the Jury was Sent out.[82]

In England there were no clear rules as to how many witnesses were needed to prove a crime. That practice was irregular is proved by an example drawn from Coke's writing and practice. In the *Third Institute*, referring to treason, where the law did require two witnesses, he noted that the rule was "grounded upon the law of God." Yet, as attorney general, he had ferociously prosecuted Sir Walter Raleigh with the evidence of but one witness who was not present at the trial.[83]

Colonial legislators and judges showed concern that there be adequate witnesses. At its first session in 1619, the Virginia House of Burgesses tried Captain Henry Spelman for having "spoken very irreverently and maliciously against the government." Though some wanted "sharpe punishments," the assembly imposed the unusual penalty of seven years servitude as an interpreter because there was only one witness and a "partial confession."[84] The Plymouth General Court ordered that the testimony of one witness, even on oath, was inadequate for conviction "without a second witnesse or concuring cercomstances."[85] Massachusetts followed the biblical rule and required two or three witnesses in capital cases.[86] Courts and juries there often wrestled with the issue of adequate evidence. Sex crimes, especially adultery, caused grave problems. Though occasionally there were witnesses to copulation, the act was by its nature private. Evidentiary requirements in cases of adultery caused dissension among the Massachusetts magistrates. Mary Latham had flaunted her infidelity, yet several magistrates had doubts about the case because there were not two "direct witnesses." During the trial, she confessed the fact and was convicted and hanged.[87] In another case, a man going to England left his family in the care of another. Two servants saw the man who had custody go twice into the woman's bedroom. The jury had trouble with this evidence, and the magistrates debated the point. The jury took the advice of the judges, who argued that the evidence was inadequate. Winthrop, one of the judges, commented: "The law requires two witnesses, but here was no witness at all, for although circumstances may amount to a testimony against the person, where the fact is evident, yet it is otherwise where no fact is apparent."[88]

In murder the body was the first essential evidence. As they have in all times and places, murderers sometimes tried to dispose of that evidence. One tried to hide the body under a pile of stones, but a pig uncovered it.[89] That there is nothing new under the sun is made clear in the case of Cornish's wife. She and a man with whom she was suspected of committing adultery tried a seventeenth-century version of the "concrete overcoat." They sunk her husband's body in a "canoe laden with clay."[90]

In the homicides the record shows confusion about what evidence was necessary to convict. It is impossible in almost half of the cases to determine what evidence was considered by court and jury. Perhaps in these cases the fact was evident. If so, Winthrop at least would have admitted circumstantial evidence. It is also possible that depositions have been lost or that clerks did not record oral testimony. Obviously judges preferred confessions and got them in 25 percent of the cases.[91] In any event, mere weight of witnesses would not necessarily convict. In Massachusetts, John Betts stood his trial before the Assistants Court for the murder of his servant, Robert Knight. Nine witnesses gave very full testimony that Betts had abused Knight badly and that on one occasion he had hit him a full blow on the back with a plow staff. But it could not be proved that any of the abuse was the proximate cause of death, and the jury refused to convict. The court refused the verdict and sent the case to the General Court, which also did not find murder, though it sentenced him to be punished severely because "the evidence brought in against him houlds forth strong presumptions & great probabilities of so bloody a fact."[92]

Dalton provided colonial magistrates with a catalog of "circumstances" that they should observe and note at the time of examination, including his and his family's "quality" and reputation, his temperament, his employment, the company he kept, his life style, his conduct at the examination, and in homicides the ancient sign that the body bled in his presence.[93] The search for and finding of this sign occurred in colonial homicides. The inquest would commonly demand that the accused touch the body to see whether it "bled anew." Though regarded as convincing evidence, by itself it would not bring a conviction.[94] Certainly colonial judges and juries considered the reputation of the accused. William Schooler's reputation helped do him in. His was an exceptional case; there had been no witnesses to his alleged crime, but to strong circumstantial evidence of murder the court added the facts that his had been "a vicious life" and that he "lived like an atheist."[95]

Trial juries had to find their verdicts by unanimous vote and were expected to give the clear general verdict, guilty or not guilty. The jury might return a verdict of guilty to a lesser crime than that alleged in the indictment, for example, guilty of manslaughter rather than murder, "incontinency" rather than rape.[96] If the jurors could not agree, presumably upon points of law rather than fact, they might return a special verdict, by which they reported what they had found, stated the reasons for their doubt, and left judgment to the court.[97] Massachusetts and Connecticut seem to have been plagued by special verdicts, though statutory attempts at remedy may have referred to civil verdicts. In Connecticut, jurors disagreeing were to ask the court for instruction and then consult again. If they still could not agree, the finding of a majority would be "a sufficient and full verdict."[98] A Massachusetts statute regulated the *non-liquet*, the special verdict in civil cases. It explained the process and problem by referring to criminal verdicts:

& so it is also in a criminal case, for in the eye of the law every man is honest & innocent unles it be proved legally to the contrary. All evidence ariseth partly from matter of fact, & partly from law or argument: The matter of fact is always seizable to be judged as well by the jury as by the Court; & concerning the law, or the point of law in reference to the case in question, it is more easy & generally knowne or more difficult to be discerned. The duty of the jury, is if they doe understand the law, not to put it off from themselves, but to find accordingly; but if any of the jury doth rest unsatisfyed what is the law in the case, the whole jury have liberty to present a speciall verdict.[99]

By the late seventeenth century, English law regarded a jury verdict as unimpeachable.[100] In practice this had been true earlier with a few notable exceptions, the most notorious having been the case of Sir Nicholas Throckmorton, wherein the jury had been fined and imprisoned for a verdict of not guilty.[101] The commentators regarded the practice as exceptional. Writing in 1565, Sir Thomas Smith remarked, "But these doings were even then of many accounted very violent, tyrannical, and contrary to the liberty and custom of the realm of England."[102] Maryland had its parallel to the Throckmorton case. John Elkin stood indicted for the murder of "a certaine Indian commonly called the king of Yowocomoco." Though Elkin had confessed the crime, the jury returned "not guilty," explaining that they did so "because the party was a pagan." The governor explained that the Indian was within the king's peace and sent the jurors back. They then returned the bizarre verdict "guilty of murther in his owne defence." The court rejected this verdict, noting that it "implied a contradiction." Out a third time, the jury returned homicide in self-defense. The governor then discharged the jury and impaneled another which found manslaughter.[103] The attorney general then prayed that the first jury "be grievously fined." The court fined George Pye, perhaps the foreman, two thousand pounds of tobacco. The attorney then made an information against Pye for contempt for having reproached the whole court "in an insolent manner" for saying "if an Englishman had beene killed by the Indians there would not have beene so much words made of it." The court fined Pye another thousand pounds of tobacco for contempt.[104]

Benefit of Clergy

After the jury had returned the verdict of guilty, the court asked the prisoner if he had any reason why judgment should not be given. The most common plea to arrest judgment was that of benefit of clergy. The origins of this curiosity are clear enough, though the history of its development is complex. In the beginning men actually in holy orders made the plea, claiming that they could not be tried in the king's courts. The judges then turned the prisoner over to the bishop to be tried in his courts. Along one line of development, the plea was gradually extended to classes of nonclerical persons. Sometime a man had pled that though he was not in orders, he was qualified to be a clerk and offered as evidence his ability to read. Over centuries, benefit of clergy was extended to all men who could read, then to women, and finally to all whether they could read or not.[105]

In the early seventeenth century, benefit of clergy was restricted to men who could read. The convicted felon asked for his book, which was, of course, the Bible. Usually the Bible opened to Psalm 51, its opening sentence being the "neck verse": "Have mercy upon me, O God, according to thy loving kindness; according unto the multitude of thy tender mercies blot out my transgressions." After the defendant had read or recited the words, the court proceeded to judgment, which consisted of branding him on the brawn of the left thumb: "M" for a homicide less than murder, usually manslaughter, and "T" for theft. He might also have been imprisoned at the discretion of the court for up to one year, but this seems to have been done rarely. The brand permanently marked the man as a convicted felon. He could have benefit of clergy only once for one class of felony. Benefit of clergy was a highly irrational and erratic means of mitigating the consequences of an exceedingly severe penal law. It saved thousands from the gallows. The other line of development was the removal or ouster of clergy from specific felonies. Treason had never been clergyable nor had arson. The other main crimes for which statutes ousted clergy were murder, rape, buggery, robbery, and burglary. By the early eighteenth century, the question of what crimes were and what were not clergyable was nearly opaque.[106]

Benefit of clergy crossed the Atlantic to Maryland and Virginia in a reasonably pure form.[107] It existed in Maryland from the beginning. Thomas Smith, convicted of piracy in the wake of the first Kent Island imbroglio, demanded his clergy. He did so after judgment. The court ruled properly that there could be no clergy in piracy and that the plea had been made too late.[108] Apparently, John Dandy was given an opportunity to make the plea in an Indian homicide.[109] In 1638, the assembly passed "An Act allowing booke to certain Felonies."[110] The law both adhered to and departed from English rules. It first established a list of felonies punishable by death: manslaughter, arson, forgery, some forms of assault and mayhem, and servants running away, described as "Stealth of ones self." The law permitted clergy for these acts though the judgment was to lose a hand or to be burned in the hand or forehead. Though there are no other examples of clergy on the record of the Provincial Court before 1660, in time the plea became common.[111] The only successful uses of the plea of clergy occurred in Virginia. In January 1628, two men were tried for felonious killings resulting from fights. The juries returned verdicts of guilty of manslaughter. In both cases the record reads, the convict "being asked what hee had to say for himselfe that he ought not to dy demanded his Clergy whereupon hee was delyvered to the ordinary."[112]

It would have been unthinkable for the Puritan colonies to admit the process of benefit of clergy into their jurisdictions. They held it as a basic truth that literacy should lead to rectitude, certainly not to an escape from the consequences of sin and crime. Yet, their desire to make punishment more rational led them to admit a part of the concept, the identifying brand. By statute a convicted burglar or robber in Connecticut and Massachusetts was branded on the forehead with the letter "B" for a first offense, branded and whipped for a second, and executed as incorrigible for a third conviction.[113] In practice judges ordered convicts branded for all types of theft. In one instance a blasphemer was branded.[114] A Plymouth case suggests the parallel with formal benefit of clergy. Found guilty of manslaughter, Robert Latham "desired the benefitt of law, viz., a psalve [Psalm?] of mercye, which was granted him."[115] Though the Rhode Island code did not mention benefit of clergy by name, it clearly intended that it could not be used in murder, robbery, arson, sodomy, and buggery cases. The code made those crimes felonies of death, "without remedy."[116]

Judgment

The men who controlled judgment on both sides of the Atlantic thought that the punishments they imposed were just and humane. They meant that English and colonial law described the form of penalty to be imposed and that the punishments were neither cruel nor unusual. Sir William Blackstone would later describe prescript penalties as "one of the glories of our English law."[117] The Massachusetts codes stated that "And for bodily punishments, we allow none that are in-humane, barbarous or cruel."[118] The wide variety and frequent use of corporal punishment makes these claims ring strange in the modern ear. But seventeenth-century Englishmen were comparing their penalties with those used in Europe and in their own distant past. Lambarde noted that "our old" law had permitted such mutilations as "pulling out the tongue," "cutting off the nose," and taking away the private parts.[119] The *Constitutio Criminalis Carolina* (1532) of the Holy Roman Empire provided for the pulling away of flesh with red hot tongs before execution and such death penalties as drowning, burial alive, and breaking on the wheel.[120] In the early stages of settlement, the standards of certainty and humaneness were sometimes violated. As has been noted, each colony went through a period when magistrates imposed penalties at their discretion. The governors of early Virginia, first under Dale's Laws and later during the 1620s, imposed brutal punishments to beat servants and "lesser men" into submission. For an aggravated contempt, Richard Barnes had his arms broken and his tongue bored through and was forced to crawl through a guard of forty men who kicked him.[121]

English and colonial punishments were all public. The spectacles of retribution were intended as dramatic examples of the consequences of crime. Penalties ranged from hanging to admonition.

The lightest possible punishment was admonition, and New England magistrates used it frequently. They might admonish a first offender who was otherwise of good reputation. They also used admonition when evidence against a person was not clear though there was a strong suspicion of guilt. They clearly regarded admonition as a formal penalty. Such use of admonition is rarely found in the Chesapeake colonies.[122]

The most common punishment was a fine payable in money or tobacco. Persons paid fines as all or a part of their punishment for a wide range of transgressions. Winthrop used fines as an example in his argument against prescript penalties. The penalty should cause pain, and a fine that would be a grievous burden to a poor man could be seen as a cheap license to err by a wealthy one.[123] The fine was commonly paid into the public treasury, but a portion of it might be assigned to a specific purpose. The Massachusetts Court of Assistants fined a man £20 for "haveing gotten a slutt with child." Half went to the colony treasury, half to the town of Salem to maintain the child.[124] Another form of monetary penalty was awards, usually in addition to a fine, to an injured party. Judges commonly made such awards in cases of assault and slander.[125] Multiple restitution in larcency and forgery was a kind of award, and courts frequently required such payments.[126] An unusual Massachusetts case apparently shows how long Magna Carta could cast its shadow. The ancient rule limited amercements so that they would not deprive a man of his means of livelihood. The Massachusetts General Court fined Marmaduke Mathewes, the teacher at the Malden church, £10 for "unsound expression in his publick teachinge." The marshal could find nothing that valuable among Mathewes's possessions except his books. The court respited the fine "til other goods appear besides books."[127]

By a variety of means short of corporal punishment, courts forced public displays of guilt. They required penance, either in court or some other public place.[128] Drunks wore the letter "D," adulterers the letter "A." Others stood in front of the church draped in white sheets. Two fornicators stood an hour in the marketplace with "a paper in great letters, on their hats."[129] Some who avoided the gallows because of lack of evidence or lack of explicit law wore a rope noose around their necks. Edward Saunders, for a rape not proved, wore a rope "openly to be seene hanging downe two foot long." Daniel Fairfield, convicted of sexually molesting young girls, had a halter put around his neck in 1642. Ten years later his wife successfully petitioned the General Court that he be permitted to take it off.[130] All punishments were ignominious, but some were designed to fit a special misdemeanor, especially slanderous gossip. A person with a loose tongue might find it clamped in a cleft stick.[131] Gossips sometimes had their mouths shut with water, were immersed from a ducking stool, or dragged through the water behind a canoe.[132]

Some forms of confinement also made possible a public display of the miscreant. Most towns had a set of stocks which served as a place of temporary confinement after arrest as well as a place of confinement later.[133] Alongside the stocks there might be a pillory, which, in addition to being a place of public confinement, also was the scene of the most frequent mutilation, usually a perjurer losing one or both ears.[134] Others were sentenced to lie for a time "neck and heels."[135]

Prisons and jails posed a problem because they were expensive to build and maintain. Although recognizing the need, a colony might go for years before actually building one.[136] Though there might be simple cages in the villages, usually a whole colony shared a single prison, and the sheriff or constable took serious offenders to it. A Maryland sheriff made his plight clear. When the court questioned him about the escape of the notorious Richard Ingle, he responded that he had "no prison but his owne hands."[137] Sentence to a term in prison occurred very rarely.[138] The Rhode Island code, explaining its deviation from English law, which required a prison sentence for riot, said that "Such long time of imprisonment . . . suits not the constitution of our place."[139] Some statutes did provide for long terms of confinement, but there is no evidence that such sentences were imposed.[140] Jails were used most commonly to hold persons accused of serious crimes before trial and to detain convicted persons until they could pay fines or make restitution.

Another form of denial of freedom as punishment was indentured servitude. Sentencing judges used the term "slavery." A person already a servant and not able to pay a fine would have his or her term of service extended. Virginia obviously used extended service to control servant behavior. In addition to being whipped, John Joyse, a runaway and a thief, served his master six more months and then was delivered to the court to serve the colony for five additional years. Henry Carman had been one of a shipload of boys sent to Virginia in 1619 by James I. A clause in their indentures provided that if they committed "any great malice" they should begin a new seven-year term of service. In 1626, with his time almost served, Carman was charged with impregnating a servant girl and was sentenced to the new term for fornication.[141] Free persons without means could be "condemned to slavery" to make restitution for theft or for other offenses.[142] Judges also used this punishment as a means of controlling those who deviated from social standards. Poor Web Abbey was an erratic hermit in Plymouth, where neither hermits nor nonconformists were wanted. For working on Sunday, disorderly living, idleness, and "nastyness," the court sentenced him to find a master, saying that if he could not the court would. Apparently he could not, so the next court assigned him to Governor Thomas Prince. Anticipating that Prince might "dislike" Web, the court said that it would find another master if necessary. Abbey soon offended again, and the court sentenced him to be whipped and, finally, out of patience, put him in jail.[143]

In both England and America, whipping was the most common corporal punishment. Usually the judge specified the number of lashes, but sometimes the sentence was simply "whipped" or "whipped severely." Massachusetts explicitly recognized the biblical rule and limited whipping to no more than thirty-nine stripes.[144] This seems to have been the rule everywhere, though there is a single example of a Virginia court ordering sixty stripes.[145] Class lines appeared clearly, and such a penalty as whipping was not to be imposed "upon a gentleman."[146] That whipping was seen as the equivalent of a fine can be seen in the Massachusetts Laws and Liberties. No man was to be whipped if he could give other satisfaction "unless his crime be very shamefull, and his course of life vitious and *profligate*."[147] The well-to-do paid; the poor suffered. Men and women were whipped most commonly for theft and fornication, but also for blasphemous expression, running away, "drinking tobacco," adultery, "lude & sodomiticall practices," "dalliance," and even for "puting his hand under a girles coates." Judges showed some mercy. A pregnant woman would not be whipped. A man suspected of adultery was to be whipped "when his health permits."[148] Dorothy Temple was to be whipped twice for having had a bastard son. Because she fainted after the first whipping, the second was not administered.[149]

In addition to other penalties, some offenders might suffer civil disabilities, disfranchisement, or at the extreme, banishment. None of these penalties was much in use in England in the early seventeenth century, nor did they become part of the law in Maryland and Virginia.[150] The New England colonies of Plymouth, Massachusetts, and Connecticut regarded those who lived in their communities as having made a free choice to do so and thus obligated to obey the rules. A man who qualified as a freeman held rights that could be forfeited if he violated the obligation. In Connecticut, a person fined or whipped "for any scandalous offence" lost his right to vote or to serve on juries.[151] A Plymouth order of 1658 barred Quakers from being freemen, but also provided that any person judged to be "grosly scandalouse as lyers drunkards Swearers &C shall lose theire freedome of this Corporation."[152] Plymouth applied the stricture of disfranchisement primarily, but not exclusively, to persons who cooperated with Quakers.[153]

From the beginning, Massachusetts banished persons who threatened church and state. A statute of 1644, though aimed at Anabaptists, described the persons who would be subject to banishment: "Incendiaries of Commonwealths . . . Infectors of persons in main matters of Religion . . . Troublers of Churches."[154] The magistrates had seen Roger Williams and the Antinomians as fitting this description and had banished them. Samuel Gorton and his company had been forced out.[155] From time to time others had been banished for speaking or writing against the government, for adultery, and for calling the Boston church "a whoare, a strumpet."[156] The most concentrated use of banishment came in the late 1650s in a concerted drive to exclude and expel the Quakers. They had arrived in Boston in 1656, and before the year was out Massachusetts recommended to the United Colonies of New England that each jurisdiction banish them. Connecticut, Plymouth, and Massachusetts all put laws on their books.[157] Only the Massachusetts law provided the death penalty if expelled Quakers returned. Quakers had Plymouth in turmoil during the years 1657–60. They actively proselytized, refused to take any oath, and acted with contempt of authority in and out of court. In 1658, the General Court appointed a day of humiliation because of the "signes of Gods displeasure." Among the signs was the "leting loose as a scourge upon us those freeting gangreinlike doctrines and persons commonly called Quakers."[158] The Plymouth courts gave Quakers forty-eight hours to get out of the jurisdiction and caused them to be whipped if they returned.[159] Massachusetts Bay pursued a sterner policy. Five or six banished Quakers returned. Quite obviously seeking martyrdom, four of them—William Robbinson, Marmaduke Stephenson, Mary Dyer, and William Ledra—died on the gallows.[160]

In England, the sentence after conviction and judgment in virtually all felonies was death. Though remnants of other modes of execution remained, the judgment was usually that the prisoner be taken to the place from whence he came and be hanged by the neck until dead. The American colonies used the same forms of judgment and execution. Authorities in both England and America meant the hangings to be spectacles so that the example of the fruits of crime could be impressed on the people. A clergyman was present at all executions to do what might be done for the soul of the doomed. In the Puritan colonies the practice developed of delivering a sermon either before the execution or at the gallows. These took the form of a recital of the confession of the condemned, usually a brief autobiography that showed how small sins had progressed inevitably to enormous crimes. The minister wove the appropriate scriptural text and comment into the sermon.[161] An attenuated account of a gallows or near gallows sermon survives from the period before 1660. Mary Martin murdered her bastard daughter, the issue of an adulterous relationship. After conviction, the ministers worked for her redemption. Reverend Wilson wrote to her in prison and

That Renowned Man, Old Mr. *Cotton* also, did his part in endeavoring that she might be renewed by Repentance; and Preached a Sermon on Ezek. 16. 20, 21. *Is this of thy Whoredoms a small matter, that thou has Slain my Children?* Whereof great notice was taken. It was hoped, that these Endeavours were not Lost: Her Carriage in her Imprisonment, and at her Execution, was very *Paenitent.* But there was this Remarkable at her Execution: She acknowledged her *Twice* Essaying to kill her Child, before she could make an End of it: and now, through the Unskilfulness of the Executioner, she was turned off the Ladder *Twice,* before She Dyed.[162]

Through the first half of the seventeenth century, Englishmen of a wide variety of persuasions condemned both the high incidence of the death penalty and the capriciousness with which it was applied.[163] They especially criticized the harshness of death as a penalty for minor larcenies. If Bacon, Coke, Cromwell, and the Levellers could agree, then indeed a broad spectrum of Englishmen felt the necessity of this reform.[164] Addressing the Parliament in 1656, Cromwell said,

> But the truth of it is, There are wicked and abominable Laws, that it will be in your power to alter. To hang a man for Six pence, thirteen pence, I know not what; to hang for a trifle, and pardon murder, is in the ministration of the Law, through the ill-framing of it. I have known in my experience abominable murders acquitted. And to come and see men lose their lives for petty matters: this is a thing that God will reckon for. . . . This hath been a great grief to many honest hearts and conscientious people; and I hope it is all in your hearts to rectify it.

Certain mitigating factors had worked to lessen the severity of the English law. Examples abound at each step of the proceedings. In the Sussex quarter sessions records there are many examples of persons being fined for "taking" items valued at more than 12d. Though I have not seen the indictments upon which these prosecutions were based, probably the accusation of felonious intent had been omitted. By whose authority prosecutors or grand juries reduced a common law felony to a trespass is an interesting question.[165] More commonly, trial juries undervalued goods. Judges accepted virtual wholesale pleas of benefit of clergy. After 1624, statutory law spared women from execution upon convictions of larcenies to the value of 10 shillings.[166] The practice of substituting military service or transportation developed after 1615.[167] The king regularly pardoned felons.

An analysis of these modes of mitigation at the assizes has led a highly competent modern historian to conclude that the assizes were not as bloody as has been assumed.[168] Trials for larceny might amount to 70 to 90 percent of the criminal calendar, and the forms of mitigation were most likely to be used in such proceedings. Of those convicted of felony, fewer than 25 percent were executed. This analysis of mitigation and execution has led James S. Cockburn to dismiss Coke's conclusion of the *Third Institute* as "pious exaggeration."[169] Coke wrote:

What a lamentable case it is to see so many Christian men and women strangled on that cursed tree of the gallows, insomuch as if in a large field a man might see together all the Christians, that but in one year, throughout England, come to that untimely and ignominious death, if there were any spark of grace, or charity in him, it would make his heart bleed for pity and compassion.[170]

Well and good to point out that but for the mitigating factors the execution rate would have been trebled. What is unknown is what criteria led to the decisions to take the life of one convicted felon and spare the lives of three. When the full weight of mitigation has been given every allowance, may it not still be asked whether Coke's doleful picture is just by any humane standard: Twenty-two persons went to "that cursed tree of the gallows" each year in Devon.[171] Eighty-five persons were "strangled" or pressed to death in Middlesex in 1649 and this against a background of about forty each year during the reign of Charles I.[172]

Valid statistical comparison of the frequency of the death penalty in England and America is difficult because we know next to nothing about how many persons lived in the jurisdictions. Regardless, the gross evidence shows that capital laws and their execution in America were much less severe and certainly much less capricious. The colonists achieved the reforms that were being fruitlessly advocated in England. Clearly, the main explanation of the difference was that colonial legislation drastically reduced the number of acts punishable by death, especially by abolishing the death penalty for crimes against property.

Mitigating factors also operated in America, but were the very rare exception rather than the rule. A jury might find manslaughter rather than murder, and an occasional convict was permitted benefit of clergy. A person convicted of a capital crime could expect to be executed. Table 2.1 lists all of the executions found in the records before 1660. All persons convicted of capital sexual crimes and witchcraft were executed. Table 4.1 sets out the details of the homicides. Of the seventeen persons (eighteen prosecutions) tried for murder (including petit treason and infanticide), sixteen were executed. Mary Parsons escaped the gallows by dying in prison. Only one convicted murderer, John Dandy, was pardoned, and he was hanged subsequently for a second murder.[173]

TABLE 2.1. EXECUTIONS IN AMERICA BEFORE 1660

	Virginia[a]	Plymouth	Massa-chusetts	Maryland	Con-necticut	New Haven	Rhode Island	Total
1621–30	larceny buggery rape petit treason	murder					none	5
1631–40		murder[b](3)	murder murder infanticide	piracy			none	7
1641–50		buggery infanticide	murder buggery murder adultery[c](2) infanticide witch			murder buggery buggery	none	12
1651–60			witch Quaker Quaker Quaker Quaker	murder[d](2) murder	witch witch witch witch witch	buggery sodomy [adultery][e]	none	16
Totals	4	6	15	4	5	6	0	40

[a] The Virginia record ends in 1632. An undetermined number of Carib Indians were executed because of fear of them (*Va. Gen. Ct.*, 155).

[b] Three executed for one murder.

[c] Both parties executed.

[d] Two executed for one murder.

[e] See the reference in Franklin B. Dexter, ed., *New Haven Town Records, 1649–1684*, 2:32.

Consequences of Judgment

The first inevitable consequence of judgment of death in English law was attainder, which implied the tainting, staining, or blackening of the convict. The consequences of attainder were forfeiture and corruption of the blood. The personal and real property of the convicted traitor or felon was forfeited to the crown. As to land and buildings, the king had "year, day, and waste." In ancient times, this had meant that the king possessed the property for a year and a day and then literally caused it to be wasted. By the seventeenth century, the king had the profits of the property without waste. After the year and the day, the property reverted to the lord of the fee, the man from whom the convict had held the land. Corruption of the blood extended the effect of judgment to the convict's family. Corruption worked both forward and backward so that none could inherit property or titles from or through the condemned person.[174] Seventeenth-century Englishmen put the abolition of forfeiture and corruption of the blood into their catalog of necessary reform.[175]

The United States Constitution bars both forfeiture and corruption of the blood.[176] The prohibition stems from the very beginnings of American law. The main exceptions to the English law of forfeiture and corruption were the customary gavelkind tenures of Kent. There sons inherited equally on the death of the father. As to forfeiture, the exception was expressed in the earthy rule, "the father to the bough, the son to the plough."[177] Several colonies explicitly barred forfeiture. The Massachusetts Body of Liberties of 1641 stated, "All of our lands and heritages shall be free from . . . yeare and day and wast, Escheats and forfeitures, upon the deaths of parents, or Ancestors, be they naturall, casuall, or Juditiall."[178] Connecticut copied this rule.[179] The Rhode Island code explained the reasons for barring forfeitures. Noting that title to land originated in the towns, which were all represented in the assembly, it followed that the towns could waive forfeiture. The assembly, "conceiving the wives and children ought not to bear the iniquities of the Husbands and Parents[,] propagate[d] that countrie proverbe in Providence Plantation, 'The Father to the Bough and the Son to the Plow.'"[180] Plymouth passed no statutory bar to forfeiture, and a single entry in a manslaughter case indicates a possible forfeiture though there is no record of such an action.[181]

Because Virginia and Maryland were organized as royal and proprietary colonies, the English rules of forfeiture could have applied there. But both court records and statutes are thin in the early period for Virginia, and practice is impossible to determine. In 1656, a statute passed which enacted that the estate of a man "condemned and executed" would remain with his wife and children.[182] In Maryland, forfeitures could have been profitable for the Calverts. The early legislative judgments against Thomas Smith and William Claiborne forfeited all their lands, goods, and chattels to the lord proprietor.[183] In 1642, a statute provided for both forfeiture and corruption of the blood in cases of treason and murder. Another law of the same session which defined ten "lesse Capitall Offences" provided for forfeiture as an optional punishment rather than as an inevitable consequence of judgment.[184]

Reprieve and Pardon

By issuing a reprieve, an English judge suspended execution for a period of time. He might do so because of a procedural flaw, inadequate evidence, or mitigating circumstances. The king could also grant reprieves. Reprieves came automatically to a condemned pregnant woman or a person judged insane. For the pregnant woman, the reprieve was usually a delay of execution until she could be delivered of the child. The reason for not executing a sentence on the insane was the belief that they would not feel the pain; hence they were not executed until they regained their sanity. A pardon was a royal act of mercy deriving from the pledge in the coronation oath to do justice and mercy. A pardon could be special or general, affecting an individual, a class of convicts, or all condemned persons. It might be absolute or conditional. By his charter of pardon the king could set aside execution and forfeiture, but only Parliament could remove corruption of the blood. Because of abuses, Parliament had several times restrained the prerogative of pardon, but a statute of Henry VIII had swept away the restrictions. Parliament could also issue pardons.[185]

The Massachusetts Body of Liberties provided that the governor might reprieve, but only the General Court could pardon "a condemned malefactor."[186] The court used this power sparingly,[187] though at times they were virtually swamped with petitions for abatement of fines.[188] Though there was no provision for pardon in the laws of Rhode Island or Connecticut, a convict doubtless could have petitioned the legislature for remission or pardon.[189] In the beginning, James I reserved the right of pardon for himself in Virginia.[190] Later commissions gave the governors the power to pardon except for treason and murder, in which cases he could reprieve until the king's pleasure could be known.[191] In Maryland, the Calverts clearly regarded the power to pardon as one of their "Royall Rights Jurisdictions and prehemencies." The proprietor delegated the authority to the governor. Because chaotic Maryland politics produced several armed revolts, the governors had ample chance to pardon, the alternative having been to hang half the population. Executive pardons of every type are on the record: for specific crimes, piracy and murder; general pardons of rebels, excepting the leaders; pardon of rebel leaders with condition that they hold no office and post large bonds; a general pardon commemorating Oliver Cromwell's installation as lord protector.[192] Except for these political pardons in Maryland, the power to pardon played virtually no role in mitigating the effects of judgment in the colonies.

Due Process

Criminal procedure in early America moved in the direction of fairness. The colonial law anticipated the form and much of the substance of modern concepts of due process. As to form, colonial legislators established durable precedent by making explicit statements concerning procedure and the rights of individuals. The Massachusetts Body of Liberties was a model for bills of rights. A composite of procedural rights can be constructed from colonial precept and practice:

1. No search or seizure without warrant.
2. Right to reasonable bail.
3. Confessions out of court invalid.
4. Right to have cause determined with reasonable speed.
5. Grand jury indictment in capital cases.
6. Right to know the charges.
7. Straightforward pleading with double jeopardy barred.
8. Right to challenge jurors.
9. Process to compel appearance of witnesses for the defense.
10. Right to confront accusers.
11. Trial by jury.
12. Limitation of punishment to the convict: no corruption of the blood or forfeiture.
13. No cruel or unusual punishment.
14. Equal protection of the law: dependent classes—women, children, and servants—have access to the courts.
15. Equal execution of the law: no capricious mitigation or application of penalties.
16. Right of appeal.

The recognition of these rights in the colonial jurisdictions extended and clarified concepts of fair procedure that, in people's imaginations at least, stretched back to Magna Carta. In the immediate context of the early seventeenth century, the articulation of some of these rights represented practical realization of one category of change being advocated by the English law reformers. For the future, they laid a comprehensive concept of due process at the base of the criminal justice systems of new societies. That these rights might sometimes be violated in practice will come as no surprise to the twentieth-century observer of the criminal law in action.

Chapter Three

Courts and Officers

In the early seventeenth century, lawmaking and judgment remained closely related in both England and the colonies. The modern editor of *De Republica Anglorum* noted that Sir Thomas Smith did not separate the legislative and judicial functions "with the sharp hatchet of a theory." Commentators and text writers referred to the High Court of Parliament. Lambarde called Parliament "our *chiefe* and *highest Court.*" Its legislation was judgment rendered to resolve issues in new cases or amend errors in old ones. In describing the means by which "absolute and definite judgment" could be given, Smith listed judgment by Parliament first, followed by judgment resulting from trial by battle or jury. Parliament could render judgment in any case "criminall or civill" by private bill but seldom did so because it was preoccupied with public affairs.[1]

Parliament continued to try or otherwise dispose of a limited number of criminal cases. A peer of the realm accused of treason or felony stood trial before the House of Lords or the Court of the Lord High Steward. The Houses of Parliament might proceed against any subject by bill of attainder. Because Parliament could define crime by statute, it could attaint a person by legislation, in effect making law and rendering judgment in the same stroke. Rarely used, this aribtrary process could reach powerful persons, usually officers of state, when a parliamentary majority thought that neither ordinary trial nor impeachment would produce a conviction.

Parliament more commonly proceeded against persons of high position by impeachment. In such proceedings, Parliament tried offenders whose actions had damaged the commonwealth. The House of Commons, acting as the grand inquest of the nation, made the charge in a bill of impeachment. The House of Lords tried the case. Though impeachments occurred with some regularity in times of high political excitement, the process was used infrequently in the early seventeenth century.[2]

In the *Fourth Institute*, Coke described the organization and jurisdiction of more than one hundred distinct courts. Of these, four courts—Kings Bench, assizes, quarter sessions, and leets—served in one way or another as models for or sources of colonial criminal jurisdiction.[3] In addition, justices of the peace, alone or in combination out of sessions, performed essential functions in the criminal justice system.

At the apex, seated at Westminster, was the Kings Bench.[4] It had originally followed the king about the country, and through it he rendered justice directly. The chief judge of Kings Bench was the chief justice of the realm. The court had a virtually unlimited original jurisdiction extending from treason through the felonies and down to the smallest misdemeanor that affected the public peace. We know most about criminal causes tried there from the records of famous cases in the *State Trials*. In the early seventeenth century, the reports of its decisions depended on selections made independently by the reporters. Kings Bench also exercised broad supervisory powers. Cases pending or determined in any court in England might be removed and brought before it by writs of error or *certiorari*.

The courts of assize[5] carried the main burden of judging serious crimes, especially felonies. The practice of sending the king's judges into the counties to administer justice was very old. By the mid-fourteenth century, England had been divided into six circuits. The judges and sergeants of the central courts rode these circuits, usually twice a year. Charged with enormous political, administrative, and judicial responsibilities in the Star Chamber before they departed from London, the assize judges were a vital instrument of crown control of the counties. They carried five commissions that empowered them to try cases. The three major criminal commissions were those of gaol delivery, oyer and terminer, and the peace. The commission of gaol delivery authorized the judges to try persons in custody; that of oyer and terminer authorized them to hear and determine, that is, to receive new indictments and try the accused. Attended on their progress with high ceremony, these judges carried with them the awesome power of life and death. They were imperious men, charged with the duty to do brutal work. A complete catalog for the Devon Assizes for the years 1589 through 1639 survives. Of all indictments tried, 70 percent were for larceny, 10 percent for homicide, and 5 percent for witchcraft. The remaining 15 percent were scattered through the rest of the felonies. During those years, 511 persons were executed at this assize, an average of 50 persons each term.[6] The work at the circuit was not only brutal but fast. The judges might determine as many as fifty crown pleas in a single day.

Within the counties, the judicial workhorse was the quarter session. These courts met four times each year, the bench consisting of the justices of the peace.[7] Appointed by the crown since 1327, these men were originally called either conservators or keepers of the peace. The old statutes prescribed that they were to be "good men and lawful" or men "of the best reputation."[8] By the end of the fourteenth century, their original police function had been transformed into a judicial one and they had become the modern justice of the peace empowered to "hear and determine at the King's suit all manner of felonies and trespasses."[9]

During the late sixteenth and early seventeenth centuries, both the quality of the men in the commissions of the peace and their functions were changing. The number of men put into the commission for each county grew rapidly. The charge was often heard that many of them were no longer "of the best reputation."[10] The commissions always designated certain justices to be of the quorum. The intent had been that those of the quorum were men of special integrity with a knowledge of the law gained either by experience or training. At least one of the quorum had to be present at the quarter sessions. In the early seventeenth century, social and political considerations intruded upon the quorum appointments to such a degree that the designation lost both its usefulness and its dignity.[11]

The justices received their authority from the commission and statutes that assigned specific responsibility to them. The statutory burden increased enormously in the Tudor-Stuart period, especially in the area of economic and social administration. The judges of the central courts gave the commission its definitive modern form in 1590. As to the criminal jurisdiction of the quarter sessions, the commission authorized the justices to "hear and determine all felonies . . . trespasses . . . and all other crimes and offences of

which such justices may or ought lawfully to inquire." This broad
authorization was conditioned by the clause that "if a case of difficulty shall arise they shall not proceed to give judgment except in
the presence of some justice of one of the benches or of assize."[12]
The "case of difficulty" clause had the effect of reducing the number of felonies tried at the quarter sessions. Yet an appreciable number of capital cases continued to be determined there; for example,
there were 109 executions at the Devon Quarter Sessions from 1598
to 1639 and 8 in Somerset between 1625 and 1640.[13] Regardless of
these figures, the responsibility of the justices in capital cases was
being reduced to original inquiry and prosecution at the assize.[14]

Justices out of sessions continued to try minor criminal offenses,
many of them summarily as provided by statute. The breadth of
their duties is indicated by the fact that the whole of Dalton's *Countrey Justice*, 372 pages, dealt only with the duties out of sessions.
Many of the statutes assigned responsibilities to two or more justices. Because it was often inconvenient for them to meet in response to specific situations, the petty sessions emerged in the early
seventeenth century. For petty sessions, justices of a defined dis-
trict of the county met at a specific time and place.[15]

Scattered all over England in 1600 were hundreds, perhaps thousands, of local courts. These courts baron and courts leet were inci-
dences of a franchise and were held either by the lord of a manor or
a borough corporation. The franchise had been created either by
prescriptive custom or royal grant. The court baron dealt with obli-
gations related to copyhold tenure and was not a court of record.
The court leet was a royal court of record. The leet had a broad
criminal jurisdiction. In it justice was done in the king's name,
though the fees and fines belonged to the holder of the franchise.
The lawyers saw court baron and court leet as two distinct tribunals. The men who owed "suit service" at the court baron were
the "homage." At the leet, men owed "suit real" and collectively
were the "jurors." Regardless of the lawyers' rule, in practice the
two courts tended to be melded together.[16] The pervasiveness of the
leet is made clear by the rule: "Everyone is in some Leet."[17]

The jurisdiction of each leet was set out in its articles of view, and
though these articles varied, they had much in common, including
view of frankpledge, which by this time meant assurance that all
had taken the oath of allegiance; matters that could be inquired into

and presented but not punished, primarily the common law felonies; matters that could be determined in the leet, among them "common annoyances," damage to the environment, certain assaults, "evil persons," breaches of the assize of ale and bread, and duties imposed by statutes regulating, among many other matters, hunting, apparel, conspiracy to raise wages, highway repair, and drunks.[18] Taken together with the courts baron, the leets had broad authority to regulate affairs between individuals and to protect the public economy, morals, and peace of those "little Commonwealths," the manor and borough.[19]

By 1660, the main features of leet procedure can be generalized,[20] though specific practice might vary. The leet might meet as often as every three weeks or as infrequently as once a year. The meeting was "law day." Its presiding officer, the steward,[21] read the articles of view, which described the duties to be discharged. The articles were addressed to ordinary suitors who bore the high-sounding name of "chief pledges." The pledges were in fact becoming petty officials, the equivalent of a constable. A jury then examined the accusations made by the pledges. These jurors were "the twelve men for the king," though if they are counted there may have been more. The jurors were drawn from among the more responsible men who had been required to attend the leet. If the jurors presented a person for felony, the case would go to the next assize for trial. If they unanimously presented a person for a lesser offense, the presentment amounted to both verdict and judgment. The presentment in a leet could not be traversed unless it affected life or freehold. Presentment was the "truth" in John Kitchin's words "as Evangelist."[22] The penalty imposed by a leet could be no more than a fine. Leet procedure created an efficient system that combined accusation, verdict, and judgment in a single agency. Its fairness depended on the conscience of the neighborhood.

Colonial Legislatures as Courts

From the beginning, colonial legislatures regarded themselves as the highest courts in their jurisdictions. The model of Parliament was obvious. The chief difference between the colonial legislatures and Parliament, as courts, was that the colonial legislatures heard ordinary criminal cases in original jurisdiction.

The only colonial bills of attainder passed before 1660 were in Maryland, where, in a turbulent time, the assembly resorted to this summary procedure. When Leonard Calvert tried to oust William Claiborne, an energetic Virginia trader, from Kent Island in Chesapeake Bay, the parties fought a small naval engagement that resulted in deaths on both sides. The assembly tried one of Claiborne's lieutenants, Thomas Smith, for piracy. In the first instance Smith was indicted, tried, found guilty, and sentenced to death. The assembly then confirmed the sentence with a regular bill that was passed by normal legislative procedure. It appeared that Smith had been twice attainted, once by conviction after trial and once by legislative bill. Because Claiborne had not been captured, the assembly proceeded against him with a bill of attainder. His prosecutors fired a scatter-gun of charges against him and noted that a grand jury had already indicted him for piracy and murder. The assembly then attainted Claiborne by bill and declared his real and personal property forfeited to Baltimore.[23] Maryland had used the exceptional and arbitrary instrument of a bill of attainder in the first, unsteady weeks of settlement to condemn expeditiously two men who could not be controlled by ordinary process. That no other colony used bills of attainder in these years perhaps reflects a prejudice against a fundamentally arbitrary procedure.

There were no formal impeachments in the colonies before 1660. Because the governor and councillors or assistants constituted the highest regular court in all colonies, these officers could only have been indicted and tried before the entire legislature instead of the upper house alone. In Maryland, such a trial would have been a gross interference with the Calverts' prerogative, and there were no impeachments there before 1660. The legislative trial of a Virginia governor or councillor would have seemed an encroachment on royal prerogative. Regardless, Virginians brought a governor to trial in a process closely resembling impeachment.

In 1635, the House of Burgesses began proceedings against Governor John Harvey because of discontent with his administration, especially his Indian policy. The lower house set out its grievances in a petition to the council. At a special session of the legislature, Harvey refused an invitation to defend himself, and the council dismissed him from office. By dismissing him, the council had gone to the limits of and probably exceeded its power. The council sent

Harvey and its charges back to England, where it apparently hoped for judgment in the Privy Council. That body took a dim view of the Virginians' action and sent Harvey back to the colony. Though exceptional, the "trial" of Harvey demonstrates the colonists' concept of the inherent and ultimate judicial powers of the legislature.[24] Because the New England legislatures elected governors and assistants, the trial of malfeasance by these officers could only be before the general courts.[25] The only trial of such an official there was that of Deputy Governor John Winthrop in Massachusetts. The charge against him was that he had exceeded his authority as a judge. The General Court acquitted.[26]

Parliament exercised no first instance jurisdiction over criminal offenses except in impeachments. Following a different course, colonial legislatures occasionally took such cases in original jurisdiction. In Virginia and Maryland, the assemblies rarely tried criminals, and the very few cases on the record appeared during the first years of settlement. The first Virginia legislature sentenced a servant to the pillory and a whipping for "neglect of his master's business and impudent abuse." At the other end of the social scale, they tried Captain Henry Spelman for illegal correspondence with the Indians and imposed the unusual punishment of seven years of service as the governor's interpreter.[27] An act of 1656 apparently confirmed the right of the burgesses to take any case in the event that it met before the regular council court, but they did not involve themselves in ordinary judicial business.[28] In Maryland, the Calverts guarded their exclusive rights of jurisdiction. Considering the one "trial" on the assembly record, it was well that they did. In 1638, after a servant had been accused of theft and flight, the members of the house were polled individually to determine punishment. One member thought that he should be hanged, but the sentiment of the majority was that he be whipped "three several times."[29]

When the general courts of New England met they had a sense of competence to do whatever business came to their attention. They heard cases in original jurisdiction and on appeal. The Rhode Island code of 1647 provided for a superior criminal court, the Court of Tryals. For nearly a decade the entire assembly convened itself into this court after it finished its legislative business.[30] The Fundamental Orders of Connecticut assigned the administration of justice

to the elected governor and magistrates. The orders were not specific in defining the power of the General Court, but declared it to
be the "supreme power," which might "deale in any other matter
that concerns the good of this commonwelth."[31] In fact, the General Court tried very few cases. Two of the five cases on the record
from 1640 to 1660 dealt with verbal criticism of government and
were, perhaps, contempt of the assembly or the equivalent of seditious libels.[32] On other occasions the court fined a man £10 for "his
many misdemeanors" and ordered the arrest of an adulterer recently arrived from Massachusetts.[33] The cases support no generalization other than that the General Court had original jurisdiction if
it chose to exercise it.

The Plymouth codes gave the governor the option to bring cases in
original jurisdiction either to the assistants or the General Court.[34]
This he apparently did as a matter of convenience, and there is no
evidence of conflict over jurisdiction between the courts. The General Court heard the majority of the criminal cases before 1660, 84
percent of the total. The governor made no distinction about the
gravity of the crime in assigning cases. Both courts tried the common offenders—drunks, fornicators, and thieves—and at the other
end of the spectrum of crime, each tried one murderer.[35]

In contrast to Plymouth and Connecticut, the assistants and
deputies in Massachusetts Bay often disputed jurisdiction. From the
beginning, the General Court occasionally tried cases that fell within
the ordinary jurisdiction of the assistants or county courts.[36] More
commonly it tried serious cases that had some special quality. For
example, the early law in relation to adultery was unclear, the death
penalty having been based in an order of the assistants. In 1636, the
Boston Quarter Court found Margaret Seale and two men guilty of
adultery. Unwilling to impose the death penalty in the absence of a
statute, the assistants referred the case to the General Court, which
ordered the offenders whipped and banished.[37] The General Court
heard several other cases of adultery before the code of 1648 settled
the law.[38] The court also tried Daniel Fairfield for having sexual intercourse with two young girls. It then passed a law providing the
death penalty for such acts.[39]

During the 1630s, the General Court conducted the great state
trials involving "Dangerous opinions," "defamation" of magistrates

and churches, "contempt & sedition," and "traducing the ministers and their ministery." For such words and actions, the court banished Roger Williams, John Wheelwright, and Anne and William Hutchinson. In 1643, the court banished Samuel Gorton, "a blasphemous enemy of the true religion" and an enemy "of all civil authority." Robert Child and his associates also stood their trials before the General Court.[40] In these cases the General Court made it clear by their actions and the rhetoric of their charges that they alone dealt with the highest crimes against the commonwealth—heresy and sedition.

The New England legislatures thus had within them all of the elements of a law court. The governor and assistants, who were the judges in the regular courts, always attended. The deputies were obviously qualified as jurors. But it is not clear how these legislative courts proceeded. Actions might begin on the complaint of an individual, usually in the form of a petition. Probably assistants and deputies could bring charges based on their own knowledge. Regular grand juries commonly attended the sessions. In Connecticut the grand jury was to present "breches of any laws" to the General Court, but this did not lead the court into much criminal business.[41] In 1635 the Massachusetts deputies ordered a grand jury to attend its sessions to present "breaches of any order, or other misdemeanors."[42] At the next General Court, Winthrop noted the presence of "the first grand jury, who presented above one hundred offenders, and, among others, some of the magistrates."[43] The record is silent as to who these persons were or what their offenses might have been, nor is the presence of grand juries at subsequent sessions apparent. In Plymouth the grand juries made the bulk of the presentments to the General Court.[44]

It is unclear whether at a trial in the New England legislatures the assistants acted as judges and the deputies as juries or whether the court followed the normal legislative process of passing orders. In Massachusetts the former seems to have been the practice. A law of 1634 provided that no sentence of death or banishment could pass except by a jury verdict or by the General Court. Before proceeding to judicial business, the deputies took an oath: "I will deale uprightly & justly according to my judgment & conscience."[45] Except on appeals, the deputies and assistants voted separately, so that the one vote might have been seen as verdict, the other as judgment. The other New England records throw no light on judicial procedure in the legislatures.

The New England general courts held supreme judicial authority and could entertain criminal appeals. The Massachusetts Body of Liberties stated the principle of broad availability of appeal in homely, nontechnical language: "everie man shall have libertie to complaine to the Generall Court of any Injustice done him in any Court of Assistants or other [court]."[46] This general rule was probably applicable to aggrieved parties in all New England jurisdictions. Plymouth did not state such a rule explicitly, perhaps because there was no hierarchy of courts there and because the General and Assistants Courts shared jurisdiction harmoniously. A Connecticut order of 1644 granted a general right of appeal, and a Rhode Island law of 1650 seemed by its language to embrace criminal as well as civil appeals.[47] The New Haven code of 1656 gave the General Court, "the highest Court within this Jurisdiction," the power to hear "all causes . . . by appeal or complaint."[48] In Massachusetts the question of judicial appeals again raised the problem of the relative power of the assistants and deputies. As long as the assistants exercised the negative vote, they could control appeals from their own court. In 1649 this possibility was eliminated by the provision that the full General Court would decide appeals.[49] The General Court also decided cases in which the magistrates and a jury disagreed about a verdict.[50] There were virtually no appeals to the New England general courts except in Massachusetts, where most of the appeals requested that fines imposed by lower courts be reduced or canceled.[51]

Because authority to try criminal causes in Virginia and Maryland came down from king and proprietor, appeals logically ought to have been to them from the council court in the colony. The record relative to appeals in Maryland is blank. The Virginia assembly regarded itself as the court of last resort, especially in cases where the law was not clear. It would hear appeals directly from a county court as well as from the general or council court. Though concerned primarily with civil cases, a statute of 1656 made it clear that the assembly would also hear criminal appeals.[52]

Superior Courts

Colonial superior courts performed the criminal functions of the English Kings Bench and assize. Whether authority derived from charter, voluntary association, or royal instructions, the superior judicial power was vested in the executive and advisers, in the governor and councillors or assistants.[53] In the Chesapeake colonies, superior courts consisted of an appointed governor and council. In their judicial capacity, these officers were called the General or Quarter Court in Virginia and the Provincial Court in Maryland. In New England, the governor and assistants made up the superior court, and they were elected by either the freemen or the legislature. Plymouth and Massachusetts styled these courts the Assistants Court, Rhode Island the Court of Tryals, Connecticut the Particular Court, and New Haven the Court of Magistrates. Massachusetts sometimes referred to its superior court as the Particular Court to distinguish a court that dealt with individuals from the General Court where the business of all came under consideration.

Though numbers varied, typically five or six magistrates made up these courts. All superior courts had regular terms, but these varied from four times a year to monthly. In Rhode Island the sessions rotated through the four main towns of the jurisdiction. Though the Virginia court normally sat at Jamestown, it met fairly frequently in other towns. Elsewhere the sessions were held in the "capital." The superior courts appear to have gone about their business with a minimum of ceremony and procedural formality. They normally sat for a single day, often a long one. In any session they heard both criminal and civil causes.

Varying concepts of jurisdiction and the state of surviving records make comparisons of the work of the superior courts as higher court difficult.[54] The Plymouth Assistants Court always exercised a general criminal jurisdiction embracing matters that normally would have been determined in lower courts. A full record for the Massachusetts Assistants Court before 1660 survives largely for the time before local courts were established. In New Haven, the record of the Court of Magistrates before 1653 is essentially that of a borough court with a general criminal jurisdiction. After the union of the towns, the volume of criminal business in that court de-

clined, an indication that the town courts were disposing of many
minor cases. In Virginia and Maryland, the General and Provincial
Courts acted originally as county as well as superior courts. The
Virginia record before 1660 exists only for the period before regular county courts were established, though there were plantation
courts during the time covered by the extant record. The Maryland
Provincial Court left the fullest, most continuous record. Even
there, the high court continued with a fair degree of regularity to
hear minor cases after the establishment of the county courts. The
records in all jurisdictions indicate that minor offenses were not be-
neath the dignity of the high courts. When the court door opened,
the magistrates did whatever business needed to be done, be it felony or misdemeanor.

Regardless of the incompleteness of and problems in the records,
certain comparisons and conclusions can be made. One is that in all
courts criminal matters amounted to only a small fraction of the
work. Civil suits, probate business, and public administration filled
the court days. Another generalization that can be made about all
higher courts is that they had exclusive jurisdiction in capital cases.
This onerous duty occurred infrequently. All of these courts also
tried lesser crimes. Drunks and fornicators headed the list in the
higher courts just as they did in the local courts. Aside from these
offenders against morals, the most common criminal was the thief.
The other major categories were cases of assault and slander, which
the judges sometimes treated as civil action, sometimes as breaches
of the peace. Other offenses are scattered randomly over the map of
the common and statutory law. Table 3.1 shows the distribution of
types of crime handled by the superior courts.

The records of superior courts in all jurisdictions show that magistrates were concerned about morality, interpersonal violence, security of property, and social order. Beyond these similarities,
several of the records evidence the values and fears of the dominant
class as mirrored by the magistracy. The Virginia magistrates were
all drawn from the entrepreneur class that engrossed land and grew
tobacco on it. Understanding that their prosperity was based in a
large and obedient labor force, the General Court dealt with servants and "all lesser men" with a severity unmatched in any other
colony. The fact that Maryland was a proprietary colony gave the
record of the Provincial Court its own special quality, that of a judi-

TABLE 3.1. DISTRIBUTION OF BUSINESS
IN COLONIAL SUPERIOR COURTS BY CLASS OF CRIME[a]
(figures are percent of total)

	Virginia General Court 1622–29 67 items	Plymouth Particular & General Court 1633–60 260 items	Massachusetts Assistants Court 1630–43 290 items	Maryland Provincial Court 1630–60 100 items	Connecticut Particular Court 1639–60 193 items	New Haven Magistrates Court 1639–56[b] 104 items
Homicide	7.4	1.1	2.4	13	2.6	.96
Theft	10.4	10.3	13.1	9	8.8	16.0
Drunkenness	16.4	11.6	26.9		11.9	20.0
Slander[c]	12.0	3.0	1.4	21	22.3	16.0
Fornication	6.0	11.0	6.9	2	2.6	8.6
Other sex crimes[d]	9.0	3.0	2.4	7	2.1	8.6
Sexual behavior[e]	1.4	8.8	9.7	7	7.8	1.9
Sedition[f]	3.0	1.6	3.5	11	.5	1.9
Contempt	18.0	5.0	9.7	12	6.9	6.7
Religion[g]	3.0	21.9	1.4	5	5.2	5.7
Witchcraft	1.5			1	2.6	2.9
Servant[h]	3.0	2.7	9.7	5	2.6	2.9
Lying		1.9	1.0	1	2.6	6.7
Assault[i]	6.0	8.6	2.4	5	5.7	
Swearing		2.7	7.2	5	2.1	
Disorderly living[j]	3.0	6.6	2.0		12.4	
Arson		.3			1.0	1.0
Piracy				2		

[a] All incidents are recorded, whether they resulted in conviction, acquittal, or dismissal.

[b] The court records for New Haven from 1643 to 1653 have been lost.

[c] Slander and defamation. The actions were sometimes civil, sometimes criminal, sometimes mixed. Several cases that probably amounted to scandulum magnatum are included.

[d] Sodomy, bestiality, rape, and incest.

[e] Actions described variously as lewd behavior, filthy dalliance, unclean carriage, and lascivious conduct.

[f] Mostly seditious words, some aggravated contempts, generally acts conceived to be against the state, "treasonable practices."

[g] Nonchurch attendance, working on Sabbath, blasphemy, scoffing, or reviling church or ministers.

[h] Mostly runaways or court discipline of unruly servants, but a few cases involving abuse of servants by masters.

[i] Includes batteries; they might be civil, criminal, or mixed.

[j] A catch-all category, including unspecified "misdemeanors," living outside approved limits, idleness, smoking in unapproved areas, and general misbehavior not covered above by specific categories.

ciary involved in violent politics. The issue of loyalty to the Calverts surfaced again and again, generating repeated charges of sedition and treason. The bench of the Massachusetts Assistants Court was manned by a chosen few who were convinced of the rectitude of their efforts to build a holy "city on a hill." Their primary concerns were to compel or expel those whom they regarded as menacing to the "twinne sisters," their church and state, and to keep the sisters free from sin. The record of the New Haven Court of Magistrates is dominated by a concern about immoral acts, especially sexual ones. It shows a near paranoic fear of sex, being in places so graphically descriptive of the filthiness of illicit sex that the modern editor omitted much detail, presumably to protect the sensibilities of the heirs of those saints. Special emphases are less apparent in the superior court records of Plymouth, Connecticut, and Rhode Island. The terse and attenuated records of the latter two colonies do not display the rhetoric that reveals values in other jurisdictions. The record of the Rhode Island Court of Tryals is a chaotic fragment, perhaps indicating that the residents of the four towns chose to do their judicial business at home rather than in the central court. The proceedings before the Connecticut Particular Court show little evidence of conflict, perhaps suggesting that the river towns were relatively homogeneous societies with agreed-upon values. The Plymouth record more than that of any other court reflects the values of one man. It bears witness to William Bradford's frustrated efforts to maintain the standards of a small, like-minded religious community in the face of rapid growth.

Creation of the Colonial Local Courts

Except in Rhode Island, the colonial superior courts discharged all judicial functions during the early years of settlement. Population growth[55] and development of new settlements forced the creation of local courts. The parceling out of judicial authority varied from colony to colony and was affected either by demographic factors or concepts of social control. For example, though Plymouth, Rhode Island, and New Haven had small populations of about the same size scattered among several towns, the distribution of judicial authority produced different court systems. In 1650, each of these colonies had a population of about fifteen hundred persons.[56] There were a dozen towns in the Plymouth jurisdiction, five in New Haven, and four in Rhode Island. In each colony the outlying towns were a considerable distance from the main town, anywhere from twenty-five to forty miles. The difference in the division of authority between central and local courts in these colonies apparently must be sought elsewhere than in simple demographic facts.

From the beginning, Bradford wished to keep Plymouth a single, compact community because he believed such a community could better defend itself, maintain church discipline, and control behavior.[57] Nevertheless, the people spread out and founded new towns. Doubtless reflecting Bradford's policy, Plymouth, more than any other colony, concentrated authority to try criminal offenses in the central General and Assistants Courts. It did not create local courts, nor did it specifically authorize individual magistrates to try minor offenders in the villages.[58] The governor and two assistants could try minor offenses, but whether they ever traveled to outlying towns to use this authority is not apparent. The selectmen held town courts to settle minor civil disputes, but they apparently had no criminal jurisdiction other than to punish violators of the prudential orders of the towns.[59]

The people of Rhode Island lived in four fiercely independent towns. The colony was characterized by a primitive federalism that recognized a large measure of local autonomy. Originally the towns had been judicially independent of one another, and they confederated reluctantly in 1647. The code of that year gave the Court of Tryals exclusive jurisdiction over capital cases and causes between towns or residents of different towns.[60] The record of the Court of Tryals is very sparse and contains less than twenty cases clearly identifiable as criminal during the years 1649 to 1660.[61] The bulk of its business seems to have involved intertown relations. Faced with a nearly blank criminal record at the superior court level, one expects to find, but does not, a large number of criminal cases in the town courts.[62] From the surviving Rhode Island record, one would conclude that the colony was virtually free from crime, an unlikely occurrence.

New Haven also confederated, but with different purposes and results than Rhode Island. The founding of the New Haven towns reflected the desire of English Puritan ministers to establish communities of their own, where they intended to apply biblical law rigorously. John Davenport's New Haven became the model for Peter Prudden at Milford, Henry Whitfield at Guilford, and Richard Denton at Stamford.[63] In 1643, these towns agreed to fundamental orders. Implicit in this agreement was the principle made explicit in the code of 1656: the first principle of the colony was "the maintenance of the purity of Religion." The agreement of 1643 permitted the "free burgesses," that is, church members, to elect "ordinary judges." The criminal jurisdiction of these town courts was limited to cases in which the punishment did not exceed whipping or a fine of £5. If a magistrate lived in the town he sat with the court. Considering the godliness of the electorate, it would seem likely that these local judges would have maintained the desired standard of morality in the towns. Regardless, the code of 1656 imposed a greater degree of central control on these tribunals, now called plantation courts, by requiring the presence of a magistrate at all sessions. He was to be assisted by elected "deputies," presumably the same men who would represent the town in the General Court of the colony. These requirements put the control of local justice in the hands of men who formulated and administered policy for the entire jurisdiction. The code also provided another type of local court. In a "remote" town, the plantation court could call in two magistrates from other towns. This court would then have jurisdiction over all civil causes and any criminal case not involving the death penalty. By these provisions, the magistrates pervaded and controlled the local courts.[64] It is now impossible to determine how business was distributed between the Court of Magistrates and the plantation courts. The surviving town records are those of New Haven,[65] and it is probable that many of its ordinary criminal cases were tried before the Court of Magistrates. That court tried all cases of witchcraft and serious sexual crime that were most menacing to the security and purity of morals.

Connecticut was also a confederation of towns. Its population was about twice as large as that of New Haven and Rhode Island, and it was spread over a somewhat larger area. It approached the problem of decentralizing its judicial system somewhat differently than any other colony. Town courts were established early. In addition to exercising a limited civil jurisdiction, these courts could punish breaches of the towns' prudential orders.[66] The General Court gave individual magistrates the power to hear and determine misdemeanors specified by statute.[67] The Particular Court heard the serious cases in its sessions at Hartford. Occasionally the General Court authorized the governor or magistrates to go to the towns to try cases. This seems to have happened when a large number of witnesses were involved in a case, thus making trial at Hartford inconvenient and costly.[68] By using this irregular type of assize, Connecticut was the only colony to try serious crime by a process that resembled the English use of the special commission of oyer and terminer.

The surge of Englishmen into Massachusetts Bay brought its population to 14,047 by 1650. This rapid expansion caused the founders to fear that "worldly men [might] prove the major part."[69] Through most of the first decade, the magistrates controlled both their fellow saints and the "worldly men" by maintaining the exclusive criminal jurisdiction of the Court of Assistants. The development of towns caused the creation of four inferior quarter or particular courts. In 1642, the colony created four counties, Suffolk, Essex, Middlesex, and Norfolk. The particular courts then became county courts, with jurisdiction over all crimes except those involving life, member, or banishment.[70] Because a magistrate always sat with the county courts, there was a fair assurance of uniform supervision. From the beginning, the governor and assistants had been regarded as justices of the peace. As individual justices, their criminal jurisdiction stemmed not from a commission for the peace but from specific statutes.[71] The continued growth of population created a burden at the local level that the assistants could not carry. In 1657, the General Court began granting the power of a magistrate to selected persons who were not assistants.[72] To meet the problem of population growth, Massachusetts had adopted in rough outline the form of the English county judicial system. The Massachusetts system served the purpose of social control and the discipline of "worldly men" because the magistrates pervaded it from top to bottom.

By 1650, 18,731 persons lived in Virginia and 4,504 in Maryland. The people did not concentrate in towns, but scattered themselves along the shores and rivers on individual farms and plantations. The Virginians thought of themselves as being in a new England, and the Calverts obviously wanted to impose older English institutions on the new land. Both colonies turned to the county form of local government. At Jamestown and St. Mary's, the governors and councils acted from the beginning as county courts for the immediate vicinity.[73] Though the practice of holding monthly courts in Virginia antedated any statute, in 1624 the assembly passed a law providing for regular monthly courts at specified localities. In 1634, the assembly divided Virginia into "shires," and by the end of the decade, a regular system of county courts had been established.[74] From the beginning, Leonard Calvert treated the eastern and western shores of Maryland as the counties of St. Mary's and Kent. In 1637, he commissioned a commander for Kent and authorized him to establish a court.[75] The governors continued to create county courts by executive commission as new counties were formed.[76] At all times, the county courts in Virginia and Maryland had two common elements: the power of officers was defined in the same way as that of the English justice of the peace, and the criminal jurisdiction of the courts extended to all cases not involving life and limb.

There was no urgent, cohesive religious purpose in the Chesapeake colonies; the governors' motivations toward central control were political and economic. Appointment of the commissioners by the governors in both colonies assured a measure of such control. In Maryland, the commander, a kind of chief justice in the county, was usually a member of the council and thus also of the central court. Virginia attempted supervision by providing that councillors attend the county courts.[77] The governor and councillors were understood to be members of every county commission even though they were not specifically listed. Rapid expansion of the counties soon made attendance of the councillor at every session impossible.

In both Virginia and Maryland, individual commissioners had about the same powers as the English justice of the peace out of session. Maryland called sessions of individual justices the hundred court, and Virginia later styled them the magistrates court. Maryland also attempted to transplant the franchise courts. The Calverts created about sixty manors during the seventeenth century, and brief parts of the records of two courts leet survive.

County Courts

Fairly extensive county court records exist in Virginia, Massachusetts, and Maryland for the period before 1660. Plymouth, Rhode Island, Connecticut, and New Haven were not then divided into counties. Plymouth differed from all other colonies in that the General or the Assistants Court acted as the only court in the colony and handled all classes of criminal business. A large part of its business, whether viewed substantively or procedurally, can be equated to county court functions elsewhere.

The county courts, together with the Plymouth courts and to a degree the Connecticut Particular Court, were a hybrid combining English quarter session and leet form and procedure.[78] As to personnel, these courts were modeled after the quarter sessions. The men who sat on those benches acted as justices of the peace, though they may have been called commissioners, conservators, or commanders. In Virginia and Maryland, this practice clearly was followed. In 1638, Leonard Calvert commissioned John Lewger to be conservator of the peace for St. Mary's County. The commission gave him "full and absolute power and authority to doe exercise and exequte all the same and the like act and acts thing and things power and powers as may be or usually are exercised and exequted by any Justice of the Peace by vertue of his Commission for the peace."[79] Another Maryland commission appointed John Evelin to be commander of Kent Island. He was to choose six others, and together they were empowered "to heare & finally determine all matters & offences whatsoever criminall . . . which may be heard and determined by any Justices of peace in England in their Court of Sessions not extending to life or member."[80] Virginia created its commissioners and county courts with a commission obviously modeled on the English documents. In 1642, Governor William Berkeley put eleven men into the commission for Accomack-Northampton County. By his royal instructions Berkeley could give the commissioners whatever criminal jurisdiction he should "thinke fitt." He chose to define their power in terms of the authority of the English justices of the peace. They were authorized "as neare as may bee according to the lawes of England to inflict punishment upon the Offenders and delinquents and to doe and execute what one Justice of peace or two or more Justices of the Peace may doe or execute such Offences only excepted as the taking away of life and member."[81] In Massachusetts the legislature created the county courts and named the judges. The title "justice of the peace" was not used in New England before 1660, but the magistrates or assistants were obviously seen as having those powers.[82]

American jurisdictions also borrowed the quorum concept from the English peace commission. The Virginia commissions usually designated three men to be of the quorum.[83] Early Maryland commissions required the presence of one specified person, but later documents resembled those of Virginia.[84] Massachusetts law required the presence of an assistant or magistrate.[85] The quorum requirement served the same purpose as it did in England, to guarantee that a responsible person with some knowledge of law would attend each session. It probably also had an additional function. In most cases, at least one of the quorum was a member of the government, either a councillor or assistant. By this device, the colony governments kept in direct contact with the local courts and did so by a much simpler process than the unwieldy English surveillance of quarter sessions by the Privy Council and assize judges.

In the extent of jurisdiction there were major differences between the English quarter sessions and the colonial county courts. The largest difference was that the colonial county courts had a civil jurisdiction which the quarter sessions did not have. The English franchise courts may have been the jurisdictional model for the colonial county courts. Although the lawyers had drawn a sharp distinction between the powers of courts baron and leet, assigning to one a civil and to the other a criminal jurisdiction, a suitor in those courts might not have perceived the difference. In practice, the two functions were often blended in an undifferentiated court.[86] Franchise court procedure as experienced by colonists probably was the model for combining criminal and civil business. Consolidating business was also a practical move that achieved a reduction of the number of courts and brought civil justice close to home, reforms being demanded in England. Another difference was that colonial county courts assumed the jurisdiction of the lower English ecclesiastical courts. A very large part of that business consisted of punishing offenses against morals, especially those of a sexual nature. A final obvious difference was competence to try capital cases. Though this power was being removed gradually from the quarter sessions in England, the colonial county courts were barred absolutely from deciding cases that involved life or limb. Despite these differences, there remained a broad similarity in that the county courts on both sides of the Atlantic dealt with ordinary trespass and misdemeanor.

Colonial county courts derived their procedure from both the quarter sessions and leets. Records in all three of these types of courts are scant, and some procedural matters were doubtless not put on the record. The most fruitful points of comparison are prosecution and judgment. In the leet, prosecution was by jury presentment. The leet presentment could not be traversed and thus amounted to conviction. At common law, both felonies and misdemeanors were prosecuted by indictment. The quarter session took indictments and either tried them by jury or sent them to the assize. In the early seventeenth century, an increasingly heavy burden of business caused the quarter sessions to use prosecution by presentment. In such a proceeding, known as trial by traverse, the justices examined interested parties and then rendered judgment.[87] Colonial county courts never took indictments. The normal mode of prosecution before these courts was by presentment, which resembled leet procedure. In addition to juries, individuals, constables, selectmen, churchwardens, and sworn presenters could make presentments.[88] Presentment amounted to conviction in the vast majority of cases, but unlike the leet, a colonial presentment could be traversed and go to trial by jury. Whether convicted by presentment or trial, the colonist received judgment from the magistrate, a practice derived from quarter sessions. From prosecution to judgment, the colonial county court blended leet and quarter session procedure.

A survey of the record of county courts in three jurisdictions—Accomack-Northampton in Virginia, Kent and Charles in Maryland, and Essex in Massachusetts—over at least a decade shows the comparative volume and nature of their business. The record of the local court for Accomack-Northampton exists from its founding in 1632. Through its first ten years it met monthly and then bimonthly. By 1640, as many as seven commissioners served the community of 650 persons, a ratio that made it likely that the justices would have knowledge of causes coming before them. The business of the court fell overwhelmingly on the civil side. Attempts to recover debts crowded the calendar. In all its civil business the court proceeded to the resolution of issues with no regard for English forms of action. The commissioners heard the parties and rendered judgment.

On the criminal side of its docket the court had little to do. The record for the years 1632 to 1645 shows only about sixty entries that could in any way be related to crime, and they are mostly for minor trespasses and misdemeanors. Slander and defamation, leading the list, amounted to one-third of all cases.[89] Seven cursers or blasphemers,[90] a dozen fornicators or adulterers,[91] and five drunks[92] came before the court. There were eight cases of assault[93] and four contempts of court.[94] There was surprisingly little larceny and that certainly petty, milking a cow "by stealth" or stealing chickens.[95] The only capital crime on the record was a charge that a man buggered a calf. In that case, the commissioners bound the accusers and the defendant over to the General Court.[96]

The commissioners appear to have been evenhanded and on the whole patient. In many cases, their role seems to have been that of counselor rather than judge. In cases of defamation and assault, they often heard persons out and either did nothing or merely required an acknowledgment of fault and an apology. In thirteen years they ordered eight persons whipped and twelve fined.[97] A few others sat in the stocks or laid neck and heels.[98] Two women slanderers suffered dunkings.[99] The record of Accomack-Northampton County is that of a law-abiding but contentious people.

The records of two Maryland county courts survive for the period before 1660, those of Kent (1648–60) and Charles (1658–60). The courts there met monthly, with four or five commissioners seated. At the Charles court, the governor or a councillor usually presided. At Kent, the commander of the island presided. As in all colonial courts, civil business dominated the calendars of these courts. Proceedings were loose to the point of disorder, the courts discharging their business with little regard for form. Taken together, the records of these two courts include sixteen years. Only fifty-two incidents that could by any standard be related to crime or control of behavior occurred. Thirty-four percent of these cases, all begun as civil actions, were for slander or defamation. Two of these cases resulted in whippings.[100] Twelve percent related to theft, and one of them produced the only other whipping, ten lashes, which was the most severe penalty imposed by these courts.[101] The only other statistically significant misdemeanor was bastardy, which amounted to about 10 percent of the "criminal" business.[102]

One comes away from these records with the clear impression that the planters expected to operate their plantations and control their families and servants without outside interference. Evidence scattered through the record indicates that private discipline could be severe, but that badly abused servants had access to the courts.[103] One planter was fined three hundred pounds of tobacco, the heaviest fine levied, for rubbing salt water on the back of a servant after a whipping.[104] Occasionally such a commotion would occur on one of the plantations that the matter would surface in court. Likely as not the trouble would have occurred at Thomas Bradnox's place. A commissioner and sometime sheriff, Bradnox was constantly before his own court for drunkenness, fighting, and abuse of servants.[105] Proceedings against Bradnox or other wayward planters took the form of extensive depositions describing the altercation. Punishment was almost never administered, the commissioners apparently believing that a public airing of the trouble would bring peace, at least temporarily.

Some Maryland criminal cases began with demands for redress by the individual harmed.[106] In effect, these seem to have been survivals of the English process of prosecution by appeal. There is no evidence of a grand jury, or, for that matter, any jury at all in criminal cases except for the inquest following a suspicious death. In Kent, the constable frequently made presentments. They were usually for drunkenness, Sabbath violation, or swearing. These accusations were attempts to enforce the laws passed during the 1650s by the Puritan-dominated assembly. The results must have been discouraging both to the constables and the assembly. Such offenders were very seldom punished.[107] Puritanism as a means of social control was reduced to pious declarations on the statute book. Marylanders did what they pleased with little prospect or fear of judicial discipline.

Essex, Massachusetts, was a large and populous county, its jurisdiction extending into a part of what is now southern New Hampshire. The Essex court met at least quarterly at Salem and Ipswich and annually at Hampton and Salisbury. Usually four or five justices made up the bench. The governor or deputy governor attended most sessions, and when their presence at the various county courts is added to their work in the General and Assistants Courts, they appear as men largely engaged in public business. When the record refers to the judges individually by name, they are "the Worshipful."

The work load created by criminal business in the Essex court was by far the heaviest of that of any court surveyed. Larceny, mostly petty taking involving food and clothing, amounted to about 8 percent of the criminal business. The Essex justices heard many cases of slander and defamation. These actions, when taken together with very frequent assaults, create the picture of argumentative and proud people. As in all other jurisdictions, Essex justices passed judgment most frequently on drunks (12.6 percent of business) and sexual offenders (11.5 percent). In this court there was no need to prove that a person had been stumbling drunk, but merely that he had imbibed excessively. Sex offenses included not only fornication and bastardy, but a wide range of sexually suggestive speech and actions. The justices demanded orderly, authorized courtships and restricted to the marriage bed any copulation or acts that might lead to intercourse. Even that sanctuary fell within the view of justice. The court gave one husband and wife the option of a fine or whipping for "defiling" it. The justices insisted that married couples cohabit and ordered separated couples to unite. An impotent husband was ordered to seek and follow the advice of a physician and report the results to the court.[108] Other behavior problems came before the court in this order of frequency: religious misconduct (absence from church and criticism of ministers, 11 percent); lying, 6 percent; swearing, 5.7 percent; disobedient servants, 4 percent; excessive apparel, 3.2 percent; taking tobacco in public, 1.5 percent; and idleness, 1 percent. In addition, the justices punished abusive speech and unnamed "misdemeanors." One comes away from this record with the clear impression that judges expended a major part of their effort keeping Essex "Puritan."[109]

Some comparisons between the Chesapeake and Essex county courts are possible. All met regularly, and high-ranking colony officers were usually present. Except in death inquests, a jury was not used in the Maryland and Virginia courts in criminal cases. In contrast, both trial and grand juries were impaneled at every session of the Essex court. Though no criminal case went to a jury trial in Essex, the grand jury played an important part in the prosecutions. A large number of cases began with grand jury presentments. Essex citizens actively participated in the judicial process; those in Maryland and Virginia did not.

All of the courts acted as safety valves for society in the area of interpersonal relations. In the large majority of cases involving slander, defamation, and assault no judgments resulted. Public airing of the case seems to have relieved pressure. Out of each 1,000 persons in each jurisdiction, 11.96 might annually appear in court in Essex, 7.09 in Kent, and 6.90 in Accomack-Northampton. The population of Essex was four and one-half times larger than Ac-

comack and seven times larger than Kent, so the Massachusetts justices clearly carried a much heavier load of criminal business than
their Chesapeake counterparts. This disparity is not to be explained
only by counting or making judgments about the proclivity toward
crime of the people of the three counties. The Chesapeake justices
must have hoped that people would settle their own differences.
They tended to let the planters maintain whatever standard of behavior suited them. They acted only when business was thrust
upon them or when some breach of the peace achieved general no-
toriety. In sharp contrast, the Essex justices embraced the duty of
punishing all crime, of maintaining the integrity of the family, and
of imposing a rigorous moral standard on the community.

Individual Magistrates

Though the English manuals set out in great detail what the justices
of the peace could and were expected to do, we know very little
about what they actually did from day to day. Few records of the
activities of individual justices have survived.[110] In the colonies the
guidelines were less clear and the record of what they did is virtually nonexistent.

The most obvious similarity between the English and American
magistrates was that they performed essential functions of local government without pay. They assumed these responsibilities as a natural consequence of social status. All were of the gentry. Though the
English justice of the peace was the model for the colonial magistracy, no colony called them by that title before 1660. The English justice derived his authority from the peace commission and
statutes. In America practice varied. Virginia and Maryland used a
brief commission that recited that the local judges had the authority
of the English justices of the peace.[111] Occasionally those colonies
gave the justices specific power by statute, for example, by giving
them a summary power to deal with drunks.[112] Several New England colonies defined the authority of their magistrates out of
court by statute without giving them a general criminal jurisdiction. In Connecticut and Massachusetts they could try swearers,
idlers, drunks, and petty thieves.[113] In Massachusetts an order of
1630 declared the governor and assistants to be justices of the
peace.[114] In both Massachusetts and Connecticut only the governor

and assistants had full magisterial power, though as population and judicial business increased, both provided for associates or assistants to aid the magistrates.[115] Plymouth law was ambiguous about the powers of individual magistrates. The code of 1636 gave the governor and assistants the basic power of the English justices to examine and commit offenders. The code required them to bring offenders before a court "with all conveniente speede." Yet, the entry defining the assistants' functions also said that they were to "have a voice in the censuring of such offenders as shall *not* be brought to public Court."[116] This may have been a clerk's error, because the same provision of the code of 1658 omitted the word "not."[117] The latter code prefaced its statement of positive criminal law with the provision that each town should build and maintain stocks and a whipping post, thus implying a magisterial jurisdiction at the local level.[118] But the code's definition of "Offences Criminal" is imprecise as to jurisdiction. In establishing penalties, the code sometimes refers to "the court" without defining which court and sometimes merely describes the punishment.[119] Without direct evidence, a good guess would be that the assistants did have discretion to punish minor offenders in their towns. Though the general and assistants courts tried many persons accused of misdemeanors, it seems unlikely that every village liar, curser, and drunk was summoned all the way to Plymouth to be tried. Only Rhode Island made any detailed rules for their conservators. Again following Dalton, the code of 1647 ordered them to bind by recognizance those who threatened the peace. It then set out what the conservators should do in cases of forcible entry and riots and described the procedures to be used in dealing with suspected felons.[120]

The criminal business done by individual magistrates in all colonial jurisdictions seems to have been related to preliminary proceedings: apprehension, examination, committal, binding, or bail. Though statutes and orders empowered magistrates to deal summarily with petty offenses, there is almost no evidence that they did so. Exceptions occurred in Essex County, Massachusetts. Several items in the record of its court indicate that individual associates brought in fines that they had levied for drunkenness, cursing, theft, and assault.[121] But the fact that the county court records are filled with cases involving minor infractions suggests that the magistrates preferred to exercise the function of judgment in court rather than taking the onus on themselves as individuals. The activities of magistrates acting out of court are unknown.

In this void there is the exception of Springfield, Massachusetts, for which the Pynchon Court Record survives. A plantation association of 1639 gave William Pynchon a broad criminal jurisdiction. The Massachusetts General Court issued commissions to Pynchon in 1641 and 1643. These confirmed the power granted by the association subject to the restriction that it not extend to life, limb, or banishment and the condition that any judgment could be appealed to Boston. With some modification, this system of one-man justice continued until 1652, when the General Court appointed three commissioners.[122] Because the Pynchon record is all that we have, it is tempting to generalize from it, but this is hazardous because of the special conditions at Springfield. In a frontier community, thinly settled and far removed from the eastern towns, Pynchon provided some of the services that would have been the business of the county court elsewhere.

Though there were some obvious differences in their situations, a comparison between Pynchon's work and that of William Lambarde as an English justice of the peace illuminates the type of business that came before justices of first instance at the local level in England and America.[123] The outstanding difference was that about 50 percent of the business coming before Pynchon was civil, whereas Lambarde was involved in no civil causes. Lambarde's most frequent activity was binding to the peace or for court appearance (42 percent). His second most frequent action was the commitment of suspected felons (22 percent). He also dealt frequently with bastardy (10 percent) and ale house regulation (6 percent). Lambarde rendered judgment only eight times, sentencing three to be whipped, one to be fined, and four to the house of correction for short terms. About 25 percent of Pynchon's business fell on the criminal side. This business was thinly scattered over the years and consisted almost exclusively of behavioral trespasses—idleness, swearing, lying, fornication, assault, misuse of tobacco. He disposed of one larceny and two cases of illegal trade with Indians. He neither bound nor committed anyone to await trial before a higher court. Pynchon proceeded to judgment eighteen times, ordering six to be whipped and twelve to be fined.

Congregations as Courts

Never popular, the English church courts came under increasingly heavy attack in the early seventeenth century.[124] The colonies left this hierarchy of courts and functionaries behind. Virginia Anglicans transferred to the civil courts the bulk of the disciplinary business that had been within the jurisdiction of the church courts. A surviving vestige of the old system was a responsibility given by the burgesses to the churchwardens to present morals offenders, but they made their accusations in the county courts.[125] No trace of ecclesiastical jurisdiction has been found in Maryland or Rhode Island.

Plymouth and the three Puritan colonies of Massachusetts, Connecticut, and New Haven might have followed Calvin's example by creating a new system of church courts. Instead, they fashioned a dual system of discipline that was logically consistent with the tenets of Congregationalism. A fundamental division of their society between those who were and those who were not church members made such a system necessary. Probably two-thirds of the people remained outside of the church. For the Puritan all crime, acts *malum in se*, was sinful. But for them the calendar of crime went beyond traditional felony and trespass to include a broad range of misconducts, acts *malum prohibitum*. All crimes were sinful and all sin was criminal. Every member of society stood responsible before the bar of public justice for criminal and sinful acts ranging from murder to idleness. The minority of church members could also expect with certainty to be judged by their own congregation.[126]

Congregational church discipline was a necessary result of the covenants. In the act of forming a church, the original members pledged "to walke in all our wayes according to the Rule of the Gospell." The individual member acknowledged his "subjection" to Christ, "my only king and lawgiver." The church responded by promising "brotherly love and holy watchfulness."[127] Brotherly watchfulness ordinarily achieved the aims of church discipline. When a member seemed in any way to be leaning toward sin, one or more of the brothers or sisters would offer counsel and warning. That failing, the pastor or an elder might privately admonish the waverer. If the member persisted in an errant course, the pastor or

TABLE 3.2   CONGREGATIONAL DISCIPLINE,
FIRST CHURCH IN BOSTON, 1638–1660
(in percent)

Religious practices/opinions	20.00
Drunkenness	18.33
Fornication/unacceptable sexual behavior	15.00
Lying	11.66
Business practices	10.00
Theft	8.33
Family relations	6.66
Adultery	6.66
Defamation	1.66
Idleness	1.66

an elder brought the case before the entire congregation. The case would have been prejudged. Though technically the congregation made the judgment, it was in fact merely ratifying the decision of the pastor or elder. Normally the congregation registered its verdict by remaining silent. On very rare occasions the elder might ask for a show of hands. The procedure was a trial only in the sense that it was an excruciating experience. The only possible defense was abject confession. Any other plea or attempted explanation automatically added contempt to existing charges. Having stood his trial, the condemned member would either receive a public admonition or be "cast out," excommunicated. In the latter baleful state, the condemned person continued to be a member. Because the system aimed at redemption, the outcast member continued to attend the services though he was barred from communion and ordinary brotherly intercourse. In time, some of the outcasts saw the light and were readmitted to the covenanted congregation.

A brief analysis of the experience of the First Church in Boston between the years 1638 and 1660 illuminates congregational discipline.[128] Only fifty cases came formally before the church during those twenty-two years. An annual rate of 2.27 miscreants suggests a saintly congregation and an effective system of brotherly watching and warning. The sinners were distributed among the various categories as indicated in Table 3.2.

In order of severity, the penalties imposed by the congregation were rebuke, public admonition, and excommunication. Penalties were applied rigorously. The congregation normally used its heaviest weapon, excommunication (72 percent). In 13 percent of the cases it approved public admonition, and in another 13 percent it approved both public admonition and excommunication. It seldom resorted to rebuke (2 percent). Men apparently sinned more often or openly than women. The church disciplined thirty-six men and fourteen women. There were only three recidivists, apparent evidence of the efficacy of the system. Thirty-four percent of those excommunicated were readmitted. Those cast out stayed out an average of thirteen months.

Congregational discipline coexisted with the system of public courts. Administratively the two systems were separate. In England, some ministers were also justices of the peace. In New England, neither ministers nor elders were magistrates. But separation did not prevent cooperation and co-option. For example, New England magistrates used formal admonition and conspicuous acts of penance as punishments; English justices did not.[129] The fact that a majority of the population were not church members limited the reach of congregational discipline. The magistrates filled the gap without hesitation by punishing misconducts that were within the jurisdiction of English church courts and colonial congregations. Though ministers and elders stood outside the system of public justice, the magistrates did not hesitate to ask them for advice.[130] The normal harmony between the officers of the two systems resulted in a finely meshed net that trapped most erring citizens.

The dual system placed church members in double jeopardy because they could suffer church discipline and public penalties for the same act. Because most of the magistrates were church members, they knew of every case instituted by the church. As to comity and rendition, the two jurisdictions followed a common sense rule: whichever found the miscreant dealt with him first or the two systems might proceed simultaneously.[131] The extent of comity is illustrated in the case of Captain John Underhill. Banished by the General Court during the Antinomian uproar, he received safe-conduct from the court so that he might reenter the jurisdiction to stand his trial before the congregation of the First Church in Boston.[132]

Sheriff and Constable

Together with the lord lieutenant, the sheriff in England remained a chief agent of the crown in the county. Always a man "of good sufficiencie," a sheriff was appointed by the king for a one-year term. Dalton, who wrote a manual for the sheriffs, described their duties under the rubrics "Absolute or Judiciall" and "Ministerial." An officer who had once heard the pleas of the crown, the sheriff's "absolute" power had shrunk to an authority to arrest and imprison suspects and take security to keep the peace. Curiously, Dalton describes the sheriff's duties to keep his tourn and the county court under the title "Ministerial."[133] The sheriff had held his tourn or court twice each year in every hundred. In the tourn, he inquired about criminal activity and punished lesser offenders. Dalton wrote that the tourn had "almost growne out of use,"[134] its business having been taken over either by leets held as franchises or by the justices of the peace. The rest of the sheriff's "ministerial" duties made up the bulk of his business. As fiscal agent he collected or seized all things of value due to the crown. He attended the assize judges on their circuit and the justices of the peace in sessions. As agent of these courts he impaneled the juries and executed all writs and orders. A member of the gentry, the sheriff left the routine work to his undersheriffs and bailiffs. The work was often badly done or not done at all.[135] Dalton ended his text with a list of over thirty allegations of corruption, malfeasance, and neglect of duty.[136]

The ancient office of sheriff crossed the Atlantic,[137] though it changed its name in several jurisdictions. As marshal in Massachusetts, Connecticut, and New Haven, messenger in Plymouth, provost marshal in Virginia, and general sargeant in Rhode Island, these men served as ministerial officers of the colony during the early years of settlement. With the establishment of counties, they usually took the familiar title of "sheriff." As in England, the American sheriff was a man of substance, "an able man of Estate."[138] In New England, the general courts and in Maryland and Virginia the governors appointed the sheriff. In Maryland he held office during pleasure, but elsewhere the appointment was made annually. The colonists left the expiring courts of the sheriff behind in England; the American counterpart was an administrative officer. Influenced by the corruption associated with the office in England, every colony except Maryland either made him a salaried officer or fixed his fees by law. Though legislative acts and commissions outline what was expected of the colonial sheriff, the record of this early period gives virtually no picture of how he executed the office.[139]

The constable was the workhorse of the English law enforcement establishment. An officer of the hundred or other units of local government, he was appointed by the justices of the peace. He served a one-year term without pay. Lambarde referred to the constables as "inferiour ministers," "unlearned men."[140] These reluctant officers were expected, on their own authority, to prevent breaches of the peace and to pacify those who broke it. If defied, they called for assistance. The larger part of their duty consisted of executing the orders of the justices of the peace. Expected to do a difficult and sometimes dangerous job, they performed erratically. As law enforcement officers they walked a narrow path, subject to fine if they exceeded their authority and penalty if they failed to exercise it. A modern historian has described their status: "Evildoers did not respect them because they were ignorant, timorous, and powerless; the justices did not respect them because they were lazy, disobedient, and negligent."[141]

The colonists brought the office of constable with them, and constables acted as the line peace officers in every jurisdiction.[142] The New England towns, following older English practice, elected their constables. In Virginia and Maryland the governors appointed them. The American constable may have been recruited from a more responsible segment of society than his English counterpart.[143] They normally served a one-year term.

Though the colonial constable's police function was patterned on the English model, overall responsibilities were larger and sometimes included duties that would have been within the sheriff's power in England. In 1658, the Massachusetts General Court gathered its scattered orders relative to the constable into a single document that amounted to a brief manual. Carrying his black staff, "that none may pleade ignorance," he was ordered to apprehend all minor offenders and suspicious persons on view. He executed the warrants and other orders of the magistrates and pursued the hue and cry. He inspected the taverns to see that they were orderly. He mounted and supervised the town watch, collected the town taxes, supervised the sealing of weights and measures, and had custody of all lost goods. He was to keep an eye out for husbands and wives living apart and to apprehend runaway servants. He acted as the town coroner and chief election official.[144] In the surviving records, the constable is seen most often making presentment of offenders to the court. Occasionally his work was unpleasant, breaking up drunken brawls or suffering the insults of persons who defied his authority.[145]

The First American Judicial System

The colonists fashioned a rational system of courts out of the old English materials. The extent of their reforms can be seen only partially in the area of criminal law. By giving all of their courts a general jurisdiction in law and equity they achieved a radical simplification of the parent models. When a colonial court door opened, its magistrates were ready to grant equitable relief, give judgment in civil suits, and hear the crown pleas.

Demographic facts, small populations, and relatively short distances made it possible to simplify the vertical structure of the courts into county courts or other local courts and a superior court. In fact, three colonies, Plymouth, Connecticut, and New Haven, disposed of virtually all criminal matters in a single central court. In the other colonies, the superior courts combined the jurisdictions of the English assize and Kings Bench. The county courts brought together the procedure and jurisdiction of leet and quarter sessions.

Standards of fairness demand that a criminal justice system comes to judgment with reasonable speed and in a uniform fashion. The early colonial courts met these standards. Courts met regularly, normally every month, and usually cleared their dockets in each session. The standard of uniformity was met in part by statutory prescription, but the structure and personnel of the courts also furthered this aim. At its inception, English common law had been defined and administered by the king in council. By the seventeenth century, the function of judgment had long since been assigned to the courts. Though the aim of commonality was served by statute, commentary, and the process of legal education, ultimate responsibility for uniform administration remained with the king and privy councillors. They administered an unwieldy system with exhortations to judges and justices and by applying political pressure all along the line of the complex judicial hierarchy. The colonial chief executive and his council were also responsible for the uniform administration of criminal justice. Governor and councillors or assistants were in fact the superior court. They also carried their standards and authority into the counties as justices of the peace. This system made possible a common criminal law for each jurisdiction and the remarkable continuity of personnel guaranteed it.

From the standpoint of administration, America has never had a more efficient or uniform system of criminal justice than it had at its beginning.

Chapter Four

Crime

Criminal activity intrudes upon and menaces a broad spectrum of personal and public values. The expression of dissident ideas either directly or by association crosses the boundary of criticism and becomes a seditious threat to the state. In societies that value material possessions highly, all forms of theft undermine the ethic of work and reward. Because the vast majority of people are neither heroic nor suicidal, crimes of violence call up the visceral fears of personal extinction. Sedition, theft, and mayhem are perceived as evil incarnate. Less deadly but nonetheless obnoxious are acts that violate standards of order and propriety, thus creating categories of behavior to be prohibited.

Whether real or vicarious, experience with crime fixes interest. News of crime, past or present, enters the morbid side of our consciousness. It does so in two ways. News of especially audacious or brutal crimes spreads rapidly through a community however simple or sophisticated its means of communication. Individual criminal acts create an explicit awareness. But there is another and cumulative consciousness of crime that grows out of perceptions of its frequency. Lack of exactness increases fear in this area of awareness and creates the assumption that crime must be close to home. It was so in the seventeenth century and it is so now.

The methods used in this chapter reflect these modes of perceiving crime. The simplest part of the business was to report specific criminal acts. To create a sense of frequency of crime was much more difficult, and the results are necessarily inexact. Some insights into the statistical dimensions of crime have been given in previous chapters, for example, Table 2.1 set out the number of executions and Table 3.1 described the distribution of business by types of crime in colonial superior courts. This chapter fills out the statistical dimensions of seventeenth-century crime in several ways. It

contains descriptive, numerical tables of all of the homicides (Table
4.1) and all of the cases of witchcraft (Table 4.2) brought to trial in
all jurisdictions before 1660. Another form of statistical information, expressed as percentages, appears in the text, for example, relative frequency of thefts committed by servants, types of things
stolen, comparisons among the jurisdictions of prosecutions for sex-
related crimes. These statistics are not documented directly. They
are based on 1,969 items in the surviving published records of all
colonial superior courts before 1660 and the county courts of
Accomack-Northampton, Virginia, Charles and Kent, Maryland,
and Essex, Massachusetts. The remaining statistical information is
set out in Table 4.3, which attempts to recreate annual crime rates
in five jurisdictions. The intrinsic difficulties and limitations in the
crime rate statistics are set out in the notes to the table.

Sedition

In the seventeenth century, the word "sedition" meant "a concerted
movement to overthrow an established government."[1] A generic
term, it covered a wide range of activities perceived to be hostile to
a government. In the American colonies charges of sedition generated a series of judicial proceedings that might fairly be called state
trials. The fact that such trials occurred primarily in the superior
courts of Massachusetts and Maryland requires examination. The
rulers of those colonies had a more fully developed concept of the
state than did those in the other colonies. Rhode Island, Connecticut, and New Haven, lacking formal charter authorization to establish polities, existed on shaky legal foundations. Virginia saw itself
as a political extension of England. Massachusetts tried persons for
seditious behavior at a rate double that of Plymouth. Any given session of the Maryland or Massachusetts courts was four times more
likely to hear cases involving persons accused of sedition than the
other four jurisdictions.

The Puritan oligarchs in Massachusetts and the Calverts in Maryland regarded their charters as virtual constitutions upon which au-
tonomous states could be built. In both cases the founders had very
concrete ideas about the character of the state they wished to
create. Although purposes in the two colonies appear to have been

different, they shared the common characteristic of being anachronistic. Both attempted to establish political systems whose time was past—the Calverts a medieval palatinate, the Puritans an Israelite state. The fact that they saw themselves building upon historical models appears to have given their concept of state a precision and definiteness lacking in other colonies. Both the rigidity and archaic quality of the governments of Massachusetts and Maryland invited criticism and opposition. The same characteristics dictated that the governors would regard seditious activity as virtually akin to treason. In both colonies the conservative leadership survived in part through use of the criminal law to suppress dissidents.

In each of the first three decades of the colony's life, the Massachusetts leadership faced a serious challenge to its authority. The 1630s brought the Antinomian crisis, the 1640s the confrontation with Robert Child, the 1650s the invasion of the Quakers. In each case, dissidents challenged the rigid orthodoxy of the established religion. Because the "twinne sisters" of church and state were so intimately bound together, the magistrates interpreted each uprising of religious dissent as a menace to the state and explicitly labeled them sedition. The same path led to heresy and treason.

The stories of the Antinomian crisis and the Child affair have been told and retold. The very name "Antinomian," used as an epithet and literally meaning against the law, smelled of sedition. Anne Hutchinson and the Reverend John Wheelwright dismissed most of the Bay Colony clergy as "legalists," pious mechanics. The Winthrop oligarchy saw the Antinomians as enthusiasts who were apt to "irrupt" and compared them to the Anabaptists of Munster who had risen in arms two centuries earlier. Child demanded toleration for Presbyterians and the political rights that would come with recognition. He threatened the oligarchy by suggesting that the English government ought to review the religious and governmental policies of the colony. In both instances the prosecutions for sedition were based on written documents, in the case of the Antinomians a petition denying that Wheelwright had been seditious, in Child's case a remonstrance that criticized the government and demanded reform. In both cases the dissidents were condemned in proceedings similar to those in the Star Chamber. A verbatim record of Anne Hutchinson's trial survives. It is a record of trial by examination, the very essence of Star Chamber method. The court banished the leading Antinomians and disarmed their followers. It imposed extremely heavy fines on Child and his associates.[2]

Puritan rectitude mixed with paranoia ultimately produced a travesty of criminal justice. Quakers began arriving in New England in 1656, bringing with them a new threat to church and state that was perceived as especially menacing. It is difficult to determine whether the magistrates feared most the Quakers' repudiation of church doctrine and polity or their concepts of social and political equality. In any event, the legal proceedings against them were more concerned with their sedition than their heresy. Authorities regarded the Quakers as carriers of a virulent plague who should be barred from entry if possible or quarantined and removed if they gained entry. Met with deep fear in all colonies and severe legal sanctions in most, their mission produced a tragedy in Massachusetts.[3] Beginning in October 1656, that colony passed a series of statutes of ascending severity against the Quakers. The original law fined captains who brought in persons known to be Quakers, punished the Quaker with whipping, imprisonment, and deportation or banishment, and fined all residents who kept Quaker books or expressed Quaker opinions. The second statute fined residents who permitted Quakers in their houses at a rate of 40 shillings per hour. It provided that upon first appearance a Quaker would suffer the loss of one ear, for a second appearance the other ear, and for a third have his or her tongue bored through with a hot iron. In 1658, the General Court took the final step by ordering the death penalty for a Quaker who returned after having been banished.[4]

Action against Quakers began during the session of the General Court that passed the first statute. The court ordered the marshal to put a group of them aboard an outbound vessel.[5] The first formal banishments came in the session that passed the death penalty law.[6] In this early phase of the repression, local converts who could not pay fines imposed in county courts were sold as servants in Virginia or Barbados.[7] The first trials for life came in 1659. William Robbinson, Marmaduke Stephenson, and Mary Dyer had returned after having been banished by the Assistants Court. The formal charge against them made no mention of their religious beliefs or advocacy. They were charged as "underminers of this government,"

their crimes having been "rebellion, sedition & presumptious ob-
truding themselves upon us." Though the record states that the
court voted only after a full hearing, it is clear that the Quakers
had been prejudged. A previous order had set the date "for theire
trialls, to suffer the poenalty of the lawe." The court took extraordinary precautions in conducting the executions, ordering one
hundred fully armed soldiers to attend. On the promise of her son
to take Mary Dyer out of the jurisdiction, the court reprieved her.
Robbinson and Stephenson were hanged eight days later. Seven
months later Mary Dyer returned and was put to death.[8]

The last Quaker to be executed was William Ledra. He first appeared in the record of the Essex County Court in 1658. Asked
why he had come into the colony, Ledra said, "to seek a godly seed
the lord god sd pase away to New England."[9] After he was banished, Ledra's mission took him to Plymouth, where he was imprisoned for an extended time. Again and again he refused to take
an oath to leave that colony, but finally the "will of God" told him
to do so.[10] Obviously seeking martyrdom, Ledra returned to Boston. Indicted for having returned from banishment "in a Rebellious
and Seditious Manner," he excoriated the magistrates as murderers.
The day before his execution, Ledra wrote a movingly poetic letter
to his friends who were still in the Boston jail: "The sweet influ-
ences of the Morning-Star, like a Flood distilling into my innocent
Habitation, hath so filled me with the joy of the Lord in the Beauty
of Holiness, that my Spirit is as it did not Inhabit a Tabernacle of
Clay, but is wholly swallowed up in the Bosom of Eternity, from
whence it had its Being."[11] Ledra was hanged March 14, 1661.

However repulsed the Puritans may have been by the religious
ideas of these sectarians, it was their rejection of authority and their
contempt of government that led the Quakers to the gallows. The
indictments of them always charged sedition. After the executions,
the magistrates felt compelled to justify their acts. The Quakers,
moved by "impetuous & fanaticke fury," aimed "to undermine &
ruine" authority. Arguing from the analogy of a man's right to defend his house and family from intruders and citing prolific biblical precedent, the magistrates saw themselves as "nursing fathers
& nursing mothers" protecting "theire subjects."[12] Writing late
in 1660 to recently restored Charles II, they said: "The Quakers

died, not because of theire other crimes, how capitoll soever, but upon theire superadded presumptuous & incorrigible contempt of authority."[13]

In each case the magistrates had come to the irrevocable act of execution with extreme reluctance: "Wee desire theire life absent rather than theire death present." The Quakers bewildered the magistrates, who, in the final analysis they saw as suicides: they "are become felons de se." It was probably no accident that the only colonial statute to bring in the common law requirement of an ignominious burial for a suicide passed in Massachusetts at this time. In the letter to Charles II, the General Court again portrayed the Quakers as suicidal. As a last resort the magistrate had, "for the defence of all," armed himself "to keepe the passage with the point of the sword held towards them." The Quakers had committed homicide by "wittingly rushing themselves thereupon."[14]

It is currently fashionable to say that the Puritans must be judged by seventeenth- rather than twentieth-century standards. At the minimum, though, it seems fair to comment that these sedition proceedings showed an extreme xenophobia. The irony is that the Puritans were perfectly aware that they had themselves fled persecution "when a wide doore was set open of liberty."[15] God had mandated that they go through that door to escape persecution, even though this might cause those who remained behind to struggle and suffer to perceive them as cowards. In Massachusetts they slammed shut the door of liberty and kept their mansion pure by a rigorous use of the criminal law. For those who disagreed with them, the options were either to use the door as an exit or die. As was to be expected, they found biblical justification for both their own flight from persecution and their forced expulsion of others: "Itt was the commandment of the Lord Jesus Christ unto his disciples, that when they were persecuted in one citty, they should flee into another, Math. 10:23." Casuists from bark to core, they could argue that the Quakers had not suffered persecution "but the due ministration of justice." This was so because the one party understood the Bible better than the other.[16]

The Byzantine politics of Maryland produced an almost continuous stream of charges of treason and sedition. In a case in 1658, the attorney general accused a man who was either a Catholic priest or a lay teacher with aiding "the attempts of foreigne or home

bred enimies."[17] From the founding of the colony such enemies of
the Calvert proprietary caused trouble. Maryland's disturbed state
resulted from a natural antagonism between a Catholic proprietor
and a predominantly Protestant population, an equally natural and
continuous friction generated by the local legislators' dislike of the
Calverts' claims of prerogative rights, the resentment of the very
presence of the colony by many Virginians who thought the creation of Maryland a violation of the charter of Virginia, Indian war,
and the confused state of English government during the Civil Wars
and Interregnum that created situations in which prudence dictated
disloyalty even to persons who had been strong supporters of the
Calverts.[18] In a bewildering variety of combinations, these factors
produced a series of sedition charges. The attorneys general of
Maryland seem to have been quick to make such charges. The relative recklessness with which charges of treason were made gives
some of the incidents a kind of comic opera quality, though they
must not have appeared that way to the participants. From out of
the maze, I have selected the cases of William Claiborne, Richard
Ingle, and Josias Fendall.

That William Claiborne did not become Calvert's nemesis was
certainly not for any lack of effort on his part. A powerful Virgin-
ian, he had established a trading post on Kent Island in Chesapeake
Bay before the first settlement in Maryland. In a small naval
engagement, Leonard Calvert defeated the Claiborne party and
gained control of the island. A leader of Claiborne's force, Thomas
Smith, had been captured. Indicted before the General Assembly
for "felonie and pyracie," he was found guilty by a jury of all the
freemen present. Sentence of death followed.[19] But Claiborne was
in Virginia, so Calvert proceeded against him by bill of attainder.
The bill, stopping short of making a charge of treason, accused
Claiborne of "contempts, insolencies and seditious acts." Further,
he had instigated persons to "committ the grievous crimes of pyracie and murther." Because it was necessary that "exemplary justice . . . be inflicted on such notorious and insollent rebels," the
act attainted him and caused his property to be forfeited to the
proprietor.[20] These proceedings guaranteed Claiborne's permanent
hostility, and he later intervened in Maryland affairs on several
occasions.

From the day that the Long Parliament first sat in 1640 until the

restoration of Charles II in 1660, Baltimore was in a difficult, ten-
uous position. Naturally loyal to the Stuarts, he attempted a pas-
sive role as the fortunes of Parliament rose. His American colony
existed through those years in a continuous state of confusion.
News of events in England often arrived in the colony in the form
of rumor and speculation. Whether and when to remain loyal to
Baltimore and thus to the king or to throw in with Parliament and
oppose the proprietor must have been a question constantly in the
minds of Marylanders.

In 1642, Leonard Calvert returned to England to counsel with
his brother. During his absence, Richard Ingle "irrupted" onto
the Maryland scene and played out the first act of what was to be a
seventeen-year drama of conspiracy and war. A ship's captain, Ingle had been trading for tobacco in the Chesapeake region. In 1643,
he returned aboard his ship the *Reformation* convinced that the future was with Parliament. Though the only overt acts committed in
America that were alleged against him were seditious words, he
may have had a large design to overthrow the proprietary and royal
governments of Maryland and Virginia or at least be on the scene if
revolts occurred. The charges of high treason against Ingle were
made by a man who may have been acting out of malice.[21] The in-
formant alleged that Ingle had said that "he was Captaine of Grave-
send for the Parliament against the King" and that he had defied an
order given in the king's name in Virginia.[22] The sheriff arrested
Ingle on a bench warrant, but through the intercession of Councillor Thomas Cornwaleys, a prominent man who had done yeo-
man service for the Calverts but who now also believed that the
future was with Parliament, Ingle was permitted to return aboard
the *Reformation*.

In the Provincial Court, Attorney General John Lewger presented three bills of indictment to the grand jury over Cornwaleys's
objection that the chief witness against Ingle was "infamous." The
first two bills were in the king's name, and it is clear that if the jury
had found them true, Ingle would have been sent to England for
trial. The first indictment charged that Ingle "rose in armes against
the kings authority" by forcibly resisting arrest in Virginia. The
second charged that he had levied war in England by accepting
a parliamentary commission. The last bill, in Baltimore's name,
charged him with "malicious & scandalous words" against Prince

Rupert, the king's commander in England. The jury returned all three bills endorsed "ignoramus." Rebuffed, the attorney general caused a second jury to be impaneled. It returned "ignoramus" a bill charging Ingle with escaping from the sheriff. Lewger then presented two more bills to the first jury. The first was a slightly more specific bill alleging the verbal attack on Prince Rupert, and it was again returned "ignoramus." A second bill charged Ingle with these traitorous words: "that the king . . . was no king neither would be king, nor could be no king, unles he did joine with the Parlament." At first the jury could not agree, but the next day they returned the bill "ignoramus." Certainly Lewger showed a familiarity with English law. Two of the bills had alleged acts that fulfilled the definition of the treason of levying war. The last bill had specifically charged that Ingle's words amounted to the treason of compassing or imagining the death of the king. One major head of the treason law remained, and Lewger tried it. He presented a bill to a third grand jury that charged the third category of treason, adhering to the king's enemies by joining the parliamentary forces. This jury was dismissed when it could not agree after deliberating all day.[23]

Having had no luck with grand juries, Lewger proceeded by a series of informations. In four of them he charged Cornwaleys, the sheriff, and five others with permitting Ingle to escape. The fifth and sixth charged Ingle with "prison break," "pyracie, mutinie, trespasse contempt & misdemeanor." Cornwaleys was fined one thousand pounds of tobacco, but it was respited. The other informations produced no results.[24] The proceedings against Ingle showed that Lewger was not only persistent, but also learned in the common law and that the Maryland jurors read the situation in England better than Calvert officials did.

The 1650s was a time of incredible confusion in Maryland. The colony had its own civil war and its own experiment with a Puritan commonwealth. By 1656, complex negotiations in England had made it clear that Baltimore would retain the proprietary. In that year he appointed Josias Fendall as governor. Fendall had recommended himself to Baltimore for his service at the battle of the Severn during the civil war. He proved to be a bad choice. Though Fendall took his office in 1657, little is known about his governorship because the records are scant. In February 1660, the Maryland assembly declared itself to be the sole authority in the colony. Fendall abandoned his commission from Baltimore and accepted one from the assembly. The motives for these actions are not apparent, but they probably reflected the dislike of the Calvert proprietary by a substantial party of Marylanders and may have been another attempt of the Puritan group to seize control of the colony.

Fendall's "rebellion" was stillborn. If it had been based on some rumor of change in England, it was completely misinformed. Two months later, Charles II returned to his throne. The king confirmed Baltimore in all of his rights and commanded the colonists to aid in the reestablishment of those rights. Baltimore appointed as governor Philip Calvert, a half-brother who had been secretary in the colony. The proprietor apparently thought that Fendall was in arms against him. In a letter to Philip he referred to "this Second Rebellion" and authorized martial law. Noting that others had thought him weak in dealing with insurgents in the past, that "I use[d] to leave my selfe a hole to gett out at," he ordered Philip "upon no tearmes to pardon Fendall so much as for life." In fact, Fendall had come into St. Mary's to submit. Before doing so, he had written to Governor Calvert and implied "menacing force" unless the governor agreed to his terms. But Fendall did submit to the council, professing a willingness to help settle "the Countrey in Peace." The council imprisoned him to await trial before the Provincial Court.[25]

The grand jury indicted Fendall for the mutiny of subverting Baltimore's authority by force and establishing an illegal government. In response to the indictment, Fendall in effect confessed his "unadvised and Indiscreete actions."[26] The court confiscated Fendall's estate and ordered him banished. He then petitioned the council (the same men who had condemned him) to remove the sentence. The council vacated the sentence but disfranchised him, barred him from any office, and took security "for his Good behaviour towards the Government." The next day the governor issued a pardon in Baltimore's name.[27]

The question comes, why did Philip Calvert pursue such a lenient policy in the face of the stern letter from Baltimore that had literally called for Fendall's head? It is possible that the proprietor had meant the letter to be a public declaration that he would no longer tolerate opposition and in private communication he authorized leniency at Philip's discretion. More likely, the governor saw that the proprietary was weak and that the execution of Fendall would trigger armed resistance. Doubtless his policy of healing and settling was the wiser one.

These early Massachusetts and Maryland cases were prophecies rather than precedents for the American use of criminal law to suppress dissent. In Maryland, political opposition, even of a violent nature, was not chastized at the gallows. In Massachusetts, ideological dissidents suffered grievous penalties.

Homicide

The frequency of inquests in the records suggests that magistrates ordered investigation of most suspicious deaths. Inquests usually found cause of death to have been accidental.[28] Because infanticides and killings of servants were fairly common, the sudden death of a child or servant would be the occasion of an inquest. One finding makes the concern clear: the child drowned "through its own weakness without the hand of any other person being any occasion or cause thereof."[29] Death by careless use of firearms would bring a finding of homicide by misadventure if no felonious intent was shown.[30] At least one-fifth of the trials for homicide began with the findings of inquests.

Table 4.1 sketches the record of the thirty homicide cases that came to trial in the period. Procedure in most cases was regular, and the trials were fully reported. Seventy-five percent of the prosecutions were by grand jury indictments, twelve of which charged killing with premeditated intent, specifically murder, infanticide, or petit treason. In two cases the charge limited the trial to the lesser degrees of homicide. When grand juries were in doubt, they charged felonious death, thus leaving the determination of the degree of homicide to the trial juries. In such cases the trial juries returned guilty verdicts for murder twice, for homicide by misadventure once, and for manslaughter three times. The three persons convicted of manslaughter were permitted to plead benefit of clergy. Charges of murder stuck. Only one jury found manslaughter where murder had been charged. Juries acquitted 25 percent of all persons accused of homicide and acquitted defendants in murder

TABLE 4.1. HOMICIDES BROUGHT TO TRIAL BEFORE 1660

Jurisdiction and Case	Prosecution	Charge	Relationship or Circumstance	Evidence	Verdict	Disposition
Connecticut						
Allyn	grand jury	manslaughter or misadventure	neighbor	confession	homicide by misadventure	£20 fine + good behavior for 12 months
Taylor	grand jury	felonious death	neighbor	unknown	special	apparently homicide by misadventure
Boston	grand jury	homicide by poison	wife-husband	unknown	not guilty	
Maryland						
Dandy[a]	inquest & grand jury	[murder]	white-Indian	unknown	guilty	pardon
Dandy[a]	inquest & grand jury	murder	master-servant	11 examinations & depositions	guilty	hanged
Elkin	grand jury	murder	white-Indian	2 depositions & confessions	manslaughter	unknown
Skighta.Mongh & Counaweza	information	murder	Indian-black servant	1 deposition & examinations	guilty	hanged
Mitchell	grand jury	foeticide	reputed father-foetus	19 depositions & examinations	fine of 5,000 lb. tobacco by court for "Adultery fornication and Murtherous intention"	
Rogers	grand jury	murder	fellow servants	unknown	acquit	
Harris	grand jury	infanticide	mother-son	5 depositions	acquit	
Massachusetts						
Williams	grand jury	murder	fellow prisoner	confession	guilty	hanged
Schooler	grand jury	murder	casual male-female relationship	reputation physical evidence	guilty	hanged
Talbie	grand jury	infanticide	mother-daughter	confession reputation	guilty	hanged

Peirce	grand jury	unknown	master-servant	unknown	acquit	
Palmer	inquest	manslaughter	male-male unknown	unknown	acquit	
Franklin	unknown	unknown	master-servant	question of intent sustained cruelty	guilty	hanged
Cornish's Wife	unknown	unknown	wife-husband	reputation body bled midwife's deposition	guilty	hanged
Martin	inquest	infanticide	mother-daughter	confession	guilty	hanged
Betts	grand jury	felonious death	master-servant	11 depositions	acquit	to gallows with rope, bond for good behavior
Cassell	grand jury	felonious death	male companions	unknown	special	strong suspicion of murder
Parsons	grand jury	infanticide	mother-child	confession	guilty	probably died before execution
Indian Maid	unknown	unknown	female Indians	unknown	not guilty of murder	whipped 10 stripes
New Haven						
Nepaupuck	unknown	unknown	Indian-white	Indian testimony	guilty	beheaded
Plymouth						
Billington	grand jury	murder	unknown	unknown	guilty	hanged
Latham	inquest & grand jury	felonious death	master-servant	unknown	manslaughter	benefit of clergy
Bishop	inquest & grand jury	infanticide	mother-daughter	confession	guilty	hanged
Peach & 2 Others	grand jury	murder	white-Indian	unknown	guilty	hanged
Virginia						
Mathews	grand jury	petit treason	servant-master	unknown	guilty	hanged
Reade	grand jury	felonious death	male companions	1 deposition testimony of accused	manslaughter	benefit of clergy
Bently	grand jury	felonious death	male companions	2 depositions	manslaughter	benefit of clergy

*Two different crimes committed by the same man, John Dandy.

trials at the same rate. Forty-eight percent of those accused of homicide in any degree suffered the death penalty. Only one convicted murderer received a pardon.

If the master-servant relationship is seen as familial, then 48 percent of the homicides occurred in the family. The one murder of a spouse was probably premeditated, and the murderess seems to have been aided by her lover.[31] The five infanticides provide standard examples of this crime. Mary Martin, a Boston servant, killed her newborn bastard daughter and hid the body in a trunk. On suspicion, a midwife examined Mary and found that she had delivered a baby. Though she claimed that the infant had been stillborn, the fact that she attempted to hide her sin by concealing the body would doubtless have convinced a jury of her guilt. But, in front of a jury, she touched the body and it bled. These were convincing pieces of evidence. She then confessed and was tried, found guilty, and executed.[32] Dorothy Talbie and Allis Bishop murdered their infant children. Talbie, clearly insane, confessed that she broke the child's neck to "free it from future misery."[33] Allis Bishop, a woman apparently plagued by depression, killed her daughter by slashing her throat.[34] One father was bound over on suspicion of murder; his case does not appear in Table 4.1 because it never came to trial. Francis Brooke, convinced that his wife was pregnant by another man, abused her badly on several occasions and finally attempted an abortion with a pair of tongs. A badly bruised child was born dead. In court, Brooke said that the delivery had occurred when his wife fell out of a peach tree. Doubtless terrified by him, she agreed to this explanation. The court warned him that though he had escaped punishment at its hand, he would yet be judged by God.[35]

The most common homicides resulted from abuse of indentured servants and apprentices, clear evidence of the extreme tensions that the master-servant relationship could generate. In several cases, long-term abuse of servants by masters preceded death. These cases caused courts and juries great agony because neither a murderous intent nor a specific causal act could be proved. Two trials before the Massachusetts Assistants Court show the nature of the crime and the difficulties of prosecution. Nathaniel Sewell, an apprentice of William Franklin, was sick and "very noisome." Franklin abused him badly and refused him water when the dying boy cried for it. The jury and magistrates struggled with the facts that Franklin's actions by themselves were not criminal and that a felonious intent could not be proved. Other magistrates argued successfully that Franklin's cruelty brought Sewell "to death by degrees." Franklin was hanged as a murderer.[36]

The case of John Betts, a repulsive one, turned out differently. Betts's servant, Robert Knight, a weaver by trade, certainly could not have been described as a good farmhand. He often shirked his work and was known as a liar and thief, behavior perhaps not unusual for such servants. After Knight fell from a ladder and bruised several ribs, Betts became very abusive, charging Knight with dissembling. While at work in the fields, Betts exploded and attacked Knight first with an ox goad and then with a heavy plow staff. The assault severely damaged Knight's back and caused internal injuries. Knight became an invalid and was visited several times by a doctor, but probably only because the physician had been called to treat Mrs. Betts. The doctor told Mrs. Betts that the young man might live for some time but that he would not be able to work. Betts continued to abuse him, calling him "wretch, rascall and bloud soucor." He dragged Knight from his bed and tied him in an upright position. Knight was incontinent and soiled his clothes. Betts made him wash his clothes and on one occasion forced his excrement into his mouth. After Knight's death, a grand jury specified the major assaults that Betts had made and presented "him for his horrible wicked Crueltys." At the Assistants Court trial, the magistrates refused to accept the jury verdict.[37] Tried again before the General Court, Betts was found not "Legally guiltie of the murderinge of his Late Servant Robert Knight: But for as much as the evidence brought in against him, houlds forth unto this Courte, strong presumptions & greate probabilities of his guilt of soe bloudy a fact, & that hee hath exercised & multiplied Inhumane cruelties uppon the said Knight, This Courte doth therefore thinke meete that the said John Betts bee sentenced." Betts was made to stand for an hour at the gallows with the noose about his neck. He was then whipped severely and bound to his good behavior for one year.[38]

In July 1657, John Dandy, a Maryland blacksmith, killed his servant, Henry Gouge. Dandy then removed the boy's clothes and threw the body into a creek to make it appear that he had drowned. Dandy's crime might have been predicted. Sixteen years before, he had shot and killed a young Indian. He had been pardoned on condition that he serve as public executioner for a term of years. The condition was removed in 1647 because he had been "behaving himself ever since uprightly."[39] Three years later, his violent temper led him to assault a visitor to his shop with a heavy hammer. After a court hearing, Dandy and his victim compromised the matter, and the court let it pass.[40] Dandy was certainly aware of his propensity to violence. Obviously Gouge irritated him and Dandy responded with abuse, on one occasion giving him a serious head wound with an ax. He had said to his wife that one day Gouge would cause him to be hanged. After the discovery of the body, Dandy fled to Virginia but was apprehended by hue and cry. Eleven deponents bore witness to his abuse of Gouge, and the court sentenced Dandy to be hanged.[41] Dandy's violent career is evidence that seventeenth-century society had no sure mechanism but the gallows to control persons with homicidal urges.

Another category of homicide was that involving Englishmen and Indians. In three cases, whites murdered Indians, in two Indians killed whites, but either way the judges confronted unusual problems. At least in time of peace, magistrates apparently wished to see English murderers of Indians prosecuted vigorously. Whether this attitude arose out of a desire to see justice done or a fear of inflaming the tribes cannot be known. Large numbers of settlers did not agree and viewed the killing of an Indian as a positive or at least excusable act rather than a crime. This dilemma is shown in Dandy's first case, when "a Great part of the Colony" petitioned for his pardon.[42] It was even more clear at John Elkin's trial, a Maryland case. Though Elkin had confessed the killing, the jury would not convict because "a pagan" was outside the king's peace, fair game for a white man. Under pressure from the governor, a second jury found manslaughter.[43] In a third case of murder of an Indian by whites, a Plymouth court and jury apparently had no problem indicting four men for highway robbery and the killing of Penowanyanguis. One of them, Daniell Crosse, escaped, but the other three, Arthur Peach, Thomas Jackson, and Richard Stinnings, were hanged.[44]

When Indians stood accused of any crime before a colonial court, the magistrates faced other dilemmas. Usually unable to understand English, the Indian must have been bewildered by the strange formalities of the colonial courts. The magistrates would have been inviting reprisal if Indians perceived procedures and penalties to be unfair. When possible, the magistrates involved other Indians, either as viewers of the trial and punishment or ideally as witnesses against the accused.

In New Haven, the sagamore of the Quillipieck Indians accused a tribal member Nepaupuck "generally" of having murdered several Englishmen. The accused admitted that Nepaupuck had killed whites, "but denyed thatt he was Nepaupuck." One of his kinsmen positively identified him and accused him specifically of murdering Abraham Finch. Nepaupuck then confessed and boasted that he, "a great captaine," had "had his hands in other English blood." He preferred to be beheaded or any form of execution except by fire because "fire was God, and God was angry with him, therefore he would nott fall into his hands." Tried the next day before the General Court, he was asked if he did not deserve to die. "[H]e answered, it is weregin [just, fated?]." The court indulged his wish and executed him by beheading.[45]

Witchcraft

The notion that the prosecution of witches was a brief spasm of judicial persecution in Salem, Massachusetts, has long been put to rest. Common to most societies, witchcraft has attracted an army of scholars who have produced a huge bibliography in history, sociology, anthropology, and psychology. No common law felony was more deeply rooted in the Bible than witchcraft, the injunctions in Exodus and Leviticus being the imperative command: "Thou shalt not suffer a witch to live."[46] The colonial cases involving witchcraft, occurring in every colony except Rhode Island, began in 1647. By 1660 there had been twenty-three cases. These are outlined in Table 4.2. The records of these cases are very uneven as to detail.

Not surprisingly, the early colonial cases support the findings of scholars who have recently applied cross-disciplinary methods to the problem.[47] The cases give insight into the type of person who was apt to be accused as a witch, the process of accusation, judicial conduct, evidence, and the methods of disposition.

A person accused of witchcraft was most likely to be a married woman or widow in her middle years. She was not from the lowest class of society. In eleven cases where status can be identified, ten

TABLE 4.2. CASES INVOLVING WITCHCRAFT BEFORE 1660[a]

Year and Case	Jurisdiction and Status	Reputation	Acts Alleged and/or Evidence	Disposition
1626; Goodwife Wright	Virginia; goodwife, midwife	"very bad woman"	foretold death; cursed hunters; threatened girl; countered other witch	8 depositions; not prosecuted
1638; Jane Hawkins	Massachusetts; midwife	malpractice of midwifery	suspicion only; had been suspected as witch in England	banished (1644)
1647; Alse Young	Connecticut; unknown	unknown	unknown	probably hanged
1648; Margaret Jones	Massachusetts; unknown	abrasive personality	caused sickness; potions; foretold events; witches mark, familiar	hanged
1648; Mary Jonson	Connecticut; unknown	convicted thief	confession of familiarity with the devil	hanged
1651; John Carrington	Connecticut; carpenter	occasional defendant in civil cases	unnatural works	hanged
1651; Joane Carrington	Connecticut; goodwife	unknown	unnatural works	hanged
1651; Goody Bassett	Connecticut; goodwife	unknown	unknown	hanged
1652; Mary Parsons	Massachusetts; goodwife	eccentric; probably demented	infanticide by witchcraft	not guilty of witchcraft; guilty of infanticide; probably died before execution
1652; Hugh Parsons	Massachusetts; sawyer, bricklayer	easily frustrated; given to anger; hard to do business with; menacing	by witchcraft caused mysterious domestic behavior of pudding, beef tongue, beer tap; caused illness & injury; had dog familiar; caused strange lights, visions of snakes; indifferent to health of child	acquit
1653; Elizabeth Godman	New Haven; gentlewoman	intrusive; garrulous	causing illness to humans & animals; familiar; knowledge of events not witnessed	3 court appearances; admonished; briefly in prison; admonished again & bound to good behavior
1653; Goody Knapp	Connecticut; goodwife			hang...

wife	New Haven; goodwife	loquacious; liar	suspected accusation by another witch; Indian gods	£10 damages & £5 costs to husband in action of slander
1654; Lydea Gilburt	Connecticut; unknown	unknown	killed a man by witchcraft; other witchcraft	probably hanged
1654; Richard Manship's wife	Maryland; goodwife	unknown	caused man to be lame	defamation; composed out of court, but publicly acknowledged
1654; Mary Lee	Maryland; unknown	unknown	witches mark; caused ship to founder; confession	executed at sea by ship's crew
1655; Nicholas Bayley & wife	New Haven	frequent court appearances for behavior	unknown	banished
1656; Anne Hibbins	Massachusetts; gentlewoman	turbulent, quarrelsome, excommunicated	unknown	hanged
1656; Eunice Cole	Massachusetts [New Hampshire]	unknown	animal familiars; witches mark	3 prosecutions; often in prison
1656; Jane Walford	Massachusetts [New Hampshire]; goodwife	unknown	caused illness; animal familiars	bound over; not prosecuted
1657; William Meaker	New Haven; unknown	unknown	accused of bewitching pigs	brought action of defamation; defendant bound to good behavior
1658; Elizabeth Garlick	Connecticut; servant	"naughty"	harm to animals; death of humans	acquitted
1659; Elizabeth Richardson	Maryland	unknown	threatened safety of a ship	hanged by seamen

[a]Wright: *Va. Gen. Ct.*, 111–13; Hawkins: *Mass. Col. Rec.*, 1:370, 2:146, Winthrop, *Journal*, 1:266, 268, 2:8; Young: John M. Taylor, *The Witchcraft Delusion in Connecticut, 1647–1697*, 145–46; Jones: Winthrop, *Journal*, 2:344–45; Johnson: Taylor, *Witchcraft Delusion*, 144–45; the Carringtons: *Conn. Hist. Soc. Coll.*, 22:93; *Conn. Col. Rec.*, 1:107, 115, 145; Bassett: *Conn. Col. Rec.*, 1:220, *N.H. Col. Rec.*, 2, 81; the Parsonses: *Mass. Col. Rec.*, 4: pt. 1, 47–48, 96. Samuel G. Drake, *Annals of Witchcraft in New England*, reprints the extensive examinations of Mary and her husband. For a rebuttal of Drake's conclusions about Commissioner Pynchon's conduct see *Pynch. Ct. Rec.*, 20, 21, 21n, 22–25, 117, 141, 219–20. She is sometimes confused with Mary Parsons of Northampton, who was involved in a defamation case at about this time. Mary Parsons of Northampton was tried for witchcraft, but not until 1675. See also Drake, *Annals*, 134–36, *Pynch. Ct. Rec.*, 24. Godman: *N.H. Col. Rec.*, 24, 29–37, 151–52; Dexter, ed., *New Haven Town Record*, 2:174, 179; Drake, *Annals*, 88, 90–95; Knapp: *N.H. Col. Rec.* 2, 81; Staples: *N.H. Col. Rec.* 2, 77–89; Gilbert: *Conn. Hist. Soc. Coll.*, 22:131, Taylor, *Witchcraft Delusion*, 148. Incredibly, she was held responsible for the death of a man who had been killed by a gun accident four years earlier. The inquest had found the verdict of death by misadventure against the man who fired. Manship: *Md. Arch.*, 10:309; Lee: *Md. Arch.*, 3:306–8; the Bayleys, Taylor, *Witchcraft Delusion*, 149; Hibbins: *Mass. Col. Rec.* 4: pt. 1, 269; Cole: Drake, *Annals*, 99–103, John Demos, "Underlying Themes in the Witchcraft of Seventeenth-Century New England," at 13, 23 citing Mass. Archives, 135:3, 13; Sally S. Booth, *The Witches of America*, 35, 37, 160, 175–76; Walford: Drake, *Annals*, 103–7, Booth, *Witches*, 37–38, 47; Meaker: *N.H. Col. Rec.* 2, 224–26, Taylor, *Witchcraft Delusion*, 149–50; Garlick: *Conn. Hist. Soc. Coll.*, 22:188, Taylor, *Witchcraft Delusion*, 119–21, Booth, *Witches*, 128, 150, Drake, *Annals*, 110–12; Richardson: *Md. Arch.*, 41:327–29.

of the women were referred to as "Goodwife" or "Mrs.," indicating a middle- or upper-class standing. Only one woman accused as a witch was a servant. Four men were charged with witchcraft. Three were accused along with their wives. The witch was a quarrelsome and combative person, viewed by others as spiteful, eccentric, and, in some cases, mad. Her contentiousness might have been shown by forcing herself upon others or into their homes when she obviously was not wanted. Some witches had appeared previously in court on a variety of charges.

In the period before 1660, the pattern of charges that later became endemic in Salem—accusations by overwrought, hysterical adolescent girls—was not apparent. A witch was usually accused by neighbors. Among frequent charges were that the accused had bewitched another person, causing illness or death; that bewitched animals had sickened and died; that accidents had occurred after a visit by or altercation with a witch; that an ordinary household process such as churning butter had failed; that the witch foretold the future or could describe events that she had not witnessed. The most serious accusation was one made by a suspected or condemned witch, the latter by itself being evidence sufficient to convict. At least one witch accused her husband. On the other hand, several husbands brought actions for slander to clear their wives' names. Most witches were formally indicted by grand juries, for example:

> Elizabeth Garlick thou art indited by the name of Elizabeth Garlick the wife of Joshua Garlick of East Hampton, that not having the feare of God before thine eyes thou has entertained familliarity with Sathan the great enemy of God & mankind & by his helpe since the yeare 1650 hath done workes above the course of nature to the losse of lives of serverall persons (with severall other sorceries) & in perticular the wife of Arthur Howell of East Hampton, for which both according to the laws of God & the established law of this Commonwealth thou deservest to dye.[48]

For a time it was fashionable to portray the magistrates who tried witches as persecutors who had prejudged the accused. In these cases, the record argues against this perception. There can be no doubt that judges truly believed in witchcraft. They appear to have proceeded with great caution. If they were in fact witch hunters, the several actions of slander brought by women or their husbands presented opportunities to conduct inquisitions and initiate prosecutions. These opportunities were not taken. To the contrary, judges were more likely to award damages to the plaintiff and punish the defendant in witch cases than in more ordinary actions of slander. In the midst of a rash of witchcraft prosecutions in surrounding Connecticut, the rigorous Puritan magistrates of New Haven might have been expected to embrace the opportunity to prosecute. Rather, two of the cases that came before their court show patient judges exercising judicial restraint. By her conduct before, at, and after the execution of Goody Knapp, Goody Staples had compromised herself. Many believed that not only Knapp, but another condemned witch named Bassett, had branded Staples as a witch. Thomas Staples brought an action of defamation against Roger Ludlow, one of Connecticut's magnates. Having heard a mass of conflicting testimony, they awarded £10 damages and £5 costs to Staples. In another series of cases, Elizabeth Godman appeared three times before these magistrates. Though she had taken the initiative to clear her name, the depositions taken, directly or by innuendo, accused her of virtually all of the acts associated with witchcraft except causing death. On the first occasion, after extensive hearings, the magistrates told her "to looke to her carriage hereafter." On another occasion she was imprisoned briefly. The last time she appeared, the magistrates bound her to good behavior and told her to "forbeare from goeing from house to house to give offenc, and cary it orderly in the family where she is."[49]

Proof of witchcraft came as a result of applying special rules of evidence. The rules had long been settled and certainly were not invented by colonial magistrates. In summarizing the case against Margaret Jones, who was hanged in 1648, Governor John Winthrop set out the main heads of evidence: she behaved in a wild manner and lied frequently; she had a "malignant touch" that caused violent illness; she administered harmless potions that nonetheless had "extraordinary violent effects"; she could foretell the future and had knowledge of events she had not witnessed; she had a familiar, an imp in the form of a phantom child who vanished when others approached; and she had a witches' teat "in her secret parts."[50]

The New Haven cases of Godman and Staples reveal again and fill out many of Winthrop's heads of evidence. Both women had intrusive personalities; both were liars. Her accusers thought that

Godman had caused a boy to be ill and a young married woman to miscarry and have fits. Godman had precise knowledge of things that she could not have seen. Neighbors held her responsible for sick chickens and pigs, beer that went bad, and butter that would not churn. She talked to herself, and this caused observers to believe that she was conversing with a familiar who was believed to suck her. The witches' teat figured in many cases. Confusion about what and where it was is shown graphically in the Staples case. When Goody Knapp had been taken down from the gallows, a group of women immediately gathered around the body. Staples pulled up Knapp's clothing and "handeled the said teates very much, and pulled them." Having done so, she declared that they were no different than her own or any other woman's. Others disagreed. The matter was settled when the midwife showed them the mark, apparently on another part of the corpse.[51]

The Staples case also illustrates the power of the most telling evidence, the accusation of a condemned witch. Many persons in Fairfield believed that Knapp had accused Staples, and much of the evidence in the depositions went to prove she had done so. This presumed accusation would explain Staples's frenzied search of Knapp's body. She wanted to prove that Knapp had not been a witch. Knapp, however, had already ended the business by coming down from the gallows before her execution to tell the most respected man in the community, the minister John Davenport, that she had no accusations to make.

A person suspected or accused of witchcraft stood about a 40 percent change of being hanged, not much different from the rate of expectation in homicide. In witchcraft, conviction guaranteed execution; there was no remedy, not benefit of clergy, not pardon. Unfortunately, surviving information tells us virtually nothing about either the evidence or the conduct of the cases that did end in hangings. In the Godman and Parsons cases, virtually every form of witchly behavior was put into evidence, but Godman was not prosecuted and the Parsonses were acquitted. Perhaps this suggests that in cases that ended in hangings, judges and juries had heard what they believed to be overwhelming evidence of guilt. It is also possible that some of the condemned confessed, although the term "confession" was used loosely in witchcraft cases. Examinations of suspect witches were extensive and detailed. What might have been called a confession would really have amounted to the accused testifying against herself. Ordinary rules that would have excluded a spouse's testimony did not control admissible evidence in witchcraft trials.

The cases are concentrated in time and place. Over 70 percent of them occurred in the seven years between 1651 and 1657, and of those, 70 percent occurred in closely related towns in Massachusetts, Connecticut, and New Haven. Jurisdictional lines were certainly not barriers to rumor and fear. From Springfield to Windsor to Hartford and on to Wethersfield, New Haven, Stratford, and Fairfield was less than one hundred easy miles by water. It is not clear what caused this cluster of cases along the Connecticut River and northwest shore of Long Island Sound. News of witch prosecutions traveled like electricity, and rumor expanded fact. Let a witch be executed, and suspicion that there were others multiplied. The glimpses we have of Goody Knapp's execution show a grim carnival scene. Everyone was there. Doubtless the ministers deepened the sense of fear. John Davenport, for example, preached at least one sermon on witchcraft during this time.[52]

Two Maryland cases show urgent fear that witches could cause immediate and serious damage. Both occurred on voyages from England to the Chesapeake. Aboard the *Charity*, the rumor ran through the crew that Mary Lee was a witch. The *Charity* was in trouble, leaking badly. The crew pressed the captain to try her "according to the Usuall Custome." He refused. The seamen then searched Lee and found the witches' mark. They tied her to the capstall, got a confession, and hanged her. On the carpet before the Maryland council, the captain made it clear that had he intervened the crew would have mutinied. In a similar case, sailors hanged Elizabeth Richardson. The owner of the ship had been aboard. The council accepted his explanation that intervention would have caused a mutiny. These are the only examples of vigilante justice in the colonies before 1660, evidence certainly of the special heinousness of witchcraft.

Theft

In England, theft was the most common crime, amounting to as much as 70 percent of the criminal business of any given court.[53]

The early colonial settlements were not plagued by large numbers of thieves, burglars, and robbers. The simple societies had a limited number of valuables to be stolen, and a successful thief would have been hard put to dispose of stolen goods. In all colonial courts, theft amounted to about 10 percent of all of the criminal business. Rates of prosecution averaged .74 per thousand persons each year and were similar in all jurisdictions. In the records surveyed, 147 entries for theft were found. In only about 100 of these was any detail given about the thief, the item stolen, or the punishment. The only status or occupation of thieves noted was servant; for example, 20 percent of the larcenies in Essex and 66 percent before the Virginia General Court were by servants. Thieves most often stole something they could consume or use. Of identifiable items stolen, 35 percent were food and 25 percent clothing. The next largest category was domestic animals and chickens (15 percent). The records revealed only five examples of theft of money or jewelry.

A convicted thief could expect to be whipped (38 percent of all punishment for theft), fined (19 percent), set in the stocks (8 percent), admonished (5 percent), required to make multiple restitution (25 percent), or suffer some combination of these penalties. There were few chronic thieves. Whether Richard Berry's wife, Allice, suffered from poverty or kleptomania cannot be known. She appeared four times before the Plymouth Assistants for stealing food and clothing before they imposed the slight punishment of a 10-shilling fine or an hour in the stocks.[54]

The more serious forms of theft occurred rarely. No robberies were recorded. The records revealed seventeen burglaries. Though quite a few cases indicate that thieves entered houses to steal, it became burglary only when there had been a breaking. Authorities regarded burglary as a more serious crime than simple larceny. Two burglars were branded, and one lost an ear. A Maryland case shows how local judges regarded burglary. In Kent County Court, Francis Bright accused his servant of "felony" for breaking into a chest and taking things. The justices handled the case as if it were very serious. Having taken examinations, they bound Bright to prosecute before the Provincial Court and sent the suspect under a sheriff's guard to jail in St. Mary's. He confessed the crime, but explained that he had put everything back when he abandoned a plan to flee to Virginia. In consideration of that fact, the court limited his punishment to twenty-five lashes.[55] Two Harvard students, sons of ministers, pulled off one of the largest heists. They stole £15 from two houses. The boys were dealt with ad hoc, Winthrop noting, "We had yet no particular punishment for burglary." Both were whipped by the college president and ordered by the court to make double restitution.[56]

The almost complete absence of the death penalty for theft makes the two cases in which that sentence was given stand out in sharp contrast. In 1623, Daniel Franke was indicted before the Virginia General Court for the theft of a calf, and George Clarke was indicted as an accessory to this "felony." Franke's indictment also charged that he had stolen a napkin and a chicken. The indictments were part of a pattern of judicial actions by which the court intended to make *in terrorem* examples among "the lesser men." The indictments described each man as "laborer." Though the items stolen by Franke doubtless brought the case over the line that divided petty and grand larceny, the indictment obviously overvalued the calf at £3 and the chicken and napkin at 10 shillings. The council reprieved Clarke, but Franke became the unfortunate exception, the only person executed for larceny in the colonies before 1660.[57]

The other sentences of death for larceny occurred in Maryland. The wife of the Jewish merchant, Simon Overzee, died in childbirth. On the day of her funeral, one of Overzee's servants, Mary Williams, opened chests in Mrs. Overzee's bedroom and stole a quantity of linen. Encouraged by Mary Clocker, the wet nurse of Overzee's newborn child, Williams stole more linen and some clothing. The women believed that Overzee would not miss the goods, though Williams's husband warned that the material would be recognized if they used it. The indictments listed fifty-two items valued at £50. In their examinations, the accused unconvincingly tried to shift the blame to one another. In effect they confessed. The court sentenced the two women and Williams to death, but the governor pardoned them.[58]

Sex-Related Crimes

Sex-related crimes and acts that seventeenth-century authorities regarded as criminal were common in all jurisdictions. They ran the gamut: rape, incest, bestiality, sodomy, lesbianism, adultery, fornication, and a wide variety of provocative behavior described as "lewd" or "lascivious." Much more concern about illicit sexual acts might be expected in New England than in the Chesapeake colonies, but bare statistics do not support the expectation. Accusations and prosecutions for sexual acts made up a significant part of the business of all courts. Such acts accounted for 22.8 percent of the criminal business in Plymouth, 19 percent in New Haven, 17 percent in Accomack-Northampton, Virginia, 16 percent in the Maryland Provincial Court, 12.5 percent in Connecticut, 12.1 percent in Essex County, Massachusetts, 11.5 percent in the Massachusetts Assistants Court, and 9.7 percent in Kent County, Maryland. The rate of these offenses per annum for each thousand persons was 1.81 in Plymouth, 1.47 in Essex, 1.19 in Accomack-Northampton, and .49 at the Massachusetts Assistants Court.

Rape, a capital felony, rarely appeared in the record. There was only one conviction on a rape charge in all of the colonies before 1660. The Virginia General Court tried nineteen-year-old Thomas Hayle on four separate indictments for rape. He was convicted and hanged. It is possible that his crime was not rape in the usual sense. The meager record speaks of his rape of "fower Mayden Childen." He may well have been tried under an Elizabethan statute that made intercourse with a girl under ten years of age a capital crime whether or not she consented.[59] The case of Robert Collens, the only trial reported in detail, showed the difficulties of a rape prosecution.[60] Jane Bond's husband had been absent for an extended period of time. Collens had forced his way into her house several times. Once she "could not save hir selfe," and on another occasion he "hardly knew hur boddy fully." On examination, Jane said that she resisted. She testified that on a fourth occasion, "after much striving and crying hee forsed her." Several witnesses had heard loud noises, and one thought that she had seen Collens in the neighborhood. Her six-year-old son identified him as "fat Robert [who] strove with his mother." Collens, who had no alibi, denied "every artickell & parte" of the indictment. The jury found him "guilty of the ackt of Incontinencie, not guilty of the forsement." The court ordered thirty-nine lashes and a fine of £10, half of which was paid to Richard Bond.

Only one case of incest appeared in the record. Thomas Atkins's daughter, Mary, accused him. Tried for his life, he admitted to having made incestuous advances while drunk, but denied the act. The jury acquitted him, and the court sentenced him to be whipped.[61]

The colonists regarded any sexual act other than intercourse between a married man and woman as both sinful and criminal. The common law and the Bible told them that bestiality and sodomy were unnatural acts. They appear to have regarded bestiality as much the more heinous perversion because they knew that there could be no conception as a consequence of sodomy, but were not certain about bestiality.

Two men did die on the gallows for sodomy. A young apprentice sailor accused Richard Williams alias Cornish of sodomizing him. Though no record of the trial before the Virginia General Court has survived, there is evidence that Cornish was executed.[62] The case of John Knight outraged the New Haven magistrates.[63] Knight had previously stood in the shadow of the gallows with a rope around his neck for illegal sexual acts. At his second trial it became apparent that Knight had continued to have sexual relations with boys and girls. Because Knight's reputation was known throughout the community, the judges assailed the parents of one girl for permitting Knight to be with her and for concealing fornication. Knight now stood charged with sodomizing his master's fourteen-year-old son. Found guilty on the testimony of witnesses, the court excoriated Knight in their judgment:

> he is a leud, prophane, filthy, corrupting, incorridgable pson, a notorious lyar, besides that sodomitticall attempt so proved, and other filthy defyling wayes, tending to the very destruction of mankinde, and this gone on in time after time, so that there seemes to be no end of his filthyness nor no meanes will reclaim him, whether publique punishment nor private warnings, wherefore the court cannot thinke him fitt to live amonge men, and therefore doe by way of sentence order, that John Knight be put to death by hanging upon the gallowes.

All other cases involving homosexual acts occurred in Plymouth, and all involved consenting adults. The Court of Assistants there found John Allexander, a man "notoriously guilty that way," and

Thomas Roberts, a servant, guilty of "lude behavior and uncleane carriage one with another by often spending their seede one upon another." The court ordered Allexander to be whipped, branded, and banished. Roberts was whipped and returned to his master.[64] In a case of lesbianism, two women stood before the Plymouth General Court accused of "lude behavior upon a bed." The court admonished one of them and forced the other to confess publicly "her unchaste behavior."[65]

Four, perhaps five, men were hanged for bestiality. William Hatchett performed the act with a cow; Thomas Graunger with a mare, a cow, two goats, several sheep, two calves, and a turkey.[66] In a rural society, the act must have been common enough. People knew that it was a capital crime. But because it was a victimless crime, one wonders why people turned suspects in. It would have to be assumed that someone spied upon Graunger over a period of time as he satisfied his desires. The depositions of a Virginia couple who discovered Nathaniell Moore buggering a heifer show their horror and awareness that it was no mere misdemeanor that they had witnessed.[67] Before 1660, New Haven tried four men for bestiality and hanged two of them.[68] The case of George Spencer shows why colonists regarded bestiality with such horror: they feared the birth of humanoid monsters. John Wakeman's sow had delivered a litter of pigs. Wakeman brought one of the litter, a badly deformed piglet, to court "to be viewed and considered."

> The monster was come to the full growth as the other pigss . . . butt brought forth dead. Itt had no haire on the whole body, the skin was very tender, and of a reddish white collour like a childs; the head was most straing, itt had butt one eye in the midle of the face, and thatt large and open, like some blemished eye of a man; over the eye, in the bottome of the foreheade which was like a childes, a thing of flesh grew forth and hung downe, itt was hollow, and like a mans instrument of generation. A nose, mouth and chinne deformed, butt nott much unlike a childs, the neck and eares had allso such resemblance. . . . Some hand of God appeared in an impression upon Goodwife Wakemans speritt, sadly expecting, though she knew nott why, some strange accedent in thatt sows pigging, and a strange impression was allso upon many thatt saw the monster, (therein guided by the neare resemblance of the eye,) that one George Spencer . . . had beene actor in unnatureall and abominable filthynes with the sow.

George Spencer had a deformed eye, and it had been this that created the "impression." Under intense examination, Spencer alternated denials with confessions. Finally convinced of his guilt, the court sentenced him to death. The sow that had borne the monster was killed with a sword within Spencer's sight before the execution.

In England adultery had been a relatively minor infraction within the jurisdiction of the church courts; all of the colonies brought the act within the jurisdiction of their civil courts. Maryland and Virginia regarded adultery as a problem of behavior and left punishment to the discretion of justices.[69] The New England colonies, strongly influenced by the Bible, regarded adultery as a very serious crime, and Massachusetts raised it to the capital level. Though by nature difficult of proof by direct evidence, the rate of conviction in adultery cases was high, about 50 percent.[70] Juries, especially in Massachusetts, were apt to find the accused innocent of the capital crime, but guilty of "adulterous practices." Most commonly the adulterers were whipped, though some were fined or banished or made to wear badges that announced their crime. In Massachusetts, James Britton and Mary Latham confessed the act and were hanged.[71] Judges appear to have been evenhanded in meting out punishment. No distinction was made between a married and an unmarried party. The man and the woman suffered about equally unless circumstances justified different treatment. For example, George Burdett, a minister of Agamenticus, Maine, indicted as "a man of ill name and fame, infamous for incontinency, a publisher and broacher of divers dangerous speeches the better to seduce that weake sex of women," paid £40 in fines. The court ordered the two women involved to do public penance.[72]

In New England, the magistrates attempted to confine premarital relations to a proper, approved courtship. Premarital sexual relations and any extramarital sexual acts were sinful and criminal. Judges, jurors, constables, and all pious citizens were constantly alert to any behavior that might lead to copulation. Occasionally they described the act: a man taking out his "instrument of nature" or putting his hands under a girl's skirt or a woman putting her hand into a man's codpiece. Usually, though, such behavior was described more generally. Judges showed how rich the English language is in certain adjectives. Sexual "carriage" might be light, lewd, lascivious, naughty, unclean, filthy, wicked, sinful, wanton, unchaste, or whorish. Such behavior brought penalties ranging from admonition to whipping.[73]

Fornication resulted in sharp punishment, usually fines or whippings. Though male and female fornicators usually received the same or similar punishment, judges apparently considered such factors as difference in age and status, reputation, and which party had been the tempter, which the tempted. Sometimes the man was whipped with the woman standing by as a witness. Though no evidence of prostitution was found, occasionally a promiscuous person appeared in court. The fact that a couple married did not save them from prosecution in cases of premarital pregnancy. The days of the term of a newly wed woman were counted. Intercourse after contract was regarded as a less serious offense than fornication before contract. The most common penalty for these acts was a 40-shilling fine. In the Chesapeake colonies the authorities apparently regarded fornication by couples who subsequently married as an ecclesiastical offense to be atoned by penance.[74]

Prudence as well as piety urged strict control of sexual intercourse between unmarried persons. Such acts could produce bastards, who reduced the efficiency of servant women and might become public charges. In most bastardy cases, the father seems to have been known. Normally, both the mother and father were whipped though if the woman was pregnant her punishment would be postponed until after her delivery. If marriage was impossible because the couple was unwilling, the mother was a servant, or one of the parties was black and the other white, the court ordered the father to maintain the child. Occasionally a man denied paternity and the woman sought civil damages, though no record of a successful action was discovered.[75]

If the law is in part a response to fear, then Englishmen in early America certainly feared the consequences of sexual acts. That such activity gave pleasure merely increased the fear—of monsters born, of a society overrun by bastards begotten by irresponsible persons, of the undermining of families, the core of their society. To these fears, real enough, was added the ultimate terror of eternal damnation, for clearly many believed that sexual sin "shutts [them] out of the kingdom of heaven."[76]

Assault and Slander

Cases of assault and slander were among the most common actions in colonial courts. Assault and slander straddled the boundary between tort and misdemeanor, which is to say that each such action might contain grounds for a civil suit for damages as well as a criminal prosecution. It is difficult, really speculative, to determine where the provincial magistrates obtained legal guidance concerning these acts. The standard manuals and commentaries offered little help. These works appear to assume that an assault is a punishable breach of the peace at common law and then go on to describe physical coercion that is justifiable, for example, the parent may chastize his child, the master his servant, the teacher his students.[77] The manuals for the justices of the peace, a prime source of information for the colonial magistrates, do not deal with slander. The exception to this dearth of information is Ferdinando Pulton's *De Pace Regis et Regni*. He began his treatise with a chapter entitled "Of Menaces, Assaults, Batteries," which he regarded as "the very root and principall cause" of breaches of the peace. Pulton made the mixed civil-criminal nature of these acts clear when he described the forms of action available to the person harmed. In slander he would have an action on the case in which were inserted the words *Ad grave damnum pisius querentis, & contra pacem nostram* (to the serious harm of the complainant and against the peace of our realm). A person menaced, assaulted, or beaten had an action of trespass, "trespass" being a word that still connoted criminality.[78]

A more likely source of guidance for colonial magistrates would have been their experience with English courts. In his manual of leet practice, Kitchin laid down the rule that "assaults were not inquirable and punishable in Leet, but bloud-shed is." He then broadened the rule to include assaults that created "common annoyance." If by the assault "the Kings people were disturbed . . . that is more than particular [private]."[79] This rule, that an assault became more than a tort if it caused bloodshed or broke the peace, was also the basis for criminal prosecution of assaults at the quarter sessions.[80]

Colonial judges followed this rule. Though in the early seventeenth century, the church courts dealt with most cases of defamation, common law judges had begun to assume jurisdiction over certain classes of slander.[81] They did this in part by issuing writs of prohibition in cases where the slanderer had said that a person had committed a crime. The king's courts also took cases of slander on the civil side if the plaintiff demanded redress of "special damage." A lay or public law of slander was emerging, but this could have been perceived only dimly. Since quarter sessions did not deal with slander, the conclusion seems reasonable that emigrating colonists had experience with slander in a church or leet court. Because they left the church courts behind in England, the public colonial court assumed entire jurisdiction over slander. Whether or not they were aware of Pulton's dictum, they proceeded as if they had been, handling cases of slander and defamation as mixed action that might harm the individual and breach the peace.

Cases of assault amounted on the average to 6 percent of the business in all colonial courts. In many cases there is no record of the disposition of the charge; only the complaint or the presentment is on the record. In such cases, the judges may have acted informally as arbitrators and thus have served the function of safety valves that permitted the release of anger and resentment. Clearly, judges regarded assaults as mixed actions, sometimes awarding damages, sometimes imposing penalties, sometimes doing both. On the criminal side, persons found guilty of assault were punished by admonition, recognizance for good behavior, ducking, stocks, forced public work, fine, and whipping.[82]

Cases of slander or defamation on the average amounted to 17 percent of the criminal business of all colonial courts. Though most of these cases began on the complaint of an individual, in effect actions on the case, many began by presentment, which clearly implied criminality. In England the use of actions on the case to seek damages for slander had threatened to inundate the courts. This led to hair-splitting semantic exercises that produced virtual dictionaries of words that were or were not actionable.[83] The extent to which colonial magistrates were aware of these classifications is difficult to determine. The Rhode Island code of 1647 did show an awareness at least of the three main rubrics of actionable words: "The cases actionable are these, for a man to say either by word or writing, and yet not able to prove it, that another is a traitor, a felon, a thief, a cutpurse, or hath stolen something . . . ; to call and be able not to prove it, an unmarried woman a whore, a young man unmarried a whoremaster . . . or that a tradesman maketh nothing but bad wares, or that a merchant or shopkeeper hath nothing but rotten and unsound wares in his house or shop."[84]

The records do not show the defamatory words uttered or the disposition of most cases of slander. Here it seems most likely that the judges often acted as safety valves to permit the venting of verbal heat. Enough detail does survive to indicate that slander fell under the three categories. As to slanderous accusations that a person was a felon, the most common was calling a woman a witch. Others were that one was a rogue or a thief.[85] Probably the most common slander was to describe a woman as a whore. Sarah Lyne, the keeper of an inn at Saco, Maine, had judgment against a man for "calling her whore & base whore & punk." Joan Andrews, "a Make bayte" suffered twenty lashes for calling Goody Mendum an "Indian Hoare." A Marylander appealed a Kent County judgment to the Provincial Court. The words had been that "Henry Clay's wife was a burnt Arse whore and had the Pox."[86] The third category, which charged incompetence or dishonesty in business or profession, included one charge that a clerk of court was incompetent to draw a will.[87]

A cause célèbre occurred in Virginia when a minister and a planter escalated a dispute into a trial before the governor and council. The minister, Mr. Pooly, was conducting a meeting. Mr. Pawlett, a planter, entering and hearing Pooly mention his name, demanded to know "*what is it you say* of Pawlett?" Pooly responded, "I say you will not paye me your Tithe Tobacco." After further exchange, Pawlett warmed to his task and called Pooly "a stonde priest, and a Perjured man," guilty of simony and bribery to boot. After Pooly called Pawlett a liar, the latter responded with "blockheded parsone" who spoke "false *latten*" and taught "false doctrines." The minister, apparently having the worst of it, responded with "base baudie fellow." Six councillors and the governor gave separate opinions as to the relative degree of guilt and the appropriate punishments. Apparently, both men paid substantial fines and acknowledged their fault in church.[88]

Magistrates awarded damages and imposed penalties for slander.

The convicted slanderer might be admonished, required to admit error and ask forgiveness publicly, be bound to good behavior, stocked, fined, or whipped.[89]

A special and confusing form of slander occurred when the person defamed was a nobleman or magistrate. In England such offending words could be punished under the obscure title of *scandalum magnatum*. This offense had its origin in the statute of Westminster I and a statute of Richard II.[90] The extremely volatile political climate of Tudor times caused Mary and Elizabeth to give *scandalum magnatum* new currency.[91] Elizabeth's statute also provided penalties for seditious words. At the same time, Star Chamber was developing the law of seditious libel, and the law dealing with spoken or written words that were critical of government officials was in a confused state.

This confusion about verbal attacks on officers and magnates was mirrored in the colonial courts, where such words were regarded alternately as slander, sedition, seditious libels, or contempts. Though the term *scandalum magnatum* was never used, some actions certainly could have been described by it. An example that would have qualified on the civil side of English *scandalum magnatum* occurred in New Haven. John Davenport, the spiritual father of the colony, certainly the equivalent of a prelate, was awarded £40 in an action of slander. Such a large judgment was obviously also a grievous penalty.[92] Other slanderers of governors or high officials were stocked or whipped.[93] In Virginia, Richard Barnes was brutalized for slandering Governor Francis Wyatt.[94] In Essex, Elizabeth Due suffered twenty stripes and wore a paper proclaiming her "A SLANDERER OF MR ZEROBABELL ENDICOTT."[95]

Colonial judges appear to have understood the distinction between slanderous words, which were spoken, and written words, which amounted to libel. Though Winthrop and the Massachusetts assistants doubtless had regarded the Child petition and remonstrance as a seditious libel, they prosecuted it as sedition, perhaps because it had not technically been published. The only published libel found occurred in Essex. There Joseph Rowlandson attached "a scandelous lybell" to the meeting house. The broadside slandered the magistrates. It read: "Turninge out all Associates which are able to corrupt justice bee the cause never so good." Rowlandson was sentenced to be fined or whipped.[96]

Misconduct

To some degree, the transatlantic migration of the English people represented a release from the standards and constraints of a traditional society. The responsibility for establishing standards of behavior in the new communities fell primarily upon the magistrates. Two large areas of control have already been examined, those of sexual behavior and of persons who threatened others with physical violence or defamatory speech. When the disciplining of drunks, idlers, cursers, abusers of tobacco, Sabbath violators, condemners of religion and ministers, game players, and those who refused to accept their place in society is added, it becomes clear that the imposition of behavioral controls was a major part of the business of the magistrates. Three intertwined factors explain the magistrates' policies: enforcement of a work ethic, control of the order of society, and maintenance of the moral standards dictated by a particular piety.

The original American experience put a high premium on the work ethic. Survival and the improvement of the standard of living required work. Inspired in part by piety, the Puritan colonies forbade idleness by statute. That enforcement of these laws was infrequent[97] is not evidence of a careless magistracy, but of a basic tenet well taught. There is some evidence[98] that the Massachusetts leaders knew Coke's philippic on the subject: "I would request, that all imployed in any place of authorities, would have an speciall care to suppresse that root of evil, from whence all mischiefs do proceed, and that is *Idleness*." Coke then made a hard and fast equation between the idler and the drunkard. The idler would sink into "the Slymie dregs of Swinelike drunkenness." The drunkard could be restored to social usefulness only by a rigorous application of the law.[99]

In every colony people drank alcohol in large quantities. Among the Pilgrim grievances against the captain of the *Mayflower* was his refusal to leave them a supply of beer. Virginians complained about the wretched quality of ale sent out by the London Company. Magistrates in all colonies would have agreed with a latter-day Puritan seer: "The wine is from God, but the Drunkard is from the Devil."[100] Whatever weight the authorities placed on the sinful aspects of drunkenness, all would have agreed that it had at least two socially undesirable results. Drunks often broke the peace, but more important, excessive drinking kept them from work. Societies that could not afford idlers would not tolerate drunks.

Drunkenness, the most common colonial misdemeanor, litters the records of most courts. An average of 12 percent of all offenders appearing in all courts were persons charged with drunkenness. The rates of appearance per thousand population per annum were 1.16 in the Massachusetts Assistants Court, .91 in Plymouth, .36 in Accomack-Northampton, and 1.52 in Essex. The most common penalty imposed on the convicted drunk was a 10-shilling fine. Fines escalated for repeaters. Chronic drunkards or especially riotous ones could expect to be whipped and in some cases to wear a badge that announced their offense to all.

A New Haven case exhibits the concerns of the Puritan magistrates.[101] James Heywood had been charged with excessive drinking aboard a Dutch vessel. When he appeared before the magistrates, he had already been cast out of the church for this act. The judges wanted evidence of his having been drunk and found it in the fact "that he had not the use of his reason, nor of his tongue, hands or feete: so that there is all the c[h]aracter of a drunken man." They preferred a confession, and Heywood obliged: "I owne my sinne and take the shame, and doe confesse the name of God hath bin dishonored and blaspheamed through mee." The presiding judge then read the lesson: "Drunkenness is among the fruits of the flesh, both to be witnessed against, both in church and civill court, and its a brutish sinne." Heywood's offense was darkened by the fact that he had been a church member, but lightened because he had not "bin given to drunkennesse." The court was asked whether it found "a disposition to drunkennesse or an act onlye." Finding the latter, they fined Heywood, but spared him a whipping.

In supervising the master-servant relationship, colonial magistrates followed the general lines of the English Statute of Labourers, which empowered the justices of the peace to inquire into breaches of the indenture by either party.[102] Such supervision combined concerns about the work ethic with those of controlling the status order of society. Indentured servants and apprentices made up a large part of the colonial labor force. If they were disciplined properly, production rose while, at least ideally, they were being trained to assume responsibilities as citizens when they had fulfilled their contract. The law expected the master to control his servants and permitted physical coercion.[103] Courts stood ready to support the master with public authority when his discipline failed. They also used their machinery to apprehend the runaway. The permission given the master to impose discipline was often abused, and extreme examples of coercion created the largest class of colonial homicides. Judges also heard servants' complaints of and presentments for masters' abuse of their authority.

Cases involving servant discipline amounted to an average of 5 percent of the criminal business in all colonial courts. Of the eighty-nine cases seen, in thirty-nine (44 percent) judges intervened to punish unruly servants, usually with a whipping and sometimes by extending their term of service. Forty percent of the cases dealt with runaways. Many of these servants were also accused of theft; punishment was almost always whipping. In fourteen cases masters were called to account for servant abuse. Though one was whipped, their penalty was usually a fine.

Offenses against established churches and their religious beliefs generated behavioral trespasses in all colonies. These acts included failure to attend church, violation of the Sabbath, disturbing church services, and reviling ministers and doctrine. Authorities in Maryland and Virginia rarely prosecuted persons for these misdemeanors.[104] Prosecutions for failing to attend church were relatively rare in New England, probable evidence that most persons went to meetings or responded to warnings by ministers and elders. Such prosecutions became much more frequent in Massachusetts and Plymouth during the late 1650s, when the magistrates used the law against those who were attracted to Quaker meetings. The New England magistrates maintained a rigorously ascetic Sabbath by punishing those who worked, traveled, or played on Sunday.[105] The knowledge that most householders would be at church was tempting to thieves, but larcenies and other crimes were punished with greater severity if they occurred on the Sabbath.[106]

At the meeting, persons were expected to be solemn and attentive, certainly not to take a nap or make a disturbance.[107] Ideally, the minister taught and led a harmonious congregation, but even a saint could not have satisfied every member. Doubtless some ministers were incompetent, but it was not wise to criticize them, as a

Salem woman did: "I Could have a boy from the Colledg that would preach better than Mr. Walton for half the wages."[108]

Another line of the law inspired by piety provided for the punishment of cursers and swearers. Swearing fell into two categories, "prophane" or "blasphemous." The curser was well advised to leave God's name out of his oath because if he used it he walked along the dangerous boundary of blasphemy, a most serious offense. To swear "by the bloud of God" or "Gods foote" or even "I vow to God" brought punishment.[109] In two cases, Puritan magistrates made it clear that utterance of such oaths was a capital crime. A Massachusetts grand jury indicted Benjamin Sawcer, a captain in Cromwell's forces, for blasphemy for uttering the words, "Jehova is the Devill, and hee [Sawcer] knew no God, but his sword, and that should save him." The trial jury refused to convict because he had been drunk. The magistrates, apparently wanting the death penalty, refused the verdict and carried the case to the General Court. Sawcer ended the business by escaping from jail.[110] In New Haven, Governor Theophilus Eaton warned George King that an oath which included the words "by God" was a most serious offense. "Its the peirceing through the name of God in passion, which is a high provokation of God, whereas the rule is, let your words be yea, yea, & nay, nay, & by a mans words he may loose his life." After this horrific warning, the court let King off with a whipping because it hoped that he had not sworn "dispitfully."[111] All colonies punished cursers and distinguished blasphemous oaths from common swearing.[112]

Lying was another form of immoral, culpable speech. In the New England jurisdictions persons were regularly presented for lying. Prosecutions for lying were often coupled with another crime. If a thief denied the act charged and it was proved, he would be punished for both lying and theft. When lying harmed another it became "notorious" or "pernicious," an example of the latter being a woman who accused two men of being the father of her child, a patent untruth.[113] There were no examples of prosecutions for lying in southern courts.

Judges exercised a wide discretion in determining the heinousness of these verbal offenses. Penalties escalated from admonition to wearing signs identifying them as cursers or liars, to confinement in the stocks, to suffering the indignity of having a cleft stick clamped on the tongue, to fines (the most common punishment), to whipping.

Prohibitions of "excessive apparel" provide the clearest example of explicit law designed to keep people in their proper place in the social order. In England all laws regulating apparel had been repealed in 1604.[114] Massachusetts and Connecticut kept such laws on their books.[115] The Connecticut order of 1641 made the purpose clear when it instructed the constables to present persons who dressed in such a way as to "exceede their conditions and ranks." In Essex County, Massachusetts, there was a rash of prosecutions in the early 1650s for wearing gold and silver lace and silk hoods.[116] If persons who dressed so splendidly came from families worth £200 they were discharged; so was a woman who had been "brought up above the ordinary rank."[117]

Crime along the Chesapeake and in New England

A historical study of crime ought to give insights into the qualities of past societies. It probably is more enlightening to turn the proposition around and say that social conditions explain the nature of crime. The most important conclusion that can be drawn about crime in all jurisdictions in America before 1660 is that there was very little of it. On the average, only one person out of every 750 appeared in court in any given year accused of any kind of crime or misconduct. From the perspective either of seventeenth-century England or twentieth-century America, this is a low rate of incidence. If only crimes against persons and property are considered, deleting misconducts, the rate of court appearance falls to one person each year out of every 2,250.

These low crime rates are explained by facts common to the societies along the Chesapeake and in New England. Total populations were small, as were the farm and village units in which the people lived. Everyone literally had a place where he or she was known to live and a similarly known place on the social scale. There were few vagabonds, and a stranger would have been recognized immediately. There was very little or no unemployment. Everyone had at least a minimum standard of food, clothing, and shelter.

TABLE 4.3.   INCIDENCE OF CRIME[a] PER THOUSAND POPULATION[b] PER ANNUM

	Massachusetts Assistants Court 1630–37 pop. 3,453 119 items	Plymouth General & Assistants Court 1633–60 pop. 1,180 229 items	Accomack-Northampton County Court, Virginia 1632–45 pop. 600 58 items	Essex County Court, Massachusetts 1636–60 834 items	Kent County Court, Maryland 1648–60 pop. 411 38 items
	Per 1,000	Per 1,000	Per 1,000	Per 1,000	Per 1,000
Homicide[c]	.14	.09	none	.01	none
Theft	.74	.81	.48	.93	.81
Drunkenness	1.16	.91	.36	1.52	.81
Slander[d]	.07	.24	1.79	2.21	2.63
Sex offenses	.49	1.81	1.19	1.47	.81
Contempt	.53	.39	.95	.22	.41
Religion[e]	.04	.73	.12	.98	.81
Assault[f]	.14	.67	1.19	1.38	.20
Behavior[g]	.74	1.15	.71	3.17	.61
Sedition	.25	.12	.12	.07	none

[a] As items appear in the record regardless of disposition.

[b] Establishing crime rates in proportion to population is fraught with difficulty. The first problem is lack of population statistics. For both England and America, population statistics are unreliable or nonexistent, especially for the counties, a major unit of criminal jurisdiction. The population statistics for Plymouth and Massachusetts have been taken from *Statistical History*, appendix Z; those for the Virginia county from the introduction to Accomack, 1632–40. The population of Kent County was taken from the introduction to volume 53 of *Maryland Archives*. The population for Essex County was estimated as follows. In conversation, David T. Konig, whose *Law and Society in Puritan Massachusetts* shows him to be most knowledgeable about the county, estimated its adult white male population in 1689 to be approximately 2,000. Applying the standard militia ratio of 1:5.3 established a total population of 10,600 for Essex in that year. The population of Massachusetts was 48,899. Thus the population of Essex was 21.7 of the Massachusetts total. Using average annual growth rates derived from *Statistical History* established an average population for Essex for the years 1636–60 of 2,744, a figure that seemed reasonable to Konig. The entire population was used as a base whether or not all persons stood at risk of committing crimes. The table is not based on convictions but on frequency of appearance of types of crime in the record. The rates are expressed as annual rates of frequency of types of crime for population units of 1,000. A second problem is uncertainty about the reach of jurisdiction of the various courts. The broad jurisdiction exercised by the superior courts confuses analysis. Some of the business done there was within the competence of county courts, but to what county should cases of simple larceny or misconduct be assigned? Except in the small number of superior court cases where there were formal indictments, the place of residence of the accused was rarely given. The courts exhibited in the table were chosen because difficulties of reach of jurisdiction were at least minimal. Plymouth had no county courts, so the record of its general and assistants courts can be assumed to include all of the crimes tried in the colony. Because the Massachusetts Assistants Court exercised an exclusive criminal jurisdiction from 1630 to 1637 its record exhibits all of the criminal cases tried in the colony during those years. Some minor crimes committed in the counties of Accomack-Northampton, Essex, and Kent may have been tried in higher provincial courts, but this has been presumed to be negligible because the superior courts were not physically located in these counties.

[c] Notice of homicides and other serious crimes appear very rarely in county courts. Unlike the English quarter sessions, colonial county courts did not take indictments in such cases.

[d] Civil, criminal, and mixed actions.

[e] Sabbath violation, nonattendance at church, reviling ministers and doctrine. Quaker discipline has been excluded from Plymouth and Essex. Had they been included the per 1,000 rates would have been 1.7 and 1.35 respectively.

[f] Civil, criminal, and mixed actions.

[g] Servant behavior and runaways, lying, swearing, tobacco abuse, idleness, excessive apparel, and disorderly living.

There was little conspicuous wealth. Such societies lacked both compelling motives and opportunities for crime. Theft was a casual act, and a career in crime was impossible.

Those tight little communities were no utopias. Social tensions generated the crimes against persons, the homicides and the assaults. On the farm or in the village, people lived in extended families. Father, mother, son, daughter, miscellaneous other relatives, and servants worked and lived together twenty-four hours a day. With little privacy in the home or at the work place and no place else to go, people lived constantly in the same small group. Such conditions created friction that could ignite interpersonal violence. Closeness generated contention. In cases of homicide for which the records are detailed, they show overwhelmingly that killings were not premeditated acts. People committed murder in a rage of frustration. Homicides were predictable explosions of violence that happened to cause death. Much less detailed information has survived for cases of assault and battery, but the acts seem not to have been calculated. The incredible frequency of slander is further evidence of abrasive human relations in small, compacted societies. The slanderer relieved frustration by hurling a hyperbolic insult at an envied or hated neighbor.

The similarity among colonies of the frequency and kinds of crimes against persons and property did not carry over into the area of misconduct. The rate of prosecutions for misconduct in Essex County, Massachusetts, was 220 percent higher than that in Accomack-Northampton County, Virginia. The statistic demonstrates the impact of Puritanism on law and law enforcement. The first obvious reason for the huge difference is that the Virginia county operated by the English rules that left much misconduct to be dealt with by the church courts. In Virginia this meant that it was not dealt with at all. Essex County operated under the rules of a Puritan legislature that penalized by statute a wide range of misbehavior. But even for acts that were punishable by public law in the two jurisdictions, Essex prosecuted at a much higher rate. For example, Essex prosecuted drunks at a rate that was 422 percent higher than that in Accomack-Northampton. Perhaps a part of this difference may be explained by the fact that an errant Puritan in Salem would be visibly drunk in the village, whereas his Virginia cousin became sotted in the solitude of a house in the clearing. But the statistics and the tone of the court records make it clear that the divergent rates are explained primarily by a difference in attitude. The Puritan magistrates sought out misconduct because it was sinful. The Chesapeake magistrates left people alone unless the pursuit of their pleasures seriously breached the peace. The fact that judicial inquiry into illicit sexual activity in Essex exceeded the Virginia rate by only 24 percent seems inconsistent with these different attitudes toward sinful behavior. Statistically, fornication was the chief problem, followed by adultery. Moral issues aside, adultery threatened family integrity and created the possibility of private violence against either party. Sharp exemplary punishment of fornicators seemed to be a wise policy. Young men and women, many of them servants, lived and worked in close quarters. If the gratification of their natural desires produced children, the new mothers were obviously less valuable as servants. If the father could not be identified, society was left with a bastard to support. These practical considerations must have had about equal weight in shaping official attitudes toward extramarital sex in all colonies.

If the success of a criminal justice system is judged by the rate of recidivism, all of the colonial jurisdictions receive high marks. Occasionally one finds a repeater: a chronic alcoholic, a boy who could not control his sexual urges, a deviant hermit, or a man obviously prone to violence. These few exceptions aside, the rate of recidivism was virtually nil. The judicial system did one of two things to convicted persons: it either inflicted penalties and returned the violators immediately to society or cut them off permanently from society by death or banishment. Those who returned to society had suffered real pain and humiliation. Apparently taught by experience and aware that they would be watched closely, they chose not to run the risk of offending and suffering again.

The Lost World of Early American Law

Where does this brief record of fifty years fit in the long history of Anglo-American jurisprudence? The noun "reception" has commonly been used to describe the process of installing English law in the American jurisdictions. Reception theory either implies or explicitly describes early American law as crude and primitive, an invention of necessity. At first, the frontier thesis, that beast of all American historical burdens, was used to explain this earliest period of law development. In time, the interpretation became established that the field of American law before 1783 was a wasteland. In America, "Blackstone mounted a waiting and empty throne." The process of reception, then, was thought to have begun after the American Revolution. This fantastic interpretation carried with it a value judgment. Good law was complex, sophisticated, technically precise, in a word, "professional." By contrast, colonial law was a bundle of miscellaneous rules. Even the raw materials out of which real law could be fashioned were missing. Witness the fact that colonial superior courts did not publish their opinions. If this reading of early American law is correct, one is left to wonder how the colonists made do at all for those 162 years before Blackstone arrived on these shores.[1]

Reception theory necessarily posits the assumption that early Americans were ignorant or that the environment made them so. By that theory, the two John Winthrops, Roger Ludlow, Samuel Gorton, Sir George Yeardley, and John Lewger were either natively stupid or were made into simpletons by the forest, a hard case to make.

Much of the confusion about reception arises from the fact that both at the beginning and the end of the colonial experience there existed radically opposed concepts of the common law. From one point of view, it was an incredibly complex and archaic system of social regulation. Viewed another way, the law itself was the main bulwark protecting the subject from arbitrary government.

If we are to understand law development in America before 1660, we need to abandon the noun "reception" and replace it with the verb "carry."[2] Emigrating Englishmen brought the law in their baggage. As immigrants always have, they left some of their possessions behind and would use some of what they carried with them for different purposes than had been intended. The law that colonists installed in the new jurisdictions was the result of conscious choice. The process of selecting from the old materials showed an awareness of the duality of the common law.

Precisely at the time when the colonists began building their law, the libertarian qualities of the common law were being illuminated as never before. As judge and Parliament man, Coke defied the Stuarts in the name of the law. In retirement, he produced his monument to the supremacy of the law, the *Second Institute*, "Coke on Magna Carta." The colonists played out the same drama on their smaller stages. The first major political struggle in America, the battle over discretionary justice, had as its issue the supremacy of law. Winthrop understood this struggle. The people who opposed him wanted laws "in resemblance to a Magna Carta." The New England codes and the statutes that Marylanders wrung out of their strife with the Calverts were evidence of the liberal tradition of the parent law: men should have known law to live by, and that law controlled all men. At the level of specifics, colonial legislators began filling out a broader definition of due process. In the common law, due process had the limited meaning of formal rules for implementing a prosecution. The colonists began what proved to be the very long struggle to equate due process with essential fairness. By positive law and practice the colonists defined due process as those explicit guarantees that were set out above in the conclusion to Chapter 2, an impressive list.

The second perception of the common law and its administration was that it was archaic, obfuscated by meaningless technicalities, inhumane, and irrational. No man who came out to America in a position of leadership could have been unaware of the agitation for law reform in England. Those emigrants did not invent reform in the forest. They brought the impulse with them and largely accomplished the changes being demanded at home. Evidence of that accomplishment has appeared in every chapter of this book. Some parts of English law they simply left behind, such as the church courts. In other cases, they made new institutions by selectively combining elements of old institutions. For example, they created out of the maze of English courts a two-level system of courts having general jurisdiction. In other instances, they acted consciously in the light of reason and humanity. Certainly it was reasonable to state the law in straightforward English and strip away the technical requirements of procedure. Certainly it was humane and rational to prefer life to property and to abolish the death penalty for theft. Certainly it was both rational and humane to restrict the consequences of judgment to the convict by barring forfeiture and corruption of the blood.

If it is true that the colonists in all jurisdictions drew their law from the same sources and selectively adopted law that either was operative in England or was being demanded by the advocates of reform, the question comes whether or not an American common law was developing. Similarities among the jurisdictions outweighed differences. The catalog of criminal acts was much the same from colony to colony, except that New England elevated the penalties for sexual misconduct. Every colony dispatched its criminal business in county and council courts. From prosecution to judgment, magistrates in those courts followed the same procedure. Crime rates showed reasonable consistency, and everywhere recidivism was rare. Some differences are obvious, the chief one being that the New England legislators generated a large body of positive law whereas those on the Chesapeake did not. Arguing from the evidence of the codes, one might conclude that a common law for New England might have developed, but it did not. Whatever similarities can be found, in 1660 seven separate bodies of law were being administered in seven distinct jurisdictions. The earliest legislators and judges laid separatism at the base of American jurisprudence. Neither English attempts at standardization after 1690 nor the amalgamation of the jurisdictions into a nation in 1789 could create a common American criminal law. Where once there were seven, now there are fifty.

To return to the question that I posed at the beginning of this conclusion and rephrase it so that it is forward-looking from the year 1660: What impact did this brief record of fifty years have on

the future development of American law? In part, the answer must
be by way of hypothesis. In the years immediately following 1660,
the process of detailed reception of the law of England began. By
the early part of the eighteenth century, that process had obliter-
ated much of the work of the earliest generation. The two chief
agencies of reception were the lawyers and the various English government boards charged with the oversight of colonial administration. As the colonies grew and prospered, the lawyers saw a fertile
but fallow field. They moved in with all their gear and planted virtually all of the old seeds. They flourished. Beginning in 1673, the
home government began to maintain agents in America. Men such
as Edward Randolph were concerned primarily with suppressing
the colonists' evasion of the laws of navigation and trade. But con-
sistently in critical reports to their superiors, they also pointed out
how far colonial law deviated from English law. The government
undertook a wholesale review of American law during the 1690s.
Its attitude toward American law was expressed in the earl of Bello-
mont's description of the laws of Rhode Island as "a parcell of Fus-
tian."[3] Some parts of the indigenous law probably survived, for
example, a restrained use of the death penalty. Regardless of such
survivals, the rational and humane law of the founders was largely
lost, swallowed up by the reception.

The lawyer-politicians who made the American Revolution and
founded the nation were largely unaware of the old native legal heritage. They were bewitched by the duality of the common law. Arguing from the libertarian side of the English law in 1728, the
senior Daniel Dulany anticipated many a polemic. The value of *The
Right of the Inhabitants of Maryland to the Benefit of the English Laws* was
that the common and statute law restrained prerogative. Beginning
with James Otis's brilliant argument against the writs of assistance
in 1761, the polemicists of the American Revolution would again
and again raise the common law as a barrier to executive prerogative and parliamentary power. Examples of the acceptance of
the obfuscated, illiberal side of the law abound. Open Alexander
Hamilton's practice manual to the first page. He began with "Process" and there they are: Latitat, Testatum Capias, Capias Pluries,
Capias Alias; further on, the plea of autrefois attaint resurrected.[4]
Consider the advice that Jeremiah Gridley gave to John Adams on
the eve of his admission to the bar: "In the study of Law the com-

mon Law be sure deserves your first and last Attention, and He has conquered all the Difficulties of this Law, who is Master of the Institutes. You must conquer the Institutes. The Road of Science is much easier, now, than it was when I sett out. I began with Co. Litt. and broke thro."[5]

Because society perceives criminal law as its first line of defense, it is tough law, highly resistant to change. Witness the failure of the English to reform their criminal law through two long centuries and the frustration that has accompanied current efforts of the Congress to reform the criminal code of the United States. The achievement of those forefathers seems remarkable. They planted old seeds in new fields and brought forth a better harvest. Can the men of those tiny communities, their law long lost, now speak to us over the gap of three hundred years? I think so. They tell us that to apply reason and humanity to the criminal law does not necessarily weaken the force of its sanctions.

Abbreviations

The following abbreviations have been used for works cited frequently.

Accomack, 1632–40	Susie M. Ames, ed., *County Court Records of Accomack-Northampton, Virginia, 1632–1640*. Washington, 1954.
Accomack, 1640–45	Susie M. Ames, *County Records of Accomack-Northampton, Virginia, 1640–1645*. Charlottesville, 1973.
B of L	The Massachusetts Body of Liberties in William H. Whitmore, ed., *A Bibliographical Sketch of the Laws of the Massachusetts Colony from 1630 to 1686*. Boston, 1890.
Conn. Col. Rec.	J. Hammond Trumbull and Charles J. Hoadly, eds., *The Public Records of the Colony of Connecticut (1636–1776)*. 15 vols. Hartford, 1850–90.
Conn. Hist. Soc. *Col.*	"Records of the Particular Court of Connecticut, 1639–1663," Connecticut Historical Society, *Collections*, vol. 22. Hartford, 1928.
Essex	Dow, G. F., ed., *Records and Files of the Quarterly Courts of Essex County, Massachusetts*. 8 vols. Salem, 1911.
Hening	William W. Hening, ed., *The Statutes at Large: Being a Collection of All the Laws of Virginia from . . . 1619*. Richmond, 1819–23.
L & L	*The Laws and Liberties of Massachusetts*. Cambridge, Mass., 1929.
Md. Arch.	William H. Browne et al., eds., *Archives of Maryland*. 66 vols. Baltimore 1883–.
Mass. Asst. Ct.	John Noble, ed., *Records of the Court of Assistants of the Colony of The Massachusetts Bay, 1630–1692*. 3 vols. Boston, 1901–28.
Mass. Col. Rec.	Nathaniel B. Shurtleff, ed., *Records of the Governor and Company of the Massachusetts Bay in New England*. 5 vols. Boston, 1853–54.
Me. Ct. Rec.	Charles T. Libby et al., eds., *Province and Court Records of Maine*. 6 vols. Portland, 1928–75.
N.H. Col. Rec. 1	Hoadly, Charles J., ed., *Records of the Colony and Plantation of New Haven from 1638–1649*. Hartford, 1857.

N.H. Col. Rec. 2	Charles Hoadly, ed., *Records of the Colony or Jurisdiction of New Haven from May 1653, to the Union*. Hartford, 1857.
Ply. Rec.	Nathaniel B. Shurtleff and David Pulsifer, eds., *Records of the Colony of New Plymouth in New England*. 12 vols. Boston, 1855–61.
Pynch. Ct. Rec.	Joseph Smith, ed., *Colonial Justice in Western Massachusetts 1639–1702: The Pynchon Court Record*. Cambridge, Mass., 1961.
R.I. Rec.	John R. Bartlett, ed., *Records of the Colony of Rhode Island and Providence Plantations, in New England*. 10 vols. Providence, 1856–65.
Va. Gen. Ct.	Henry R. McIlwaine, ed., *Minutes of the Council and General Court of Colonial Virginia*. Richmond, 1924.

Notes

Chapter One: Substantive Criminal Law

1. Joan R. Kent, "Attitudes of Members of the House of Commons to the Regulation of 'Personal Conduct' in Late Elizabethan and Early Stuart England," 39–71; Donald Veall, *The Popular Movement for Law Reform, 1640–1660*; G. B. Warden, "Law Reform in England and New England, 1620–1640," 668–90; Barbara Shapiro, "Law Reform in Seventeenth Century England," 280–321. Some of the pamphlets of the advocates of law reform are in volumes 2, 4, 5, and 8 of the *Harleian Miscellany*; William Haller and Godfrey Davies, eds., *The Leveller Tracts, 1647–1653*; and Sir Francis Bacon, *Law Tracts*.
2. The data upon which the charts in this chapter are based may be found in Appendix Tables A and B. The references to the statutes are in the notes to these appendixes.
3. Edmund S. Morgan, *American Slavery, American Freedom*, 123–28, 149–53.
4. *Ply. Rec.*, 11:72.
5. William Bradford, *Of Plymouth Plantation, 1620–1647*, 234; "Governor Bradford's Letter Book," Massachusetts Historical Society, *Collections*, 1st ser., 3:37; Ply. v. John Billington.
6. *Ply. Rec.*, 11:72.
7. Charles M. Andrews, *The Colonial Period of American History*, 2:11–17; Samuel Gorton, *Simplicities Defense against Seven-headed Policy*, title page, 22, 39, 41, 57, 65–66, in Peter Force, *Tracts and Other Papers*, vol. 4.
8. Roger Williams, *The bloody Tenent yet more bloody*, in James H. Trumbell et al., eds., *The Complete Writings of Roger Williams*, 4:485–88; Edmund S. Morgan, *Roger Williams: The Church and the State*, 90–94, 102–3; The First Epistle of Paul the Apostle to Timothy, 1:9–10.
9. Some of the colonists, for example William Bradford, used the Geneva Bible (Elizabeth's Bible). Others, for example John Winthrop, used the Authorized Version (King James' Bible); see P. Marion Simms, *The Bible in America*, 90, 93. Biblical citations in the New England law texts have been checked against the 1594 version of the Geneva Bible and the 1616 edition of the Authorized Version. Usually the citations in the codes accurately reflect the biblical text. The Puritans felt the need to base every mandatory death penalty on the authority of the Bible. The crime of rape obviously caused problems. The text is Deuteronomy 22:23–29 and the two versions of the Bible are in harmony.

The concern there is with intercourse between a man and a betrothed virgin. If copulation occurred in the city, both the man and the woman were executed. If the act occurred in the fields, only the man died. The rationale for the difference was that a woman being raped would cry out. She would be heard in the city but not in the country. Massachusetts, with New Haven following, avoided the difficulty by following the common law. Because no precise biblical text supported the common law of rape, those colonies made the death penalty optional in all cases of nonconsensual intercourse whether or not the woman was betrothed. Ignoring the distinction between the rural and urban settings, Connecticut demanded the death penalty in cases where the woman raped was betrothed or married. The Massachusetts and New Haven codes required the death penalty for a homicide committed "suddenly in anger, or cruelty of passion." By excluding premeditation, this definition approximated the English crime of manslaughter, a clergyable offense. The Puritan codes rest primarily on Leviticus 24:17, which requires the execution of him who "killeth anie man." Connecticut did not follow the Massachusetts example. It based the homicide provisions of its codes primarily in Exodus 21:12, 13, 14. Though the text is not perfectly clear, the requirement of premeditation for a capital homicide may be inferred. See *L & L*, 6; *N.H. Col. Rec. 2*, 578; *Conn. Col. Rec.*, 1:77. For the unsuccessful prosecutions of manslaughter in these jurisdictions see Table 4.1

10. See below, Chapter 4.
11. Shapiro, "Law Reform."
12. A few men in all colonies had legal training, but virtually none practiced law. The active colonial prejudice against lawyers reflected the opinion of some English advocates of reform; see, for example, William Cole, *A Rod for Lawyers*, in *Harleian Miscellany*, vol. 4; *B of L*, 16; Hening, 1: 495; Anton-Herman Chroust, *The Rise of the Legal Profession in America*, 1: 268–71.
13. Sir Edward Coke, *The Third Part of the Institutes of the Laws of England*, 58.
14. *N.H. Col. Rec. 2*, 577.
15. C. H. Firth and R. S. Rait, eds., *Acts and Ordinances of the Interregnum, 1642–1660*, 2:387–89.
16. Hening, 1:69.
17. *Mass. Col. Rec.*, 1:91–92, 198, 202–3, 300, 335; John Winthrop, *Winthrop's Journal "History of New England,"* ed. James K. Hosmer, 1:263, 2:12–14, 161–63; *B of L*, 94.9.
18. *R.I. Rec.*, 1:173.
19. *Ply. Rec.*, 11:12.
20. Michael Dalton, *The Countrey Justice*, 32–33; William Lambarde, *Eirenarcha or the Office of the Justice of the Peace*, 270; 18 Eliz. c.3 (1576); 7 James I c.4 (1610).
21. Lyon G. Tyler, ed., *Narratives of Early Virginia, 1606–1625*, 271–72; Hening, 1:438–39.
22. *Md. Arch.*, 1:159, 312–13; *R.I. Rec.*, 1:173.
23. *Conn. Col. Rec.*, 1:78.
24. Ibid., 1:527; *L & L*, 23; *Ply. Rec.*, 11:12, 46.

25. Emil Oberholzer, Jr., *Delinquent Saints*, 127–51; see below Chapter 3.
26. Kent, "Attitudes to Regulation of 'Personal Conduct.'"
27. Christopher Hill, *Society and Puritanism in Pre-Revolutionary England*, 298–343.
28. See Coke's philippic on the subject, *The Lord Coke His Speech and Charge*, H2–H3.
29. John Bond arguing against a bill mandating church attendance in the session of 1601, quoted in Kent, "Attitudes to Regulation of 'Personal Conduct.'"
30. Forestall: to intercept goods on the way to market; regrate: to buy and sell the same goods in the same market; engross: to buy food products at the place of production. The intent in each case was to drive up prices.
31. Contempt: resistance or threat of resistance to officers or process; embracery: corruptly influencing a jury; barratry: stirring up suits for profit; champerty: maintaining the cost of the suit of another in return for a share of the award.
32. Mass. v. Benjamin Sawcer; N.H. v. George King (1646).
33. *Virginia Magazine of History and Biography* 7 (1899–1900): 129–30; 11(1903–4): 505; 16 (1908–9): 121–22.
34. Francis N. Thorpe, ed., *The Federal and State Constitutions, Colonial Charters, and Other Organic Laws of the States, Territories, and Colonies Now or Heretofore Forming the United States of America*, 3: 1679–81.
35. For the main episodes of this long conflict, *Md. Arch.*, 1:31, 39, 82–83, 146–64, 241–43, 262–72, 300, 317.
36. Va. v. Daniel Franke; Md. v. John & Mary Williams; Morgan, *American Slavery*, 108–30.
37. The Plymouth code left a great deal of discretion with the judges.
38. John Calvin, *Institutes of the Christian Religion*, ed. John T. McNeill, 2: 1489–92, 1502.
39. For modern analyses of the political crises of the 1640s see Robert E. Wall, Jr., *Massachusetts Bay*, and Kai T. Erikson, *Wayward Puritans*, 71–114.
40. Winthrop, *Journal*, 1:211–18; Allyn B. Forbes, ed., *Winthrop Papers*, 4: 468–84.
41. *Conn. Col. Rec.*, 1:21, 25, 78.
42. *Mass. Col. Rec.*, 1:passim; Carol F. Lee, "Discretionary Justice in Early Massachusetts," 120–39.
43. *Mass. Col. Rec.*, 1:94, 108, 132–33, 177, 212–13.
44. The proceedings against these people are scattered through the first volume of *Mass. Col. Rec.* and Winthrop, *Journal*. They are dealt with extensively in the secondary sources. Details of the process may be seen in the trial of Anne Hutchinson, in Thomas Hutchinson, *The History of the Colony and Province of Massachusetts-Bay*, 2: appendix, and the trial of Samuel Gorton, *Simplicities Defense*, 62–75.
45. Winthrop, *Journal*, 1: 151.
46. Howard M. Chapin, ed., *Documentary History of Rhode Island*, 1: 32.
47. *R.I. Rec.*, 1:288.
48. Connecticut Historical Society, *Collections* 1(1906): 20–21.
49. Forbes, ed., *Winthrop Papers*, 4:53–54, 81.

50. The replacement of communal agencies of social control (church and township) with more formal institutions (explicit law and public courts) as population became larger and more diverse is a main theme of David T. Konig, *Law and Society in Puritan Massachusetts, Essex County, 1629–1692*, and William E. Nelson, "The Larger Context of Litigation in Plymouth, 1725–1825," which is the introduction to David T. Konig, ed., *The Plymouth Court Records.* See also William E. Nelson, *Dispute and Conflict Resolution in Plymouth County, Massachusetts, 1725–1825*; William Bradford, *Of Plymouth Plantation*, 252–54, 316–17; William Bradford, "A Descriptive and Historical Account of New England in Verse," 81.
51. Winthrop, *Journal*, 1:335–38.
52. *R.I. Rec.*, 1:157.
53. *L & L*, 1; *Conn. Col. Rec.*, 1:509; *N.H. Col. Rec. 1*, 571–72.
54. J. Spedding, et al., eds., *The Works of Francis Bacon*, 8:102.

Chapter Two: Judicial Proceedings

1. Dalton, *Countrey Justice*, 298–300; Lambarde, *Eirenarcha*, 16; 34 Edw. IV c.1; M. J. Ingram, "Communities and Courts: Law and Disorder in Early Seventeenth Century Wiltshire," in James S. Cockburn, ed., *Crime in England, 1550–1800*, 111–13, describes English use of recognizance that is strikingly similar to colonial practice.
2. *Md. Arch.*, 4:19; other examples: ibid., 131–32; *Ply. Rec.*, 1:63, 119; *Me. Ct. Rec.*, 1:272–73.
3. *Md. Arch.* 4:35.
4. *Me. Ct. Rec.*, 1:75; *Mass. Col. Rec.*, 1:298.
5. *Mass. Asst. Ct.*, 2:134, 137, 138.
6. *Me. Ct. Rec.*, 1:176.
7. For examples of forfeited recognizances: *Ply. Rec.*, 2:112, 113, 127. Robert Hutchinson, for an open contempt of court, forfeited a good behavior bond for a previous adultery, *Va. Gen. Ct.*, 119.
8. William S. Holdsworth, *A History of English Law*, 2:393.
9. John Langbein, *Prosecuting Crime in the Renaissance*, 66.
10. Dalton, *Countrey Justice*, 136–37.
11. Ibid., 20.
12. *B of L*, 18; *L & L*, 28, 36; *Conn. Col. Rec.*, 1:539–40; *R.I. Rec.*, 1:162–63, 232; Veall, *Popular Movement for Law Reform*, 136.
13. *Mass. Col. Rec.*, 1:108, 132—33; *Va. Gen. Ct.*, 19–20; *Ply. Rec.*, 2:24, 25.
14. For examples of contempts and punishments: *Mass. Col. Rec.*, 1:84, 86, 94, 97, 100, 177, 219–20, 245, 249, 261, 265, 286, 296, 300; *Ply. Rec.*, 2:136, 175; *Me. Ct. Rec.*, 1:87, 118, 177, 266; *Conn. Col. Rec.*, 1:44, 155; *Va. Gen. Ct.*, 57; *Md. Arch.*, 11:36.
15. *R.I. Rec.*, 1:162–63.
16. *Mass. Col. Rec.*, 1:121–23.
17. John P. Kennedy and Henry R. McIlwaine, *Journal of the House of Burgesses, 1619–1659*, 1:86–87, 117.

18. *Ply. Rec.*, 11:12.
19. Ibid., 2:111, 112, 113, 127, 140; *Pynch. Ct. Rec.*, 230–31.
20. Hening, 1:71.
21. Ibid., 167, 193–94; *Mass. Col. Rec.*, 2:100; *Md. Arch.*, 1:159; 4 Jac. I c.5 (1608).
22. *Mass. Col. Rec.*, 1:109, 140, 2:180, 193, 195, 281; *R.I. Rec.*, 1:186; *L & L*, 25–26, 31, 35–38, 45; *Conn. Col. Rec.*, 1:528, 537–38, 547; *Md. Arch.*, 1:159, 286, 344, 375; Hening, 1:167, 194; *R.I. Rec.*, 1:185.
23. Dalton, *Countrey Justice*, 300–306.
24. Ibid., 65; Ferdinando Pulton, *De Pace Regis Regni*, 152–56.
25. *Md. Arch.*, 1:60; *Mass. Col. Rec.*, 2:150–51, 3:157, 170; *Ply. Rec.*, 11:10.
26. Winthrop, *Journal*, 2:191–93.
27. *Va. Gen. Ct.*, 135. This is the only reference to the general warrants. No source was found describing the authorization for or nature of these warrants.
28. *R.I. Rec.*, 1:168–69; Cf., William Cuddihy and B. Carmon Hardy, "A Man's House Was Not His Castle: Origins of the Fourth Amendment to the United States Constitution," 371–400. The authors dismiss statements of Coke, Pratt, Pitt, and Otis as rhetoric that has hidden nearly universal use of discretionary writs and warrants, especially in cases of seditious libel, recusancy, excise, and customs. Their American evidence is drawn largely from the period after 1660. It may be that pre-1660 colonial statutory restraints on search were mere rhetoric, but it may also have been an example of concern for fair procedure in "the lost world" of early seventeenth-century American law. The evidence as to practice is so thin that no conclusive judgment can be made.
29. *B of L*, 21; *L & L*, 49.
30. *R.I. Rec.*, 1:167, 194; Hening, 1:483; *L & L*, 13; *Mass. Col. Rec.*, 1:150–51; *Md. v. John Dandy* (3); see also *Essex*, 2:192.
31. 1 & 2 Ph. & M. c.13 (1554); 2 & 3 Ph. & M. c.10 (1555); In *Prosecuting Crime in the Renaissance*, John H. Langbein makes it clear that the statutes were not an attempt to introduce Continental inquisitorial processes. The bail statute aimed to end abuses by the justices. The commitment statute began to shift the burden for prosecuting at the assize onto the justices of the peace (Part I, "The Marian Statutes").
32. Langbein, *Prosecuting Crime*, 25–26; Dalton, *Countrey Justice*, 269–77.
33. Dalton, *Countrey Justice*, 286–97.
34. By statute in Massachusetts, *B of L*, 18; *L & L*, 28, and elsewhere in practice.
35. Lambarde's *Ephemeris*, in Conyers Read, ed., *William Lambarde and Local Government*, 67–149.
36. Dalton, *Countrey Justice*, 364–65; Lambarde, *Eirenarcha*, 383–402; Pulton, *De Pace Regis Regni*, 169–79.
37. Lambarde, *Eirenarcha*, 403–9.
38. Dalton, *Countrey Justice*, 226–27; Sir Edward Coke, *Second Institute*, 739.
39. *R.I. Rec.*, 1:198–99; *L & L*, 32; *Conn. Col. Rec.*, 1:536; Hening, 1:304; *Me. Ct. Rec.*, 1:43, 73; *Ply. Rec.* 11:11, 32; *Pynch. Ct. Rec.*, 228–29.

40. For the technical requirements of English indictments, see Sir Matthew Hale, *Historia Placiforum Coronae: Pleas of the Crown*, 2:168–93. Examples: Md. v. John Elkin; Md. v. SkightamMongh & Counaweza; Md. v. John Dandy (3); Va. v. Daniel Franke; Va. v. George Clarke; Va. v. William Reade; Va. v. William Bently.
41. Mass. v. John Betts; Mass. v. Benjamin Sawcer; Mass. v. Robert Collins; Mass. v. Gregory Cassell.
42. For procedure by presentment, see these examples: *Ply. Rec.*, vols. 2 and 3, there are presentments at every session; see also *Essex*, passim.
43. See especially Md. v. Richard Ingle, where the attorney general had been frustrated by several grand juries' unwillingness to find bills.
44. *B of L*, 57; *L & L*, 16. Examples: *R.I. Rec.*, 1:163; *Md. Arch.*, 4:9–10, 139, 255, 10:52, 73–74; *Conn. Col. Rec.*, 1:42, 103; *Mass. Col. Rec.*, 1:78, 81; *Pynch. Ct. Rec.*, 246, 249, 267, 282–83; *Ply. Rec.*, 1:39, 88, 2:151, 174–76, 3:15, 28, 39, 40, 70, 93, 109, 146–47, 148, 158, 159–60, 172, 195–96, 11:6.
45. *Mass. Col. Rec.*, 1:78; Winthrop, *Journal*, 1:223.
46. *Pynch. Ct. Rec.*, 249; also *Md. Arch.*, 4:139; *Va. Gen. Ct.*, 38.
47. *Md. Arch.*, 4:9–10; *Ply. Rec.*, 1:88.
48. *Va. Gen. Ct.*, 53–54; another example, Forbes, ed., *Winthrop Papers*, 4:285–86.
49. Lambarde, *Eirenarcha*, 415–26.
50. This description oversimplifies a very complex business. Had the colonial magistrates wished to bring English process with them, no seventeenth-century manual, text, abridgement, or commentary would have set out a complete set of rules for them. The forms of process were in Latin. Dalton sets out the forms as they "seem to be" in *Countrey Justice*, 367–69. The efficacy of the system depended upon sheriff and constable. These officers might easily have become confused about the endorsements they were to make, among others: *nihil habet* (He has nothing), *non est inventus* (He is not found), *cepi corpus* (I have taken the body). In the text I have followed Lambarde, *Eirenarcha*, 417–18, 438–41, 445–46. For a full discussion of process and the difficulty of installing the old forms in a provincial jurisdiction, see Julius Goebel, Jr., and T. Raymond Naughton, *Law Enforcement in Colonial New York*, 384–484.
51. *Mass. Col. Rec.*, 3:185.
52. *L & L*, 49.
53. *Me. Ct. Rec.*, 1:90; see also *Md. Arch.*, 41:151.
54. Examples of traverse: *Ply. Rec.*, 2:5, 11–12, 112, 140.
55. Pulton, *De Pace Regis Regni*, 222–23; John H. Langbein, *Torture and the Law of Proof*, 74–77; John C. Jeaffreson, ed., *Middlesex County Records*, 3:xxi–xxii.
56. Mass. v. Dorothy Talbie.
57. *B of L*, 42.
58. Md. v. Giles Brent.
59. Mass. v. Benjamin Sawcer.
60. Mass. v. William Ledra.

61. N.H. v. George Spencer.
62. *Ply. Rec.*, 3:82, 91, 177–79, 180; *Mass. Col. Rec.*, 1:93, 219, 287; *Mass. Asst. Ct.*, 2:121.
63. Winthrop, *Journal*, 1:313.
64. *Mass. Col. Rec.*, 2:241.
65. 33 Edw. I c.4 (1305).
66. Pulton, *De Pace Regis Regni*, 198–204.
67. Ibid., 206; Lambarde, *Eirenarcha*, 431–34; Dalton, *Countrey Justice*, 273–74.
68. *Ply. Rec.*, 11:3.
69. John Hammond, *Leah and Rachel*, 16; the Massachusetts "Parallels" in William H. Whitmore, ed., *A Bibliographical Sketch of the Laws of the Massachusetts Colony from 1630–1686*, 66–68.
70. *Md. Arch.*, 1:151; examples of jury trials in noncapital cases in *Pynch. Ct. Rec.*, 230–31; *Mass. Col. Rec.*, 1:118; *Ply. Rec.*, 2:11–12, 111, 112, 140.
71. *Md. Arch.*, 4:379.
72. Rhode Island followed a broader rule requiring property of any kind worth £40 (*R.I. Rec.*, 1:199–200).
73. *Mass. Col. Rec.*, 2:109.
74. Md. v. SkightamMongh & Counaweza.
75. *R.I. Rec.*, 1:199–200; *L & L*, 51; examples of challenges: Md. v. John Elkin; Md. v. Thomas Smith. In Md. v. Capt. William Mitchell, a man was given opportunity to challenge members of a grand jury. See also *Md. Arch.*, 4:156, 181, 41:207; *Essex*, 1:7.
76. *R.I. Rec.*, 1:200–201; *B of L*, 26.
77. *R.I. Rec.*, 1:202–4.
78. Sir John Fortescue, *De Laudibus Legum Angliae*, C.XXI, C.XXVI, and see the conclusion in J. F. Stephen, *A History of the Criminal Law of England*, 1:334–36.
79. Md. v. John Dandy (3).
80. Va. v. William Reade.
81. Langbein, *Prosecuting Crime*, 29–31; Lambarde, *Eirenarcha*, 434.
82. Md. v. John Dandy (3).
83. Coke, *Third Institute*, C.2, 25; *Raleigh's Case*.
84. *Calendar of State Papers, Colonial, 1574–1660*, 22.
85. *Ply. Rec.*, 3:107.
86. *B of L*, 47.
87. Mass. v. Mary Latham.
88. Winthrop, *Journal*, 2:259.
89. Ibid., 218–19.
90. Case of Cornish's Wife.
91. See the table of homicides, below, Chapter 4.
92. Mass. v. John Betts.
93. Dalton, *Countrey Justice*, 275–76.
94. Mass. v. Mary Martin; Case of Cornish's Wife; Md. v. John Dandy (3).
95. Mass. v. William Schooler.

96. Md. v. John Elkin; Case of Robert Collins; *Mass. Asst. Ct.*, 2:121.
97. Pulton, *De Pace Regis Regni*, 206–7; Stephen; *Criminal Law*, 1:305.
98. *Conn. Col. Rec.*, 1:84–85.
99. *Mass. Col. Rec.*, 3:424–25.
100. Bushell's Case.
101. Throckmorton's Case; Stephen, *Criminal Law*, 1:325–29.
102. Stephen, *Criminal Law*, 1:302; Thomas Smith, *De Republica Anglorum*, 211.
103. Md. v. John Elkin.
104. *Md. Arch.*, 4:182–84.
105. Main relevant statutes: 9 Edw. II c.15 (1316); 1 Edw. VI c.12 (1547); 18 Eliz. c.7 (1576); 21 Jac. I c.6 (1624); Pulton, *De Pace Regis Regni*, 207–18.
106. Hale, *Historia Placitorum Coronae*, c.43–45.
107. An amateur book of uneven quality on the subject is George W. Dalzell, *Benefit of Clergy in America and Related Matters*.
108. Md. v. Thomas Smith.
109. Md. v. John Dandy (1).
110. *Md. Arch.*, 1:72.
111. Peter Yackel, "Benefit of Clergy in Maryland," 383–97.
112. Va. v. William Reade; Va. v. William Bently.
113. *Conn. Col. Rec.*, 1:513–14; *L & L*, 4–5.
114. *Mass. Col. Rec.*, 1:64, 101, 163, 203, 2:21, 3:257; *Ply. Rec.*, 1:64, 132, 143, 3:69.
115. Ply. v. Robert Latham.
116. *R.I. Rec.*, 1:164, 167–68, 172–73.
117. On exactness of punishment, Sir William Blackstone, *Commentaries on the Laws of England*, 4:371–72.
118. *B of L*, 46.
119. Lambarde, *Eirenarcha*, 68.
120. Langbein, *Prosecuting Crime*, 303.
121. Va. v. Richard Barnes.
122. *Ply. Rec.*, 2:137, 147, 161, 162, 172, 174, 3:5, 10, 138, 159, 168, 185–86; *Mass. Col. Rec.*, 1:193, 233, 2:2; *Pynch. Ct. Rec.*, 255; *Mass. Asst. Ct.*, 2:122, 124, 131, 135.
123. Winthrop, *Journal*, 2:475.
124. *Mass. Asst. Ct.*, 2:137.
125. *Pynch. Ct. Rec.*, 246, 247; *Mass. Col. Rec.*, 3:299–300; *Ply. Rec.*, 1:12, 26, 41; *Md. Arch.*, 22; Va. v. John Heney; Councillors' opinions in Case of Pooly & Pawlett (Va.).
126. *R.I. Rec.*, 1:174; *Conn. Col. Rec.*, 1:115, 203; *Md. Arch.*, 1:344, 10:424; *Ply. Rec.*, 1:143; *Mass. Asst. Ct.*, 2:118, 131; *Mass. Col. Rec.*, 1:194, 203.
127. *Mass. Col. Rec.*, 3:236–38.
128. Va. v. John Heney; Case of Pooly & Pawlett; *Ply. Rec.*, 2:163; *Mass. Asst. Ct.*, 2:124.
129. Examples: *Mass. Col. Rec.*, 1:107, 112, 172, 248, 268; *Me. Ct. Re.*, 1:73–75; *Ply. Rec.*, 1:132, 2:28, 3:4, 23, 112; *Mass. Asst. Ct.*, 2:124; *Md. Arch.*, 10:487; *Accomack 1632–40*, 711, *1640–45*, 235–36.

130. *Mass. Col. Rec.*, 3:364; Mass. v. Daniel Fairfield, other examples: *Mass. Col. Rec.*, 1:335; Winthrop, *Journal*, 2:317–18; *Ply. Rec.*, 1:132; *Mass. Asst. Ct.*, 2:121, 3:25.
131. *Mass. Col. Rec.*, 1:177, 233, 313.
132. *R.I. Rec.*, 1:185; *Va. Gen. Ct.*, 119, 153; *Accomack, 1632–40*, 20, 88.
133. Examples: *L & L*, 30; *Mass. Asst. Ct.*, 2:134, 135; Mass. Col. Rec., 1:76–77; *Ply. Rec.*, 1:12, 164, 2:9, 74, 3:4, 159; *Md. Arch.*, 1:159, 4:445; *Va. Gen. Ct.*, 108.
134. Examples: *R.I. Rec.*, 1:180–82; *Conn. Col. Rec.*, 1:168; *Md. Arch.*, 1:350, 4:445; *Va. Gen. Ct.*, 12, 14; *Mass. Col. Rec.*, 1:295, 4:pt. 2, 11.
135. *Ply. Rec.*, 3:175, 199; *Va. Gen. Ct.*, 57, 58, 85; *Accomack, 1632–40*, 24, 60, 114; *1640–45*, 307–8.
136. Problems with prisons: *R.I. Rec.*, 1:213, 391–92; Providence Record Commission, *Early Records of the Town of Providence*, 2:130–31; *Conn. Col. Rec.*, 1:47; *Mass. Col. Rec.*, 2:230; *Ply. Rec.*, 1:75, 115, 142, 2:23, 11:35.
137. *Md. Arch.*, 4:258.
138. But, some examples: *Mass. Col. Rec.*, 1:177, 249; *Conn. Col. Rec.*, 1:142.
139. *R.I. Rec.*, 1:170.
140. *R.I. Rec.*, 1:173; *L & L*, 37; *Conn. Col. Rec.*, 1:78.
141. *Va. Gen. Ct.*, 105, 117.
142. Examples of "slavery": *Ply. Rec.*, 1:157; *Mass. Col. Rec.*, 1:100, 154, 246, 269, 284, 297, 2:21; *Mass. Asst. Ct.*, 2:118, 122. On at least one occasion, real slavery, see the case of the Indian, Chausop, *Mass. Col. Rec.*, 1:181.
143. *Ply. Rec.*, 1:86, 87, 91, 92, 2:36, 42.
144. *L & L*, 50.
145. Va. v. John Heney.
146. *Md. Arch.*, 1:184; *B of L*, 43.
147. *L & L*, 50.
148. *Mass. Col. Rec.*, 3:349.
149. *Ply. Rec.*, 1:127; other examples: ibid., 2:30; Md. v. Susan Warren; *N.H. Col. Rec. 1*, 435.
150. Lambarde, *Eirenarcha*, c.12, 67–68; a Maryland exception, loss of suffrage for a third conviction of drunkenness, *Md. Arch.*, 1:375.
151. *Conn. Col. Rec.*, 1:138, 389.
152. *Ply. Rec.*, 11:101.
153. Ibid., 3:101, 167, 176–83, 188–89, 198–99.
154. *Mass. Col. Rec.*, 2:85; *L & L*, 2.
155. *Mass. Col. Rec.*, 1:207, 2:51, 52, 57.
156. Ibid., 1:88, 91, 159, 225, 335.
157. *Ply. Rec.*, 11:100–101; *Conn. Col. Rec.*, 1:283–84.
158. *Ply. Rec.*, 3:151.
159. Ibid., 3:123–24, 127, 139–40, 176, 178–79, 184, 197, 199.
160. *Mass. Col. Rec.*, 4:pt.1, 383–90, 419; *Mass. Asst. Ct.*, 3:68–70; Mass. v. William Ledra.
161. See, for example, Cotton Mather, *Pillars of Salt*, a collection of execution sermons.

162. Ibid., 60–62. For other evidence of a gallows sermon in this period, see Mass. v. Dorothy Talbie, also a case of infanticide.
163. Veall, *Popular Movement for Law Reform*, 1–5, 101, 103, 117, 121, 127–31; Warden, "Law Reform."
164. Coke, *Third Institute*, Epilogue; Oliver Cromwell, *Speeches of Oliver Cromwell, 1644–1658*, 244; Haller and Davies, eds., *Leveller Tracts*, 152, 325–26.
165. B. C. Redwood, ed., *Quarter Sessions Order Book, 1642–1649*, xiv, 45, passim.
166. 21 Jac. I c.6 (1624).
167. Abbot E. Smith, "The Transportation of Convicts in the American Colonies in the Seventeenth Century," 232—49.
168. James S. Cockburn, *A History of English Assizes, 1558 to 1714*, 94–96, 125–33.
169. Ibid., 131.
170. Coke, *Third Institute*, Epilogue.
171. Cockburn, *Assizes*, 96.
172. Jeaffreson, ed., *Middlesex County Records*, *3 : xvii–xix*.
173. See the table of homicides in Chapter 4.
174. The general rules are stated here. The law was very complex in relation, *inter alia*, to various tenures. See Pulton, *De Pace Regis Regni*, 216–39; Coke, *Third Institute*, c.102.
175. Veall, *Popular Movement for Law Reform*, 114, 122, 131; Haller and Davies, eds., *Leveller Tracts*, 326.
176. Art. III, sec. 3, 2.
177. Pulton, *De Pace Regis Regni*, 216.
178. *B of L*, 10.
179. *Conn. Col. Rec.*, 1 : 536–37.
180. *R.I. Rec.*, 1 : 162.
181. Ply. v. Robert Latham.
182. Hening, 1 : 398.
183. *Md. Arch.*, 1 : 17, 39.
184. Ibid., 158.
185. Pardon was enmeshed in technicalities and was set out in a confusing fashion by commentators. See Coke, *Third Institute*, c. 105, 106; Pulton, *De Pace Regis Regni*, 218–21. Whatever restrictions remained after 27 H. VIII c.25 (1536) could apparently be avoided by changing the words or form of the pardon.
186. *B of L*, 72.
187. *Mass. Col. Rec.*, 2 : 241.
188. Ibid., 166, 261.
189. *Conn. Col. Rec.*, 1 : 118.
190. Hening, 1 : 70.
191. Evarts B. Greene, *The Provincial Governor in the English Colonies of North America*, 214–18.
192. *Md. Arch.*, 2 : 52, 96, 179, 182, 187, 195, 305, 395, 406–9, 4 : 441–42. Several colonies also provided for pardon in cases of homicide by misadventure; see *R.I. Rec.*, 1 : 165–66; *Journal of the House of Burgesses*, 96.

Chapter Three: Courts and Officers

1. L. Alston, introduction to Smith, *De Republica*, xxxiv, and the text, 64; William Lambarde, *Archeion or a Discourse upon the High Courts of Justice in England*, 140; Charles H. McIlwain, *The High Court of Parliament and Its Supremacy*, ch. 3.

2. An extensive modern treatment of English impeachments in Raoul Berger, *Impeachment*, 1–72, is misleading. Cf. Clayton Roberts, "The Law of Impeachment in Stuart England."

3. Though Star Chamber had some transatlantic influence, I have excluded consideration of it here and dealt with its precedents in specific parts of the text where it is relevant.

4. A great many modern studies have dealt with the courts of medieval England. Until recently, little work had been done in the sixteenth and seventeenth centuries. A modern work on the Kings Bench remains to be written; for it, see Sir Edward Coke, *Fourth Institute*, c.7, 70–76; Holdsworth, *History of English Law*, 1:204–31.

5. A modern work of great value is Cockburn, *Assizes*, on which my description is based. See Coke, *Fourth Institute*, c.28, 30, pp. 161–65, 167–69; Smith, *De Republica*, c.23.

6. Table of the Devon Assizes in Cockburn, *Assizes*, 94–96.

7. On justices and the quarter sessions in this period see J. H. Gleason, *The Justices of the Peace in England, 1558 to 1640*, which provides excellent analysis of the men who were commissioned. Also very helpful is Thomas G. Barnes, *Somerset, 1625–1640*. I believe that these later scholars have passed too harsh judgment on Charles A. Beard, *The Office of the Justice of the Peace in England, in Its Origin and Development*, which is a good description of the office. I have also used the brief description in Stephen, *Criminal Law*, 1:111–116, and, of course, throughout the book the manuals by Lambarde and Dalton.

8. 1 Edw. II c.16 (1307); 18 Edw. II c.2 (1325); 4 Edw. III c.2 (1331).

9. 34 Edw. III c.1 (1361).

10. John Hawarde, *Les reportes del cases in Camera Stellata, 1593 to 1609*, 20, 21, 102, 106, 350–56, 368, 477; Cockburn, *Assizes*, 103–4; Kent, "Attitudes to Regulation of 'Personal Conduct,'" 51–52; Beard, *Justice of the Peace*, 145–46; William B. Willcox, *Gloucestershire*, 56–60.

11. Barnes, *Somerset*, 46; J. P. Dawson, *A History of Lay Judges*, 141; Langbein, *Prosecuting Crime*, 112–16.

12. The commission is in Dalton, *Countrey Justice*, 13–16.

13. Cockburn, *Assizes*, 96; Barnes, *Somerset*, 52.

14. Langbein, *Prosecuting Crime*, 34–44. For the difficult cases clause, Lambarde, *Eirenarcha*, 452; Barnes, *Somerset*, 50–53; Cockburn, *Assizes*, 90–93. Cf. Dalton, *Countrey Justice*, 42.

15. Barnes, *Somerset*, 80–85.

16. I have relied on Fossey J. C. Hearnshaw, *Leet Jurisdiction in England*, and on Dawson, *Lay Judges*, esp. 208–63. I have also used the most widely available

manual of the times, John Kitchin, *Jurisdiction, or the Lawful Authority of Courts Leet.* Though the common lawyers disliked these courts (see Coke's truncated description in *Fourth Institute*, c.54 (pp. 261–65), Coke himself wrote a manual, *Compleate Copy-holder*; Willcox, *Gloucestershire*, 289.

17. Kitchin, *Jurisdiction*, 67.
18. Hearnshaw, *Leet Jurisdiction*, 43–63, gives twelve examples of medieval articles of view. He describes the modern articles, pp. 83–130. Kitchin sets the articles out as a model steward's charge in *Jurisdiction*, 16ff.
19. Dawson, *Lay Judges*, 214.
20. Hearnshaw, *Leet Jurisdiction*, 79–83, 131–40.
21. The rule of the lawyers was that the steward was judge in the leet. They probably felt it necessary to assert this rule to distinguish the leet, a royal court, from the private and popular courts. See Coke, *Compleate Copy-holder*, sec. 25; *Fourth Institute*, c.54 (261). Presentment by the jury amounted to conviction and stated the penalty, thus reducing the steward's role to a formality. In addition to presiding, he would act as law "expert" if one were needed, which was seldom (Dawson, *Lay Judges*, 224–28).
22. Kitchin, *Jurisdiction*, 86.
23. *Md. Arch.*, 1:16–19, 21, 23–24. The indictment before the Provincial Court is in ibid., 4:21–23. The more regular course would have been to pursue Claiborne to an outlawry, but the attainder was certainly more efficient than this slow and uncertain process.
24. Peter C. Hoffer and N. E. H. Hull, "The First American Impeachments," 653–67.
25. *Mass. Col. Rec.*, 1:38; *Conn. Col. Rec.*, 1:25; and by inference certainly, *N.H. Col. Rec. 2*, 570.
26. Winthrop, *Journal*, 2:275–81; *Mass. Col. Rec.*, 3:18–25; Robert E. Wall, Jr., *Massachusetts Bay*, 93–120.
27. Tyler, *Narratives of Early Virginia*, 275.
28. Philip A. Bruce, *Institutional History of Virginia in the Seventeenth Century*, 1:693.
29. *Md. Arch.*, 1:35–36.
30. Andrews, *Colonial Period*, 2:38.
31. *Conn. Col. Rec.*, 1:25.
32. Ibid., 51, 252, 253.
33. Ibid., 125, 186.
34. *Ply. Rec.*, 11:7, 158.
35. Ibid., passim.
36. For example, forgery, buggery, drunkenness: *Mass. Col. Rec.*, 1:295, 339, 344, 2:3, 3:349, 364.
37. Ibid., 1:198, 202–3, 225.
38. Ibid., 243, 2:127; Winthrop, *Journal*, 2:12–14.
39. Mass. v. Daniel Fairfield.
40. *Mass. Col. Rec.*, 1:189, 205ff.; see Chapter 4.
41. *Conn. Col. Rec.*, 1:91.
42. *Mass. Col. Rec.*, 1:143.

43. Winthrop, *Journal*, 1:157.
44. *Ply. Rec.*, vols. 1 and 2, passim.
45. *Mass. Col. Rec.*, 1:118; 2:9–10; *L & L*, 32.
46. *B of L*, 36.
47. *Conn. Col. Rec.*, 1:118; *R.I. Rec.*, 1:222.
48. *N.H. Col. Rec. 1*, 169–70.
49. *Mass. Col. Rec.*, 2:285.
50. *L & L*, 32; *Mass. Col. Rec.*, 3:179–80, 4:pt.1, 73, 96, 145, 193–94, 212–13, 269.
51. *Mass. Col. Rec.*, 2:227, 3:167, 190, 192, 194, 206–7, 214, 232, 233, 235, 257, 271, 278, 289, 299–300, 304, 428.
52. Bruce, *Institutional History of Virginia*, 1:690–93; Hening, 1:272.
53. The best secondary descriptions of the courts are, for Massachusetts, Joseph Smith, ed., *Colonial Justice in Western Massachusetts, 1639–1702*, 65–88; Virginia, Bruce, *Institutional History of Virginia*, 1:pt. 3, "Legal Administration"; Maryland, Joseph H. Smith, "The Foundations of Law in Maryland: 1634–1715," 92–115; Connecticut, William M. Maltbie, "Judicial Administration in Connecticut Colony before the Charter of 1662," 147–58; New Haven, Henry H. Townshend, "Judicial Administration in New Haven Colony before the Charter of 1662," 210–34; Plymouth, Julius Goebel, Jr., "King's Law and Local Custom in Seventeenth Century New England"; Rhode Island, John T. Farrell, "The Early History of Rhode Island's Court System," 9:65–71, 103–17, 10:14–25.
54. The record of the Plymouth General and Assistants Court is continuous for the period 1633–60 (*Ply. Rec.*, vols. 1, 2, 3, 7). The record of the Virginia General Court before 1660 survives only for the years 1622–32 (*Va. Gen. Ct.*). The record of the Massachusetts Court of Assistants is quite full for 1629–60, though the years 1643–60 have been filled in with fragments and records from other courts. The record of the Maryland Provincial Court is also fairly full (*Md. Arch.*, vols. 3, 10, 41). The Connecticut Particular Court records are continuous, but sparsely reported (*Conn. Col. Rec.*, vol. 1; Conn. Hist. Soc. *Coll.*, 22). The record of the New Haven Court of Magistrates is detailed, but the years 1643–56 are missing (*N.H. Col. Rec. 1, 2*). The record of the Rhode Island Court of Tryals is a mere fragment covering the years 1647–62 (*Records of the Court of Tryals of the Colony of Providence Plantations, 1647–1662*, vol. 1).
55. I have taken figures for total populations of all colonies from *The Statistical History of the United States from Colonial Times to the Present*, a volume prepared under the direction of the United States Bureau of the Census with the cooperation of the Social Science Research Council and published in 1965. The data may be found at pages 743 and 756. Other estimates have drastically reduced some of these estimates; for example, Arthur E. Karinen in "Maryland Population," 365–407, estimates the population in 1650 at only 1,410. I have used the figures from the *Statistical History* because they are the only extant statistics known to me that have established populations for all colonies by the same method. Thus those figures seemed more valid for purposes

of comparison. Other estimates that have come to my attention are mentioned in the notes.

56. Sainsbury, ed., *Statistical History*, 756. The population of New Haven is not given, but it appears likely that it was about fifteen hundred.

57. Bradford, *Of Plymouth Plantation*, 188, 252–54.

58. Individual magistrates may have had discretion to try minor statutory offenses in the towns.

59. *Ply. Rec.*, 1:12, 83, 103, 158, 214, 217–18, 223.

60. *R.I. Rec.*, 1:191.

61. *Records of the Court of Tryals of the Colony of Providence Plantations, 1647–1662*, passim.

62. Clarence S. Brigham, ed., *The Early Records of Portsmouth*; Providence Record Commission, *Early Records of the Town of Providence*, I; and Howard M. Chapin, ed., *The Early Records of the Town of Warwick*, have been searched.

63. Andrews, *Colonial Period*, 2:158–64.

64. *N.H. Col. Rec. 1*, 112–16, 2:567–71.

65. Franklin B. Dexter, ed., *New Haven Town Records, 1649–1684*.

66. *Conn. Col. Rec.*, 1:36–37.

67. Ibid., 514, 528, 533, 538, 547, 558.

68. Ibid., 86, 125–26, 226–27, 233, 249, 257.

69. Hutchinson, *History of Massachusetts*, 1:493–95.

70. *Pynch. Ct. Rec.*, 69–71; *Mass. Col. Rec.*, 1:169, 175, 2:38, 41, 227; *L & L*, 15–16.

71. *Mass. Col. Rec.*, 1:2, 13, 19–20, 24, 30–31, 35, 44–45, 52; *Pynch. Ct. Rec.*, 72–73.

72. *Mass. Col. Rec.*, 4:pt. 1, 288.

73. For the establishment of county government, see Bruce, *Institutional History of Virginia*, 1:484–97; Newton D. Mereness, *Maryland as a Proprietary Province*, 230–32.

74. Hening, 1:125, 224.

75. *Md. Arch.*, 3:59.

76. Ibid., 237, 257–58, 348.

77. Hening, 1:224.

78. See Goebel's seminal essay, "King's Law and Local Custom"; Francis S. Philbrick's introduction to Ames, *Accomack, 1632–1640*, xv–xvi.

79. *Md. Arch.*, 3:61.

80. Ibid., 59.

81. *Accomack, 1640–45*, 177–79.

82. *Mass. Col. Rec.*, 1:74; *Pynch. Ct. Rec.*, 79.

83. *Accomack, 1640–45*, 177–79.

84. *Md. Arch.*, 3:62, X, 413.

85. *Mass. Col. Rec.*, 1:169, 175.

86. Goebel, "King's Law and Local Custom."

87. Lambarde, *Eirenarcha*, 438–41; Barnes, *Somerset*, 54.

88. In *Pynch. Ct. Rec.*, 129, Smith lists six forms of presentment used in Massachusetts.

89. *Accomack, 1632–40*, 2, 20, 28, 60, 86, 88, 117, 118, 119, 146; *Accomack, 1640–45*, 28–29, 104, 172–73, 190, 235–36, 287–313, 316–17, 351, 392–93.
90. *Accomack, 1632–40*, 15, 24; *Accomack, 1640–45*, 184, 202, 235, 236, 317.
91. *Accomack, 1632–40*, 19, 20, 22–23, 25, 151; *Accomack, 1640–45*, 117, 287, 290–91, 293.
92. *Accomack, 1632–40*, 114, 121, 134.
93. Ibid., 15, 84, 121; *Accomack, 1640–45*, 84, 104, 119, 201, 205–7, 298–300.
94. *Accomack, 1632–40*, 24, 114, 115; *Accomack, 1640–45*, 307–8.
95. *Accomack, 1632–40*, 38, 53, 111.
96. *Accomack, 1640–45*, 371–73, 376.
97. *Accomack, 1632–40*, 15, 24, 86, 114, 118, 121; *Accomack, 1640–45*, 104, 172–73, 184, 202, 212, 235, 236, 317, 393.
98. *Accomack, 1632–40*, 24, 28, 60, 111, 114, 134; *Accomack, 1640–45*, 307–8.
99. *Accomack, 1632–40*, 20, 88.
100. *Md. Arch.*, 53:21–22, 54:122.
101. Ibid., 53:28.
102. Ibid., 3:4, 28–33, 37, 38, 78, 54:113, 121.
103. Ibid., 54:9, 167–69, 178–79, 184.
104. Ibid., 9.
105. Ibid., 9, 116–21, 173, 178, 179.
106. Ibid., 53:4, 54–55, 78, 54:69, 116–21, 163–64.
107. Ibid., 54:41, 59, 78, 121, 160, 161.
108. *Essex*, 1:221, 305.
109. The source of the statistics is explained at the beginning of chapter 4.
110. Lambarde, *Ephemeris*, in Read, ed., *Lambarde*, 15–52; H. W. Saunders, ed., *The Official Papers of Sir Nathaniel Bacon of Stiffkey, Norfolk as Justice of the Peace, 1580–1620*, 1–65; Graville Leveson-Gower, "Note Book of a Surrey Justice," 161–232. Ernst Axon, ed., *Manchester Sessions*, has a misleading title. It consists largely of matters that came before Justice of the Peace Oswald Mosley out of sessions.
111. See above, Chapter 2.
112. *Md. Arch.*, 1:375; Hening, 1:167, 193–94.
113. *Pynch. Ct. Rec.*, 72–75; *Conn. Col. Rec.*, 1:514, 528, 533, 538, 547, 558.
114. *Mass. Col. Rec.*, 1:74.
115. *Pynch. Ct. Rec.*, 75; *Conn. Col. Rec.*, 1:226–27, 233, 252, 257. The word "assistant" was here used in its ordinary sense of "aide."
116. *Ply. Rec.*, 11:7–9, italics added.
117. Ibid., 159.
118. Ibid., 172.
119. Ibid., 172–76.
120. *R.I. Rec.*, 1:192–94.
121. *Essex*, 1:287, 2:167, 212.
122. *Mass. Col. Rec.*, 1:171, 321–22, 4:pt. 1, 115, 118.
123. The comparison is based on one hundred consecutive items of business taken from two records. Lambarde's business fell within three years, 1583–85;

Pynchon's stretched over twenty years, 1639–59. Pynchon was holding court; Lambarde was dealing with problems out of court, either alone or together with fellow justices. Pynchon was on a frontier; Lambarde worked in a populous area of eastern Kent. The items were taken from *Ephemeris*, 36–52, and *Pynch. Ct. Rec.*, 204–40.

124. Hill, *Society and Puritanism*, 298–381; Carl Bridenbaugh, *Vexed and Troubled Englishmen, 1590–1642*, 259–62; Veall, *Popular Movement for Law Reform*, 139.

125. Hening, 1:126, 157, 240, 309–10.

126. In this section I have relied heavily on Oberholzer, *Delinquent Saints*. George L. Haskins, "Precedents in English Ecclesiastical Practices for Criminal Punishments in Early Massachusetts," 321–36, is a broader treatment of congregational discipline than the title suggests. Konig, *Law and Society in Puritan Massachusetts*, 28, 30, 32, 91, 92–98, 101, 124, 125.

127. Richard D. Pierce, ed., *The Records of the First Church in Boston, 1630–1868*, 1:10, 12.

128. Ibid., 20–58.

129. Haskins, "Precedents in English Ecclesiastical Practices."

130. For example, on the definition of sodomy and the nature of evidence, Bradford, *Of Plymouth Plantation*, 404–13; on the criminal jurisdiction of the courts, *Mass. Col. Rec.*, 2:90–96; Winthrop, *Journal*, 1:211–18.

131. For examples of double jeopardy: Pierce, ed., *Records of the First Church in Boston*, 1:21–22, 25, 26, 34, and compare *Mass. Col. Rec.*, 1:207, 246, 259, 269, 281, 336; N.H. v. James Heywood.

132. *Mass. Col. Rec.*, 1:237–51.

133. I have taken this brief description of the sheriff from Michael Dalton, *Officium Vicecomitum. The Office and Authority of Sherifs*.

134. Ibid., 157.

135. See Barnes, *Somerset*, ch. 5.

136. Dalton, *Office of Sherifs*, 193–95.

137. A pioneering comparative work is Cyrus H. Karraker, *The Seventeenth-Century Sheriff*.

138. *R.I. Rec.*, 1:198.

139. Basic legislation and commissions: ibid.; *Mass. Col. Rec.*, 2:200; *L & L*, 38; *Md. Arch.*, 1:148, 2:61, 96–97, 117, 137; *Ply. Rec.*, 11:18–19, 45, 53; Hening, 1:223–24; *Va. Gen. Ct.*, 130; *Conn. Col. Rec.*, 1:398, 540. In Maryland, the appointment was made by the "chief justice," that is, the governor.

140. William Lambarde, *The Duties of Constables, Borsholders, Tithingmen, and such other low Ministers of the Peace*, 3, 4.

141. Barnes, *Somerset*, 76–77; for some of the constable's difficulties see Willcox, *Gloucestershire*, 48–55.

142. For the basic legislation and commissions: *L & L*, 13, 49; *Md. Arch.*, 2:60; *Ply. Rec.*, 11:10; *Mass. Col. Rec.*, 2:150–51, 3:157, 170, 200; *Conn. Col. Rec.*, 1:521–22.

143. As suggested in Winthrop, *Journal*, 2:191–93; Bruce, *Institutional History of Virginia*, 1:602–3.

144. *Mass. Col. Rec.*, 4:pt. 1, 324–27.

145. Winthrop, *Journal*, 2:191–93; *Mass. Col. Rec.*, 3:233; *Conn. Col. Rec.*, 1:13, 136; *Ply. Rec.*, 3:10, 68, 74, 123, 124; *Md. Arch.*, 41:18, 44:171; *Essex*, 1:4, 34, 101, 140.

Chapter Four: Crime

1. *Oxford English Dictionary.*
2. For modern analysis of these well-known events, see Emory Battis, *Saints and Sectaries*, and Wall, *Massachusetts Bay.* Charles Francis Adams reprinted the documents of the Antinomian crisis including Anne Hutchinson's trial in *Antinomianism in the Colony of Massachusetts Bay, 1636–1638.* For the persistent awareness of the Munster outbreak, see Perry Miller and Thomas B. Johnson, eds., *The Puritans*, 1:xxii.
3. See Chapter 1 for the sanctions of all colonies.
4. *Mass. Col. Rec.*, 4:pt. 1, 277–78, 308–9, 345–47.
5. Ibid., 278.
6. Ibid., 349.
7. Ibid., 366.
8. Ibid., 383–84, 419.
9. *Mass. Asst. Ct.*, 3:97; *Essex*, 2:103–4.
10. *Ply. Rec.*, 3:176, 178, 184.
11. *Mass. Asst. Ct.*, 3:110.
12. The justification was published, *Mass. Col. Rec.*, 4:pt. 1, 384–90.
13. Ibid., 451.
14. Ibid., 385, 386, 432, 451.
15. Thomas Shepard, *A Defence of the Answer*, in Miller and Johnson, eds., *The Puritans*, 1:119.
16. *Mass. Col. Rec.*, 4:pt. 1, 389–90.
17. Md. v. Francis Fitzherbert.
18. The older histories of Maryland are partisan. There is no adequate modern history, but see Andrews, *Colonial Period*, 2:314–23, and Matthew P. Andrews, *History of Maryland*, 33–171.
19. Md. v. Thomas Smith.
20. *Md. Arch.*, 1:23–24.
21. Ibid., 4:248.
22. For the Virginia incident, see *Accomack, 1640–45*, 270, 301–2, 304–5.
23. *Md. Arch.*, 4:237–39, 245.
24. Ibid., 245–52.
25. Ibid., 3:396–97.
26. Ibid., 41:428–29.
27. Ibid., 3:406–9.
28. Examples: *Ply. Rec.*, 3:15, 16, 28, 92–93, 97, 148, 158, 159–60, 195–96; *Pynch. Ct. Rec.*, 249, 282–83; *Md. Arch.*, 10:456–58.
29. *Ply. Rec.*, 2:174–76, 3:92, 146–47; *Pynch. Ct. Rec.*, 246, 249; *Md. Arch.*, 4:139; *Essex*, 2:119, 222–23.
30. Winthrop, *Journal*, 1:223; *Me. Ct. Rec.*, 1:108–9; *Md. Arch.*, 10:141–43.

31. Case of Cornish's Wife.
32. Mass. v. Mary Martin. Concealment alone had been made sufficient evidence by 21 Jac. I c. 27 (1624). For a thorough analysis of this statute and infanticide in England and America, see Peter Hoffer and N. E. H. Hull, *Murdering Mothers*.
33. Mass. v. Dorothy Talbie. Talbie had previously been chained to a post for beating her husband and for contempt and had been whipped for "misdemeanors" against her master (*Essex*, 1:6, 9).
34. Ply. v. Allis Bishop.
35. Md. v. Francis Brooke.
36. Mass. v. William Franklin.
37. The verdict is not given in the record.
38. Mass. v. John Betts.
39. *Md. Arch.*, 2:98, 146, 187. Md. v. John Dandy (1).
40. Md. v. John Dandy (2).
41. Md. v. John Dandy (3).
42. *Md. Arch.*, 3:98.
43. Md. v. John Elkin. A similar view of the status of Indians was expressed by John Hawthorne, an associate of the Essex, Massachusetts, County Court. Writing in support of an Indian woman named Mall, he said, "First the law is undeniable that the Indian may have the same distribusion of Justice with our selves; there is as I humbly conseive not the same argument as amongst the negroes for the light of the gospell is a begineing to appeare amongst them—that is the indians" (*Essex*, 2:240–41).
44. Ply. v. Arthur Peach et al.
45. N.H. v. Nepaupuck. For other homicides by Indians, see *Conn. Col. Rec.*, 1:294; *Mass. Col. Rec.*, 3:395.
46. Exodus 22:18; Leviticus 20:27; Edwin Powers, *Crime and Punishment in Early Massachusetts, 1620–1692*, ch. 14.
47. Two recent essays of great merit are, for England, A. D. J. MacFarlane, "Witchcraft in Tudor and Stuart Essex," and for the colonies, John Demos, "Underlying Themes in the Witchcraft of Seventeenth-Century New England."
48. Conn. Hist. Soc. *Coll.*, 22:188.
49. For another example, see Joseph Smith's rescue of William Pynchon from the aspersions cast on him for his examination of Hugh and Mary Parsons, *Pynch. Ct. Rec.*, 20–25.
50. Winthrop, *Journal*, 2:344–45.
51. After the Salem trials, Thomas Brattle wrote of the teat or mark, "And I wonder what person there is, whether man or woman, of whom it cannot be said but that, in some part of their body or other, there is preternatural execresence. The term is a very general and inclusive term" (quoted in Miller and Johnson, eds., *The Puritans*, 2:760–61).
52. N.H. Col. Rec. 2, 29.
53. Given as 45 percent at Wiltshire Quarter Sessions, 1615–24 (Ingram, "Communities and Courts," 110–34); 73 percent at Essex, Hertfordshire, and Sus-

sex assizes in late Tudor and early Stuart times (J. S. Cockburn, "The Nature and Incidence of Crime in England, 1559–1625," 49–71); 33 percent at Worcestershire Quarter Sessions, 1633–37 (J. W. Willis Bund, ed., *Worcestershire County Records. Calendar of the Quarter Sessions Papers 1591–1641,* 505–654).

54. *Ply. Rec.*, 3:28, 36, 75, 82.
55. *Md. Arch.*, 10:291–92.
56. Winthrop, *Journal*, 2:169–70.
57. Va. v. Daniel Franke; Morgan, *American Slavery, American Freedom*, 124–26.
58. Md. v. Mary Williams et al.
59. Va. v. Thomas Hayle.
60. Me. v. Robert Collens. For other charges of rape: *Mass. Col. Rec.*, 1:177, 2:121; *Md. Arch.*, 10:499–500, 54:69; *N.H. Col. Rec. 2*, 134–36.
61. Ply. v. Thomas Atkins.
62. Va. v. Richard Williams alias Cornish.
63. N.H. v. John Knight.
64. Ply. v. John Allexander and Thomas Roberts. Other examples: *Ply. Rec.*, 1:137, 143, 153, 2:29, 146–47, 3:37.
65. *Ply. Rec.*, 2:137, 163.
66. Mass. v. William Hatchett; Ply. v. Thomas Graunger; and perhaps John Nubery in Connecticut, see *Conn. Col. Rec.*, 1:159. For a false accusation of buggery see *Mass. Asst. Ct.*, 3:66–67.
67. *Accomack, 1640–45*, 371–73, 376.
68. N.H. v. George Spencer, N.H. v. Thomas Hogg; N.H. v. Walter Robinson; N.H. v. John Ferris.
69. *Md. Arch.* 54:1, 9–10, 20, 116–119; 53:4; *Accomack, 1632–40*, 20, 22–23; *Accomack, 1640–45*, 117, 287, 290–91, 293; *Md. Arch.*, 10:506, 558; *Va. Gen. Ct.*, 139, 140–42, 148.
70. Cases of adultery that came to trial in New England: Mass. v. James Britton and Mary Latham; *Mass. Col. Rec.*, 1:91, 198, 202–3, 225, 335, 2:243, 3:127, 349; Winthrop, *Journal*, 1:108, 2:13–14, 259; *Me. Ct. Rec.*, 1:146, 176; *Conn. Col. Rec.*, 1:45; *Ply. Rec.*, 1:132, 2:28, 3:110–13, 131.
71. Mass. v. James Britton and Mary Latham.
72. Me. v. George Burdett.
73. For examples of this type of behavior: *Ply. Rec.*, 2:36, 37, 165, 174, 3:11, 36, 41, 75, 93, 159; *Mass. Asst. Ct.*, 2:48, 65, 81, 86, 89, 94, 95, 108, 121, 126, 139; *N.H. Col. Rec. 1*, 38, 81, 84; *Essex*, 1:3, 8, 17, 60, 83, 91, 107, 152, 174, 205, 220, 244, 269, 280, 286, 347, 348, 2:3, 39, 101, 236, 242.
74. Examples of fornication: *Mass. Col. Rec.*, 1:102, 123, 163, 177, 184, 246, 269, 287, 296, 297; *Va. Gen. Ct.*, 154; *Conn. Col. Rec.*, 1:129; *Ply. Rec.*, 1:12, 93–94, 127, 132, 162, 164, 2:36–42, 75, 86, 109–10, 112, 135, 172, 3:5, 6, 42, 47, 75, 93; *Mass. Asst. Ct.*, 2:30, 60, 64, 65, 79, 87, 94, 121, 124, 131, 132; *Accomack, 1632–40*, 151; *N.H. Col. Rec. 1*, 88, 89, 259, 327, 435, 469–70, 2:122–24, 201–2, 263–68; *Essex*, 1:39, 56, 71, 80, 82, 174, 179, 180, 196, 220, 224, 243, 250, 286, 287, 305, 323, 337, 347, 360, 361, 380, 404, 414, 420, 2:10, 54, 67, 69, 136, 151, 152, 156, 179, 247.

75. Examples of bastardy cases: *Mass. Col. Rec.*, 1:285; *Me. Ct. Rec.*, 1:1; *Conn. Col. Rec.*, 1:129; *Va. Gen. Ct.*, 155; *Ply. Rec.*, 1:93, 94, 103, 127, 161, 165; *Mass. Asst. Ct.*, 2:95, 137; *Md. Arch.*, 54:78, 85, 113, 121, 53:29–33, 33–34, 78; *Essex*, 1:196, 210–12, 323, 2:1, 50, 58.

76. *N.H. Col. Rec. 1*, 435.

77. Dalton, *Countrey Justice*, 161–62.

78. Pulton, *De Pace Regis Regni*, 1–3.

79. Kitchin, *Jurisdiction*, 45, 74–75; Hearnshaw, *Leet Jurisdiction*, 47, 49, 59, 112; William M. Marcham and Frank Marcham, eds., *Court Rolls of the Bishop of London's Manor of Hornsey, 1603–1701*, passim.

80. Bund, ed., *Worcestershire*, passim, 95 indictments for assault; Jeaffreson, ed., *Middlesex County Records*, passim, 42 prosecutions for assault.

81. Theodore F. T. Plucknett, *A Concise History of the Common Law*, 427–45; Van Vechten Veeder, "The History of the Law of Defamation," 446–73; Ronald A. Marchant, *The Church under the Law*, 9, 19–20, 54, 57, 61, 63, 65, 71–75, 80, 189, 192–94, 244.

82. Assaults resulting in criminal penalties: *Essex*, 1:25, 49, 57, 113, 115, 170, 174, 179, 208, 235, 244, 250, 287, 397, 422, 2:10, 11, 35, 50, 212, 225, 235; *Conn. Hist. Soc. Coll.*, 22:152, 213; *Va. Gen. Ct.*, 118; *Accomack, 1632–40*, 15, *1640–45*, 84; *Ply. Rec.*, 1:26, 75; *Mass. Asst. Ct.*, 2:78–79.

83. Plucknett, *Concise History*, 439.

84. *R.I. Rec.*, 1:184.

85. Slanderous charges of being a witch: *Essex*, 1:199, 202, 204, 276, 301; *Md. Arch.*, 4:18–19, 300, 392, 430, 434, 450, 10:399; *Pynch. Ct. Rec.* 219, 238, 244; *N.H. Col. Rec. 2*, 122; of crime: *Va. Gen. Ct.*, 18–20, 169; *Ply. Rec.*, 1:12.

86. *Me. Ct. Rec.*, 1:76, 85–87; *Md. Arch.*, 4:149–50, 181, 183, 258, 10:234–35, 402–3; *Pynch. Ct. Rec.*, 236–37; *Conn. Col. Rec.*, 1:134.

87. *Accomack, 1640–45*, 28–29.

88. Case of Pooly & Pawlett.

89. Criminal penalties in cases of slander: *Md. Arch.*, 4:487; *Conn. Col. Rec.*, 1:142, 193; *Conn. Hist. Soc. Coll.*, 22:134, 157; *N.H. Col. Rec. 1*, 35, 327; *Ply. Rec.*, 1:41–42, 106, 132, 3:52; *Md. Arch.*, 53:13, 21–22, 54:122; *Accomack, 1632–40*, 60, 86, 117, 146; *Essex*, 1:50, 158, 173, 179, 196, 201, 222, 2:196.

90. Westminster I, c.34 (1275); 2 R. II st.1 c.5 (1378); Plucknett, *Concise History*, 429–30.

91. 1 & 2 Ph. & M. c.3 (1554); 1 Eliz. c.6 (1558); John C. Lassiter, "The Defamation of Peers."

92. *N.H. Col. Rec. 1*; 280.

93. Examples of prosecutions equivalent to *scandalum magnatum*: *Essex*, 1:182, 185, 186, 380, 2:35; *Md. Arch.*, 54:2; *Va. Gen. Ct.*, 14, 136; *Accomack, 1640–45*, 313, 316–17, 351, 392; *Md. Arch.*, 4:439–40, 59, 515; *Conn. Hist. Soc. Coll.*, 22:140.

94. Va. v. Richard Barnes.

95. *Essex*, 1:380.

96. Ibid., 234–35.

97. Ibid., 20, 34, 36, 51, 58, 59, 174, 414; *Mass. Asst. Ct.*, 2:70, 126; *Ply. Rec.*, 2:170.

98. At the conclusion of Coke's *The Lord Coke His Speech and Charge*, delivered at the Norwich Assize and published in 1607, he reminded his audience that "the life and strength of the Laws, consisteth in the execution of them." Though this may have been a common aphorism, the only other place I have seen it is in the Massachusetts Laws and Liberties, where it comes near the end of the text of the epistle and is expressed: "The execution of the law is the life of the law" (*L & L*, epistle).

99. *The Lord Coke His Speech and Charge*, H2–H3.

100. Increase Mather, *Wo to Drunkards*. See also Powers, *Crime and Punishment*, chap. 11, "The Colonial Drunkard."

101. *N.H. Col. Rec. 1*, 306–7.

102. 5 Eliz. c.4 (1563); George Haskins, *Law and Authority in Early Massachusetts*, 156–57; Dalton, *Countrey Justice*, 68–75.

103. Reasonable physical punishment was exempt from the law of assault (Dalton, *Countrey Justice*, 161; Pulton, *De Pace Regis Regni*, 7).

104. *Va. Gen. Ct.*, 107–8; *Md. Arch.*, 54:27, 41, 59, 78, 195, 258, 414; *Accomack, 1632–40*, 28.

105. Examples of nonattendance and Sabbath violation: *Essex*, 1:50, 52, 75, 134, 135, 138, 174, 183, 184, 244, 365, 414, 423, 2:39, 49, 103, 220, 225; *N.H. Col. Rec. 1*, 337, 455; *Mass. Asst. Ct.*, 2:9, 118; *Ply. Rec.*, 1:75, 2:140, 156, 165, 3:5, 15; *Conn. Col. Rec.*, 1:193; Conn. Hist. Soc. *Coll.*, 10:99, 103, 128, 137, 166, 169, 191.

106. *Essex*, 1:20, 27, 49, 60, 113, 387, 2:11, 38.

107. *Pynch. Ct. Rec.*, 276.

108. *Essex*, 1:378; other examples of criticizing or reviling ministers or doctrine: ibid., 34, 69, 70, 156, 168, 178, 222, 306, 360, 2:36; *Accomack, 1632–40*, 28; *N.H. Col. Rec. 1*, 39, 173; *Mass. Asst. Ct.*, 2:121; *Ply. Rec.*, 2:17.

109. *Mass. Asst. Ct.*, 2:177, 249; *Essex*, 2:106.

110. Mass. v. Benjamin Sawcer.

111. New Haven v. George King. A case of blasphemy not involving an oath occurred in Maryland. Jacob Lumbrozo, a Jew, became involved in a conversation about the miracles performed by Jesus and the resurrection of Christ. He was understood to say that Jesus was not a divine being, but a magician. In court, Lumbrozo answered lamely that he had spoken of Moses and the magicians of Egypt. He was never prosecuted (*Md. Arch.*, 41:203).

112. *Md. Arch.*, 54:51, 161, 166, 178; *Accomack, 1632–40*, 15, 24, *1640–45*, 184, 202, 212, 235, 236, 317; *Conn. Col. Rec.*, 1:140; Conn. Hist. Soc. *Coll.*, 22:86; *Essex*, 1:25, 36, 59, 133, 134, 138, 156, 160, 173, 184, 204, 287, 2:50, 60, 106, 168, 192; *Ply. Rec.*, 2:9, 37; *Mass. Asst. Ct.*, 2:50, 53, 64, 77, 87, 98, 102, 133, 135.

113. *Essex*, 1:361; examples: *Conn. Col. Rec.*, 1:177; Conn. Hist. Soc. *Coll.*, 22:119, 126; *N.H. Col. Rec. 1*, 56, 162, 170, 455, 469, 488; *Essex*, 1:5, 7, 25, 58, 61, 83, 99, 101, 110, 113, 128, 132, 150, 156, 168, 177, 179, 182, 184, 185, 188, 219, 224, 225, 227, 265, 269, 307, 313, 322, 347, 361, 370, 2:39,

40, 59, 68, 70, 155, 220; *Ply. Rec.*, 3:129, 131, 133, 159; *Mass. Asst. Ct.*, 70, 83, 118.

114. 1 Jac. I c.25 (1603).
115. *Conn. Col. Rec.*, 1:64; *Mass. Col. Rec.*, 1:126, 274–75, 4:pt. 2, 41–42.
116. *Essex*, 1:266, 270, 272, 275, 276, 279, 285, 304.
117. Ibid., 276, 278, 303.

Conclusion: The Lost World of Early American Law

1. For an analysis of various reception theories, see Goebel and Naughton, *Law Enforcement*, xvii–xxxix, 759–61; the quotation is from Walton Hamilton, "The Law and Mr. Blackstone," *Columbia Law Review* 39 (1939): 736.
2. See Joseph H. Smith & Thomas G. Barnes, *The English Legal System: Carry-over to the Colonies*.
3. *R.I. Col. Rec.*, 3:393.
4. Julius Goebel, Jr., ed., *The Law Practice of Alexander Hamilton*, 1:55, 243–49.
5. Lyman H. Butterfield, ed., *Diary and Autobiography of John Adams*, 1:55.

Selected Cases

There were no printed court records and reports and therefore no formal citation of specific cases in early colonial courts. The scholar might be aided by a list identifying a body of colonial case law, and it is possible that a modern lawyer would have occasion to use such cases to prove the antiquity of a point. The form of citation causes problems. Virginia cases were brought in the name of the king, Maryland cases in the name of the lord proprietor, Massachusetts cases usually in the name of the commonwealth. During the period of the English civil wars, Commonwealth, and Protectorate, the forms of citation became even more confusing. I have chosen to cite the cases by the jurisdiction because this form would be most useful to anyone wishing to locate and use the cases. The notation indicates points of interest about each case. This list of cases represents only a small fraction of the cases used in the book. It is not meant to be statistically representative. It is weighted heavily on the side of the capital cases. Some of the cases have been included because they illuminate procedure. Others have been listed because they are fully enough reported to give insight into social conditions.

Connecticut

Conn. v. Thomas Allyn (1651): homicide by misadventure. Conn. Hist. Soc. *Coll.*, 22:106.

Conn. v. Goody Bassett (1651): witchcraft, death penalty. *Conn. Col. Rec.*, 1:220; *N.H. Col. Rec. 1*, 81.

Conn. v. Katherine Boston (1658): homicide by poison. Conn. Hist. Soc. *Coll.*, 22:194.

Conn. v. John and Joane Carrington (1651): witchcraft, death penalty, indictments. Conn. Hist. Soc. *Coll.*, 22:93.

Conn. v. Lydea Gilburt (1654): witchcraft, death penalty. Conn. Hist. Soc. *Coll.*, 22:131.

Conn. v. Mary Jonson (1648): witchcraft. *Conn. Col. Rec.*, 1:171.

Conn. v. Goody Knapp (1654): witchcraft, death penalty. *N.H. Col. Rec. 2*, 81.

Conn. v. William Taylor (1654): felonious death. Conn. Hist. Soc. *Coll.* 22:144.

Maryland

Md. v. John Nevill & Susanna Atcheson (1657): adultery, depositions. *Md. Arch.*, 10:558.

Md. v. Thomas Bradnox (1648): cattle theft, evidence. *Md. Arch.*, 4:444, 447.

Md. v. Giles Brent (1642): sedition, procedure. *Md. Arch.*, 4:126.

Md. v. Francis Brooke (1656): infanticide. *Md. Arch.*, 10:464, 488.

Md. v. Mary Butler (1657): bigamy. *Md. Arch.*, 10:515.

Md. v. Judith Catchpole (1656): infanticide, jury of women. *Md. Arch.*, 4:456.

Md. v. William Claiborne (1637): murder, piracy, attainder. *Md. Arch.*, 4:21.

Md. v. Mary Clocker (1658): accessory to larceny, presentment, evidence. *Md. Arch.*, 41:207.

Md. v. John Dandy (1) (1643): Indian homicide. *Md. Arch.*, 4:255, 260.

Md. v. John Dandy (2) (1650): assault. *Md. Arch.*, 10:31.

Md. v. John Dandy (3) (1657): murder of servant, hue and cry, indictment, evidence, forfeiture. *Md. Arch.*, 10:524, 536.

William Eliot v. John Salter (1655): larceny, depositions. *Md. Arch.*, 54:42.

Md. v. John Elkin (1642): Indian homicide, murder/manslaughter, jury verdict. *Md. Arch.*, 4:177, 180.

Md. v. Josias Fendall (1660): seditious practices. *Md. Arch.*, 41:428.

Md. v. Francis Fitzherbert (1658): seditious practices, depositions. *Md. Arch.*, 41:144.

Md. v. Richard Galey et al. (1659): piracy, jurisdiction. *Md. Arch.*, 41:310.

Md. v. Elizabeth Harris (1660): infanticide, depositions. *Md. Arch.*, 41:430.

Md. v. Robert Holt (1658): bigamy, indictment, outlawry. *Md. Arch.*, 41:149.

Md. v. Blanch Howell (1648): perjury, pillory, loss of ears. *Md. Arch.*, 4:445.

Md. v. Richard Ingle (1643): treason, modes of prosecution. *Md. Arch.*, 4:231, 237.

In re Catherine Lake (1660): homicide inquest, evidence. *Md. Arch.*, 41:385.

Md. v. James Langworth (1650): manslaughter. *Md. Arch.*, 10:141.

Md. v. Jacob Lumbrozo (1658): blasphemy, evidence. *Md. Arch.*, 41:203.

Md. v. Capt. William Mitchell (1652): blasphemy, adultery, fornication, attempted murder, function of jury. *Md. Arch.*, 10:170; *Md. Arch.*, 3:250, 264, 294.

Md. v. Naughnongis (1658): larceny by an Indian. *Md. Arch.*, 41:186.

Md. v. Simon Overzee (1658): homicide by chance medley, black servant, depositions. *Md. Arch.*, 41:190, 204.

Md. v. Jane Palladin (1658): bastardy, depositions. *Md. Arch.*, 41:14.

Md. v. Elizabeth Robins (1658): abortion, jury of women. *Md. Arch.*, 41:20.

Md. v. Hanna Rogers (1660): murder. *Md. Arch.*, 41:429.

In re John Salter (1658): assault, depositions. *Md. Arch.*, 54:116.

Peter Sharpe v. Robert Harwood (1657): appeal of rape. *Md. Arch.*, 10:499.

Md. v. SkightamMongh & Counaweza (1653): murder of a black servant by Indians, procedure, death penalty. *Md. Arch.*, 10:294.

Md. v. Thomas Smith (1638): piracy, procedure, benefit of clergy. *Md. Arch.*, 1:16.

Sarah Tailer v. Thomas Bradnox (1659): assault, depositions. *Md. Arch.*, 54:167.

Md. v. Susan Warren (1652): fornication, depositions. *Md. Arch.*, 10:170.

Md. v. John & Mary Williams (1658): larceny, examinations, death penalty, pardon. *Md. Arch.*, 41:207.

Massachusetts

Mass. v. John Betts (1653): murder of servant, evidence, punishment. *Mass. Asst. Ct.*, 3:24.

[Mass.]* v. John Bonithon (1645): assault, resisting process, outlawry. *Me. Ct. Rec.* 1:90.

[Mass.]* v. George Burdett (1640): fornication and adultery. *Me. Ct. Rec.*, 1:73.

Mass. v. Gregory Cassell (1657): murder. *Mass. Asst. Ct.*, 3:59.

Case of Robert Child et al. (1646): seditious practices. Winthrop, *Journal*, 2:271.

[Mass.]* v. Robert Collens (1650): rape, indictment, evidence, verdict. *Me. Ct. Rec.*, 1:140.

Case of Cornish's Wife (1644): murder, evidence, death penalty. Winthrop, *Journal*, 2:218.

Mass. v. Mary Dyer (1659): Quaker, banished, death penalty. *Mass. Col. Rec.*, 4:pt. 1, 383, 419; *Mass. Asst. Ct.*, 3:68.

Mass. v. Nathaniel Eaton (1639): assault, confession. Winthrop, *Journal*, 1:313.

Mass. v. Daniel Fairfield (1642): fornication with young girls, punishment. *Mass. Col. Rec.*, 1:12.

Mass. v. William Franklin (1644): murder, criminal intent, death penalty. Winthrop, *Journal*, 1:187.

Mass. v. Samuel Gorton et al. (1643): blasphemy, sedition, banishment. *Mass. Col. Rec.*, 2:5, 52, 57.

Mass. v. William Hatchett (1641): buggery, death penalty. *Mass. Col. Rec.*, 1:344.

Mass. v. Ann Hibbins (1656): witchcraft, death penalty. *Mass. Col. Rec.*, 4:pt. 1, 269.

Anne Hutchinson's Case (1637): traducing ministers, examination, banishment. *Mass. Col. Rec.*, 1:207; Adams, *Antinomianism*.

Mass. v. Margaret Jones (1648): witchcraft, evidence, death penalty. Winthrop, *Journal*, 2:345.

Mass. v. Mary Latham & James Britton (1644): adultery, death penalty. Winthrop, *Journal*, 1:161.

Mass. v. William Ledra (1660): Quaker, banished, death penalty. *Mass. Asst. Ct.*, 3:93.

Mass. v. Mary Martin (1648): infanticide, death penalty. Winthrop, *Journal*, 2:317; Mather, *Pillars of Salt*.

Mass. v. Marmaduke Mathews (1651): unsound religious teaching, limits on execution of judgment. *Mass. Col. Rec.*, 3:236.

Mass. v. Mary Parsons (1651): witchcraft, infanticide, evidence, death penalty. *Mass. Col. Rec.*, 3:229; Drake, *Annals*, 218.

Mass. v. Hugh Parsons (1651): witchcraft, evidence. *Mass. Col. Rec.*, 3:229; Drake, *Annals*, 218.

Mass. v. Marmaduke Peirce (1639): murder, evidence. *Mass. Col. Rec.*, 1:269, 283.

Mass. v. Robert Quimby (1657): murder, evidence. *Mass. Col. Rec.*, 3:63.

Mass. v. William Robbinson (1659): Quaker, death penalty. *Mass. Asst. Ct.*, 3:68; *Mass. Col. Rec.*, 4:pt. 1, 383, 419.

Mass. v. Edward Saunders (1654): rape. *Mass. Col. Rec.*, 3:364, 389.

Mass. v. Benjamin Sawcer (1654): blasphemy, indictment requirements, plea. *Mass. Asst. Ct.*, 3:34; *Mass. Col. Rec.*, 3:368.

Mass. v. William Schooler (1637): murder, evidence. *Mass. Col. Rec.*, 1:202; Winthrop, *Journal*, 1:235.

Mass. v. Marmaduke Stephenson (1659): Quaker, banished, death penalty. *Mass. Col. Rec.*, 4:pt. 1, 383, 419; *Mass. Asst. Ct.*, 3:68.

Mass. v. Dorothy Talbie (1638): infanticide, death penalty. *Mass. Col. Rec.*, 1:246; Winthrop, *Journal*, 1:282.

Case of John Wheelwright (1637): sedition, banishment. *Mass. Col. Rec.*, 1:89.

Mass. v. John Williams (1637): murder, confession, death penalty. *Mass. Col. Rec.*, 1:202; Winthrop, *Journal*, 1:235.

Mass. v. Robert Wyar et al. (1652): filthy dalliance, evidence, confession. *Mass. Asst. Ct.*, 2:121.

*[Maine cases have been listed under Massachusetts. Some of them occurred in courts that were under the jurisdiction of Sir Ferdinando Gorges.]

New Haven

N.H. v. William Ellit (1655): rape, evidence. *N.H. Col. Rec. 2*, 134.

N.H. v. John Ferris (1657): buggery. *N.H. Col. Rec. 2*, 223.

N.H. v. John Frost (1656): arson, sentence. *N.H. Col. Rec. 2*, 169.

In re Elizabeth Godman (1653): witchcraft, examinations. *N.H. Col. Rec. 2*, 29, 151.

N.H. v. Thomas Hogg (1646): buggery. *N.H. Col. Rec. 1*, 295.

N.H. v. John Knight (1655): sodomy, death penalty. *N.H. Col. Rec. 2*, 137.

N.H. v. Jacobus Loper (1660): arson, sentence. *N.H. Col. Rec. 2*, 384.

N.H. v. Nepaupuck (1639): murder by Indian, death penalty, mode of execution. *N.H. Col. Rec. 1*, 22.

N.H. v. Walter Robinson (1654): buggery, death penalty. *N.H. Col. Rec. 2*, 132.

N.H. v. George Spencer (1641): buggery, examination, confession, death penalty. *N.H. Col. Rec. 1*, 62.

Thomas Staples v. Roger Ludlow (1654): defamation, witchcraft, depositions. *N.H. Col. Rec. 2*, 77.

N.H. v. John Uffoote (1657): adultery, examinations. *N.H. Col. Rec. 2*, 201.

N.H. v. George Wood (1656): larceny, banishment. *N.H. Col. Rec. 2*, 187.

Plymouth

Ply. v. Thomas Atkins (1660): incest. *Ply. Rec.*, 3:197.

Ply. v. John Billington (1630): murder, death penalty. Bradford, *Of Plymouth Plantation*, 87–88, 156–57, 234.

Ply. v. Allis Bishop (1648): infanticide, evidence, death penalty. *Ply. Rec.*, 2:132.

Ply. v. Thomas Graunger (1642): buggery, death penalty. *Ply. Rec.*, 2:44.

Ply. v. Robert Latham (1655): manslaughter, inquest, benefit of clergy. *Ply. Rec.*, 3:71, 82, 143.

Ply. v. Francis Linceford & Thomas Bray (1641): adultery, punishment. *Ply. Rec.*, 2:28.

Ply. v. Mary Mendame & Tinsin (1639): adultery with Indian, punishment. *Ply. Rec.*, 1:132.

Ply. v. Arthur Peach et al. (1638): murder of an Indian, death penalty. *Ply. Rec.*, 1:96.

Virginia

Va. v. Richard Barnes (1624): criticism of government, cruel and unusual punishment, banishment. *Va. Gen. Ct.*, 14.

Va. v. William Bently (1628): manslaughter, depositions, benefit of clergy, *Va. Gen. Ct.*, 190.

Va. v. Henry Carman (1626): fornication, sentence. *Va. Gen. Ct.*, 117.

Va. v. George Clarke (1623): accessory to larceny, death penalty, reprieved. *Va. Gen. Ct.*, 4.

Case of Richard Williams alias Cornish (1625): sodomy, death penalty. *Va. Gen. Ct.*, 93.

Va. v. Daniel Franke (1623): larceny, indictment, death penalty. *Va. Gen. Ct.*, 4.

In re Thomas Hall (1629): court determination of a person's sex. *Va. Gen. Ct.*, 194.

Va. v. Thomas Hayle (1627): rape, death penalty. *Va. Gen. Ct.*, 149.

Va. v. John Heney (1625): contempt, punishment. *Va. Gen. Ct.*, 85.

Case of Margaret Jones (1626): assault, punishment. *Va. Gen. Ct.*, 119.

Va. v. William Mills (1627): larceny, examination, depositions. *Va. Gen. Ct.*, 159.

Case of Pooly & Pawlett (1625): slander. *Va. Gen. Ct.*, 88.

Va. v. William Reade (1628): manslaughter, depositions, benefit of clergy. *Va. Gen. Ct.*, 183.

In re John Verone (1625): suicide, deodand. *Va. Gen. Ct.*, 53.

Case of Goodwife Wright (1626): witchcraft, depositions. *Va. Gen. Ct.*, 111, 112, 114.

Appendix

Table A identifies the sources of colonial substantive law. The sources of some laws, especially in the categories "English" and "Biblical," were obvious. "Indigenous" means that no clear biblical source or source in the English law as it then existed was apparent. "None" indicates that no law in that category was found. Much of the law categorized as indigenous reflected the demands of the English advocates of law reform and/or the desires of those Englishmen who wished the public law to control misconduct. Both the definition of the act described as criminal and the punishments authorized affected the distributions. Crimes against property in Maryland furnish examples of the method used. In recognizing burglary and robbery as distinct kinds of theft, Maryland followed the English example. By giving the judge a wide discretion as to punishment, the colony deviated from parent precedents. The entries Eng 60 percent and Ind 40 percent have been made. In defining larceny, Maryland did not follow English law. The entries Ind. 60 percent and Bib. 40 percent have been made because restitution as punishment was probably biblically inspired.

It is difficult to assign a statistical value to text and practice. It would have been possible to explain each distribution (406 in all), but this would have defeated the purpose of the tables, which was to avoid a detailed description of each crime. The percentages are based on the author's choice and discretion and thus are arbitrary. Doubtless some readers will quarrel with some of the distributions. In the aggregate, though, they probably exhibit a fair picture of the sources and means of expressing early American law.

Table B shows the means used in each jurisdiction to express the law: usage, statute, or code. The entry "none" means that no code provision, statute, or prosecution was found. Not every expression of the substantive law has been noted. If statutory law later became embodied in a code, only the entry "code" has been used. The percentages represent the choice of method. In most cases the mode of expression was obvious. In those for which the method used to express the law was less than obvious, the percentages assigned reflect the author's judgment. For example, the Plymouth codes and Maryland statutes merely mentioned many crimes by name. In these cases a low percentage was assigned to "statute" or "code" because the definition of the crime and its punishment had been left largely to the judges.

TABLE A. SOURCES OF THE LAW
(figures indicate percent of total)

Eng = English   Ind = Indigenous   Bib = Biblical

	Virginia	Maryland	Massa-chusetts	Connect-icut	New Haven	Plymouth	Rhode Island
Treason	Ind 100	Eng 100	none	none	none	Eng 100	Eng 100
Murder	Eng 100	Eng 100	Eng 100	Eng 100	Eng 100	Eng 100	Eng 100
Man-slaughter	Eng 100	Eng 60 Ind 40	Eng 40 Bib 60	none	Eng 40 Bib 60	Eng 100	Eng 100
Homicide by Misadventure	Eng 100	Eng 60 Ind 40	none	none	none	none	Eng 100
Rape	Eng 100	Eng 60 Ind 40	Eng 60 Ind 40	Bib 100	Eng 60 Ind 40	Eng 100	Eng 100
Witchcraft	Eng 100	Eng 60 Ind 40	Eng 50 Bib 50	Eng 50 Bib 50	Eng 50 Bib 50	Eng 100	Eng 100
Arson	none	Eng 100	Eng 70 Bib 30	Eng 70 Bib 30	Eng 70 Bib 30	Eng 100	Eng 100
Burglary	none	Eng 60 Ind 40	Eng 20 Ind 80	Eng 20 Ind 80	Eng 20 Ind 80	none	Eng 100
Robbery	none	Eng 60 Ind 40	Eng 20 Ind 80	Eng 20 Ind 80	Eng 20 Ind 80	none	Eng 100
Larceny	Eng 10 Ind 90	Ind 60 Bib 40	Ind 30 Bib 70	Ind 30 Bib 70	Ind 30 Bib 70	Ind 60 Bib 40	Eng 10 Ind 70 Bib 20
Sedition	Ind 100	Ind 100	Ind 50 Bib 50	Ind 100	Ind 50 Bib 50	Ind 100	Ind 100
Riot	none	none	none	none	none	none	Eng 100
Assault	Eng 100	Eng 100	Eng 100	Eng 100	Ind 70 Bib 30	Eng 100	Eng 100
Apostasy/ Heresy	none	Ind 100	Bib 100	Bib 100	Bib 100	Ind 100	none
Blasphemy	none	Ind 100	Bib 100	Bib 100	Bib 100	none	none
Man Stealing	none	none	Bib 100	Bib 100	Bib 100	none	none
Incorrigible Children	none	none	Bib 100	Bib 100	Bib 100	none	Ind 100
Adultery	Eng 50 Ind 50	Ind 100	Bib 100	Bib 100	Bib 100	Ind 100	Eng 100
Buggery/ Sodomy	Eng 100	Eng 60 Ind 40	Eng 50 Bib 50	Eng 50 Bib 50	Eng 30 Ind 20 Bib 50	Eng 100	Eng 100
Defamation	Eng 100	Eng 100	Eng 100	Eng 100	Ind 70 Bib 30	Eng 100	Eng 100
Offenses against Trade	Eng 100	Eng 70 Ind 30	Eng 80 Ind 20	Eng 80 Ind 20	Eng 80 Ind 20	Eng 40 Ind 60	none
Offenses against Justice	Eng 100	Eng 50 Ind 50	Eng 80 Ind 20	Eng 80 Ind 20	Eng 100	Eng 100	Eng 100
Drunkenness	Eng 100	Eng 60 Ind 40	Eng 100	Eng 100	Eng 100	Eng 100	Eng 100
Fornication/ Bastardy	Eng 100	Ind 100	Ind 50 Bib 50	Ind 50 Bib 50	Ind 50 Bib 50	Eng 100	Eng 100
Cursing	Eng 100	Eng 100	Eng 100	Eng 100	Eng 100	Eng 100	Eng 100

TABLE A.—*Continued*
(figures indicate percent of total)
Eng = English   Ind = Indigenous   Bib = Biblical

	Virginia	Maryland	Massa-chusetts	Connect-icut	New Haven	Plymouth	Rhode Island
Lying	none	none	Bib 100	Bib 100	Bib 100	Ind 100	none
Idleness	none	none	Eng 50 Ind 50	Eng 50 Ind 50	Eng 50 Ind 50	Eng 50 Ind 50	none
Apparel	none	none	Ind 100	Ind 100	none	none	none
Sabbath Violation	Eng 100	none	Eng 50 Bib 50	Eng 50 Bib 50	Eng 50 Bib 50	Eng 50 Bib 50	none
All Crimes	Eng 81.1 Ind 18.9	Eng 54.6 Ind 43.6 Bib 1.80	Eng 41.2 Ind 20.0 Bib 38.80	Eng 38.8 Ind 21.2 Bib 40.0	Eng 34.8 Ind 22.4 Bib 42.8	Eng 59.0 Ind 36.7 Bib 4.30	Eng 86.2 Ind 12.9 Bib 0.90

TABLE B. MODES OF EXPRESSING THE LAW
(figures indicate percent of total)

	Virginia	Maryland	Massa-chusetts	Connec-ticut	New Haven	Plymouth	Rhode Island
Treason	statute 100	statute 100	none	none	none	usage 80 code 20	code 100
Murder	usage 100	usage 80 statute 20	code 100	code 100	code 100	code 100	code 100
Manslaughter	usage 100	usage 80 statute 20	code 100	none	code 100	code 100	code 100
Homicide by Misadventure	usage 100	usage 80 statute 20	none	none	none	none	code 100
Rape	usage 100	usage 80 statute 20	code 100	code 100	code 100	usage 80 code 20	code 100
Witchcraft	usage 100	usage 80 statute 20	code 100	code 100	code 100	usage 70 code 30	code 100
Arson	none	statute 100	statute 50 code 50	code 100	code 100	code 100	code 100
Burglary	none	usage 80 statute 20	code 100	code 100	code 100	none	code 100
Robbery	none	usage 80 statute 20	code 100	code 100	code 100	none	code 100
Larceny	usage 100	usage 80 statute 20	code 100	code 100	code 100	usage 60 statute 20 code 20	code 100
Sedition	statute 100	statute 100	code 100	code 100	code 100	code 100	code 100
Riot	none	none	none	none	none	none	code 100
Assault	usage 100	usage 100	usage 100	usage 100	code 100	usage 100	code 100
Apostasy/ Heresy	none	statute 100	code 100	code 100	code 100	code 100	none
Blasphemy	none	statute 100	code 100	code 100	code 100	none	none
Man Stealing	none	none	code 100	code 100	code 100	none	none
Incorrigible Children	none	none	code 100	code 100	code 100	none	code 100
Adultery	usage 80 statute 20	usage 80 statute 20	code 100	code 100	code 100	code 100	code 100
Buggery/ Sodomy	usage 100	usage 80 statute 20	code 100	code 100	code 100	usage 80 code 20	code 100
Defamation	usage 100	usage 100	usage 100	usage 100	code 100	usage 100	code 100
Offenses against Trade	statute 100	statute 100	code 100	code 100	code 100	statute 100	none
Offenses against Justice	usage 100	statute 100	code 100	code 100	code 100	usage 70 code 30	code 100
Drunkenness	statute 100	statute 100	code 100	code 100	code 100	code 100	code 100
Fornication/ Bastardy	usage 80 statute 20	usage 80 statute 20	code 100	code 100	code 100	code 100	code 100
Cursing	statute 100	statute 100	code 100	code 100	code 100	code 100	statute 100
Lying	none	none	code 100	code 100	code 100	code 100	none
Idleness	none	none	code 100	code 100	code 100	statute 50 code 50	none
Apparel	none	none	statute 100	statute 100	none	none	none
Sabbath Violation	statute 100	none	code 100	code 100	code 100	code 100	none

TABLE B.—*Continued*
(figures indicate percent of total)

	Virginia	Maryland	Massa-chusetts	Connec-ticut	New Haven	Plymouth	Rhode Island
All Crimes	usage 64.4	usage 49.1	usage 7.6	usage 8.0	usage 0.0	usage 35.2	usage 0.0
	statute 35.6	statute 50.9	statute 5.7	statute 4.0	statute 0.0	statute 8.1	statute 4.8
	code 0.0	code 0.0	code 86.5	code 88.0	code 100	code 56.7	code 95.2

SOURCES OF DATA IN TABLES A AND B

TREASON: 25 Edw. III c.2 (1351); Coke, *Third Institute*, 1–18; Hening, 1:359–61; *Md. Arch.*, 1:158; *Ply. Rec.*, 11:12; *R.I. Rec.*, 1:161. MURDER: Coke, *Third Institute*, 48–52; Dalton, *Countrey Justice*, 217; *Md. Arch.*, 1:158; *L & L*, 5; *Conn. Col. Rec.*, 1:77; *N.H. Col Rec. 1*, 576; *Ply. Rec.*, 11:12; *R.I. Rec.*,1:164–65. MANSLAUGHTER: Coke, *Third Institute*, 54–57; Dalton, *Countrey Justice*, 222–23; *Md. Arch.*, 1:158; *L & L*, 5; *Conn. Col. Rec.*, 1:77; *N.H. Col. Rec. 1*, 576; *Ply. Rec.*, 11:12; *R.I. Rec.*, 1:164–65. HOMICIDE BY MISADVENTURE: Coke, *Third Institute*, 55–56; Dalton, *Countrey Justice*, 224; *Md. Arch.*, 1:158; *R.I. Rec.*, 1:165. RAPE: Coke, *Third Institute*, 60–61; Dalton, *Countrey Justice*, 233–34; *Md. Arch.*, 1:158; *Ply. Rec.*, 11:12; *L & L*, 6; *Conn. Col. Rec.*, 1:77; *N.H. Col. Rec. 1*, 578; *R.I. Rec.*, 1:173. WITCHCRAFT: 33 H. VIII c.8 (1542); 5 Eliz. c.16 (1563); 1 Jac. I, c.12 (1603); Coke, *Third Institute*, 44–47; *Md. Arch.*, 1:158; *Ply. Rec.*, 11:12; *L & L*, 5; *Conn. Col. Rec.*, 1:77; *N.H. Col. Rec. 1*, 576; *R.I. Rec.*, 1:166. ARSON: Coke, *Third Institute*, 65–67; Dalton, *Countrey Justice*, 245–46; *Md. Arch.*, 1:158; *L & L*, 23; *Mass. Col. Rec.*, 3:264; *Conn. Col. Rec.*, 1:526; *N.H. Col. Rec. 1*, 589; *Ply. Rec.*, 11:12; *R.I. Rec.*, 1:168. BURGLARY: Coke, *Third Institute*, 63; Dalton, *Countrey Justice*, 231–34; *Md. Arch.*, 1:158; *L & L*, 4–5; *Conn. Col. Rec.*, 1:513–14; *N.H. Col. Rec. 1*, 575; *R.I. Rec.*, 1:167. ROBBERY: Coke, *Third Institute*, 67–69; Dalton, *Countrey Justice*, 234–37; *Md. Arch.*, 1:158; *L & L*, 4–5; *Conn. Col. Rec.*, 1:513–14; *N.H. Col. Rec. 1*, 575; *R.I. Rec.*, 1:167. LARCENY: Coke, *Third Institute*, 106–10; Dalton, *Countrey Justice*, 237–45; *Md. Arch.*, 1:158; *L & L*, 4–5; *Conn. Col. Rec.*, 1:513–14; *N.H. Col. Rec. 1*, 575–76; *Ply. Rec.*, 11:12, 172; *R.I. Rec.*, 1:163–64. RIOT: Dalton, *Countrey Justice*, 97–108; Lambarde, *Eirenarcha*, 172–83, 228–42; *R.I. Rec.*, 1:169–70. ASSAULT: Pulton, *De Pace Regis Regni*, 1–68; Lambarde, *Eirenarcha*, 135–44; *N.H. Col. Rec. 1*, 585–86. APOSTASY/HERESY: Coke, *Third Institute*, 39–43; 1 Eliz. c.1 (1558); *Md. Arch.*, 1:244–46; *L & L*, 5; *Conn. Col. Rec.*, 1:77; *N.H. Col. Rec. 1*, 576. BLASPHEMY: *Md. Arch.*, 1:244–46; *L & L*, 5; *Conn. Col. Rec.*, 1:77; *N.H. Col. Rec. 1*, 577. MAN STEALING: *L & L*, 6; *Conn. Col. Rec.*, 1:77; *N.H. Col. Rec. 1*, 577. INCORRIGIBLE CHILDREN: *L & L*, 6; *Conn. Col. Rec.*, 1:77; *R.I. Rec.*, 1:173. ADULTERY: Dalton, *Countrey Justice*, 172; Firth and Rait, eds., *Acts and Ordinances of the Interregnum*, 2:387–89; Hening, 1:433; *Md. Arch.*, 1:286; *L & L*, 6; *Conn. Col. Rec.*, 1:77; *N.H. Col. Rec. 1*, 577; *Ply. Rec.*, 11:12, 95, 172; *R.I. Rec.*, 1:173. BUGGERY/SODOMY: Coke, *Third Institute*, 106–10; Dalton, *Countrey Justice*, 250; *Md. Arch.*, 1:158; *L & L*, 5; *Conn. Col. Rec.*, 1:77; *N.H. Col. Rec. 1*, 576–77; *Ply. Rec.*, 11:12; *R.I. Rec.*, 1:184. OFFENSES AGAINST TRADE: Coke, *Third Institute*, 195–96; Pulton, *De Pace Regis Regni*, 99–100; Lambarde, *Eirenarcha*, 263, 349–50; 5 & 6 Edw. VI c.4 (1552); Hening, 1:150–51, 166, 172, 190, 194–95, 217, 245; *Md. Arch.*, 1:161–62, 294; *L & L*, 3, 6, 32–34, 43, 51; *Conn. Col. Rec.*, 1:515–16, 541; *N.H. Col. Rec. 1*, 574, 578, 597; *Ply. Rec.*, 11:29. OFFENSES AGAINST JUSTICE: Coke, *Third Institute*, Pulton, *De Pace Regis Regni*, 48–55, 56–60; Dalton, *Countrey Justice*, 31–32, 274; Lambarde, *Eirenarcha*, 321–42; *Md. Arch.*, 1:158–59; *L & L*, 3–4, 23, 36; *Conn. Col. Rec.*, 1:512, 526. 540; *N.H. Col. Rec. 1*, 574, 585; *Ply. Rec.*, 11:175; *R.I. Rec.*, 1:168–69, 178, 181–82. DRUNKENNESS: 4 Jac. I c.5 (1607); 21 Jac. I c.7 (1624); Dalton, *Countrey Justice*, 172; Hening, 1:167; Lyon G. Tyler, ed., *Narratives of Early Virginia*, 263; *Md. Arch.*, 1:159, 312–13; *L & L*, 30; *Conn. Col. Rec.*, 1:533; *N.H. Col. Rec. 1*, 596–97; *Ply. Rec.*, 11:17, 96, 113, 173, 197; *R.I. Rec.*, 1:185–86. FORNICATION/BASTARDY: Dalton, *Countrey Justice*, 32–33; 18 Eliz. c.3 (1576); 7 Jac. I c.4 (1610); Tyler, *Narr. Early Va.*, 271–72; *Md. Arch.*, 1:286, 312–13; *L & L*, 23; *Conn. Col. Rec.*, 1:527; *N.H. Col. Rec. 1*, 590; *Ply. Rec.*, 11:12, 172; *R.I. Rec.*, 1:173. CURSING: 21 Jac. I, c.20 (1624); Hening, 1:126, 167, 194, 433; *Md. Arch.*, 1:159; *L & L*, 45; *Conn. Col. Rec.*, 1:547; *N.H. Col. Rec. 1*, 606; *Ply. Rec.* 11:172; *R.I. Rec.*, 1:314. LYING: *L & L*, 35; *Conn. Col. Rec.*, 1:547; *Ply. Rec.*, 11:95–96, 173. IDLENESS: Dalton, *Countrey Justice*, 111–16; 39 Eliz. c.4 (1597); 1 Jac. I c.7 (1603) [rogues & vagabonds]; *L & L*, 24, 35–36; *Conn. Col. Rec.*, 1:527–28; *N.H. Col. Rec. 1*, 601; *Ply. Rec.*, 11:66, 96, 168, 173. APPAREL: 1 Jac. I c.25 (1603); *Mass. Col. Rec.*, 1:126, 274–75; *Conn. Col. Rec.*, 1:64; SABBATH VIOLATION: 1 Car. I c.1 (1625); 3 Car. I c.2 (1628); Hening, 1:144, 240, 261, 434; *L & L*, 20; *Conn. Col. Rec.*, 1:524; *N.H. Col. Rec. 1*, 588; *Ply. Rec.*, 11:177.

Bibliography

Primary Sources

Legislative and Judicial Records

Ames, Susie M., ed. *County Court Records of Accomack-Northampton, Virginia, 1632–1640.* Washington, 1954.
————. *County Court Records of Accomack-Northampton, Virginia, 1640–1645.* Charlottesville, 1973.
Axon, Ernst, ed. *Manchester Sessions, Notes of Proceedings before Oswald Mosley (1616–1630), Nicholas Mosley (1661–1672) and Sir Oswald Mosley (1734–1739) and Other Magistrates.* Manchester, 1901.
Bartlett, John R., ed. *Records of the Colony of Rhode Island and Providence Plantations, in New England.* 10 vols. Providence, 1856–65.
Browne, William H., et al., eds. *Archives of Maryland.* 66 vols. Baltimore, 1883–.
    Vol. 1: *Proceedings and Acts of the General Assembly, 1637/8–1664.* 1883.
    Vol. 3: *Proceedings of the Council, 1636–1667.* 1885.
    Vol. 4: *Proceedings of the Provincial Court, 1637–1650.* 1887.
    Vol. 10: *Proceedings of the Provincial Court, 1650–1657.* 1891.
    Vol. 41: *Proceedings of the Provincial Court, 1658–1662.* 1922.
    Vol. 53: *Proceedings of the County Court of Charles County, 1658–1666, and Manor Court of St. Clements' Manor, 1659–1672.* 1936.
    Vol. 54: *Proceedings of the County Courts of Kent, 1648–1676, Talbot, 1662–1674, and Somerset, 1665–1668, Counties.* 1937.
Bund, J. W. Willis, ed. *Worcestershire County Records. Calendar of the Quarter Sessions Papers, 1591–1641.* Worcester Historical Society Publications, vol. 11. Worcester, 1900.
Coke, Sir Edward. *The Lord Coke His Speech and Charge with a Discoverie of the Abuses and Corruption of Officers.* London, 1607.
Connecticut Historical Society. "Records of the Particular Court of Connecticut, 1639–1663." Connecticut Historical Society, *Collections,* vol. 22. Hartford, 1928.
Cushing, John D., ed. *The Earliest Acts and Laws of the Colony of Rhode Island and Providence Plantations, 1647–1719.* Wilmington, Del., 1977.
Dow, G. F., ed. *Records and Files of the Quarterly Courts of Essex County, Massachusetts.* 8 vols. Salem, 1911.

Firth, C. H., and Rait, R. S., eds. *Acts and Ordinances of the Interregnum, 1642–1660.* 3 vols. London, 1911.

Great Britain. *The Statutes of the Realm.* 11 vols. London, 1819–22.

Hall, Huburt. "Some Elizabethan Penances in the Diocese of Ely." *Transactions of the Royal Historical Society.* 3d ser., 1 (1907):236–77.

Hawarde, John. *Les reportes del cases in Camera Stellata, 1593 to 1609.* Edited by William P. Baildon. London, 1894.

Hening, William W., ed. *The Statutes at Large: Being the Laws of Virginia from the First Session of the Legislature in the Year 1619.* 13 vols. Richmond, 1819–23.

Hoadly, Charles J., ed. *Records of the Colony and Plantation of New Haven from 1638–1649.* Hartford, 1857.

———. *Records of the Colony or Jurisdiction of New Haven from May 1653, to the Union.* Hartford, 1857.

Howell, Thomas B., ed. *A Complete Collection of State Trials.* 31 vols. London, 1816–31.

Jeaffreson, John C., ed. *Middlesex County Records.* 4 vols. London, 1886–92.

Kennedy, John P., and McIlwaine, Henry R., eds. *Journals of the House of Burgesses, 1619–1659.* 13 vols. Richmond, 1905–13.

Leveson-Gower, Graville. "Note Book of a Surrey Justice." *Surrey Archaelogical Collections* 9 (1888):161–232.

Libby, Charles T., et al., eds. *Province and Court Records of Maine.* 6 vols. Portland, 1928–75.

McIlwaine, Henry R., ed. *Minutes of the Council and General Court of Virginia.* Richmond, 1924.

Marcham, William M., and Marcham, Frank, eds. *Court Rolls of the Bishop of London's Manor of Hornsey, 1603–1701.* London, 1929.

Massachusetts. *The Laws and Liberties of Massachusetts.* Introduction by Max Farrand. Cambridge, Mass., 1929.

Noble, John, ed. *Records of the Court of Assistants of the Colony of Massachusetts Bay, 1630–1692.* 3 vols. Boston, 1901–28.

Read, Conyers, ed. *William Lambarde and Local Government: His "Ephemeris" and Twenty-nine Charges to Juries and Commissions.* Ithaca, 1962.

Redwood, B. C., ed. *Quarter Sessions Order Book, 1642–1649.* Lewes, 1954.

Rhode Island. *Records of the Court of Tryals of the Colony of Providence Plantations, 1647–1662.* 2 vols. Providence, 1920–22.

Saunders, H. W., ed. *The Official Papers of Sir Nathaniel Bacon of Stiffkey, Norfolk as Justice of the Peace, 1580–1620.* London, 1915.

Shurtleff, Nathaniel B., and Pulsifer, David, eds. *Records of the Colony of New Plymouth in New England.* 12 vols. Boston, 1855–61.

Shurtleff, Nathaniel B., ed. *Records of the Governor and Company of the Massachusetts Bay in New England.* 5 vols. Boston, 1853–54.

Smith, Joseph, ed. *Colonial Justice in Western Massachusetts, 1639–1702: The Pynchon Court Record.* Cambridge, Mass., 1961.

Trumbull, J. Hammond, and Hoadly, Charles T., eds. *The Public Records of the Colony of Connecticut (1636–1776).* 15 vols. Hartford, 1850–90.

Whitmore, William H., ed. *A Bibliographical Sketch of the Laws of the Massachusetts Colony from 1630 to 1686.* Boston, 1890.
————. *The Colonial Laws of Massachusetts.* Boston, 1887.

Commentaries, Manuals, Law Texts

Blackstone, Sir William. *Commentaries on the Laws of England.* 4 vols. Oxford, 1765–69.
Bracton, Henry de. *De Legibus et Consuetudinibus Angliae.* Translated by Samuel E. Thorne. Cambridge, Mass., 1968.
Coke, Sir Edward. *Compleate Copy-holder . . .* London, 1644.
————. *The Fourth Part of the Institutes of the Laws of England: Concerning the Jurisdiction of the Courts.* London, 1797.
————. *The Second Part of the Institutes of the Laws of England: Containing the Exposition of Many Ancient and Other Statutes.* 2 vols. London, 1797.
————. *The Third Part of the Institutes of the Laws of England: Concerning High Treason, and Other Pleas of the Crown and Criminal Causes.* London, 1797.
Dalton, Michael. *The Countrey Justice, Containing the Practise of the Justices of the Peace out of Their Sessions . . .* London, 1619.
————. *Officium Vicecomitum. The Office and Authoritie of Sherifs . . .* London, 1623.
Fortescue, Sir John. *De Laudibus Legum Angliae.* Translated and edited by S. B. Chrimes. Cambridge, Eng., 1942.
Hale, Sir Matthew. *Historia Placitorum Coronae: The History of the Pleas of the Crown.* 2 vols. London, 1736.
Kitchin, John. *Jurisdiction, or The Lawful Authority of Courts Leet . . .* London, 1675.
Lambarde, William. *Archeion or a Discourse upon The High Courts of Justice in England.* Edited by Charles H. McIlwaine and Paul L. Ward. Cambridge, Mass., 1957.
————. *The Duties of Constables, Borsholders, Tithingmen, and such other low ministers of the peace.* London, 1583.
————. *Eirenarcha or the Office of the Justice of the Peace.* London, 1581.
Pulton, Ferdinando. *De Pace Regis Regni Viz A Treatise declaring which be the great and generall offences of The Realme, and the chiefe impediments of the peace of The King and The Kingdom . . .* London, 1609.
St. Germain, Christopher. *The Dialogue in English, between a Doctor of Divinitie and a Student in the Lawes of England.* London, 1604.
Smith, Thomas. *De Republica Anglorum.* London, 1583; reprint, Menston, 1970.

Pamphlets and Tracts

Anon. *The Laws Discovery.* In *The Harleian Miscellany*, vol. 2. 8 vols. London, 1744–46.
Bacon, Sir Francis. *Law Tracts.* No. 1: "A Proposition for Compiling and Amendment of Our Laws." No. 3: "The Elements of the Common Law of England." London, 1741.
Chidley, Samuel. *A Cry against a Crying Sin.* In *The Harleian Miscellany*, vol. 8. 8 vols. London, 1744–46.

Child, John. *New-Englands Jonas Cast up at London* . . . In Peter Force, ed., *Tracts and Other Papers Relating Principally to the Origin, Settlement, and Progress of the Colonies in North America from the Discovery of the Country to the Year 1776*, vol. 4. 4 vols. Washington, 1836–46.

Cole, William. *A Rod for Lawyers*. In *The Harleian Miscellany*, vol. 4. 8 vols. London, 1744–46.

Dulany, Daniel. *The Right of the Inhabitants of Maryland to the Benefit of the English Laws*. Annapolis, 1728.

Gorton, Samuel. *Simplicities Defense against Seven-headed Policy*. In Peter Force, ed. *Tracts and Other Papers* . . . vol. 4. 4 vols. Washington, 1836–46.

Haller, William, and Davies, Godfrey, eds. *The Leveller Tracts, 1647–1653*. New York, 1944.

Hammond, John. *Leah and Rachel* . . . In Peter Force, ed., *Tracts and Other Papers* . . ., vol. 4. 4 vols. Washington, 1844–46.

Hurste, Thomas. *The Descent of Authority or The Magistrates Patent from Heaven. Manifested in a Sermon Preached at Lincolnes Assizes, March 13, 1636*. London, 1637.

Lechford, Thomas. *Plain Dealing; or Newes from New-England*. London, 1642.

Mather, Cotton. *Pillars of Salt. An History of some Criminals Executed in this Land for Capital Crimes, with some of Their Dying Speeches* . . . Boston, 1699.

Mather, Increase. *Wo to Drunkards. Two Sermons Testifying against the Sin of Drunkenness*. Cambridge, Mass., 1673.

Peters, Hugh. *A Word for the Army, and Two Words to the Kingdom*. In *The Harleian Miscellany*, vol. 5. 8 vols. London, 1744–46.

Warr, John. *Corruption and Deficiency of the Laws of England*. In *The Harleian Miscellany*, vol. 3. 8 vols. London, 1744–46.

Williams, Roger. *The bloody Tenent yet more bloody*. In James H. Trumbull et al., eds., *The Complete Writings of Roger Williams*, vol. 4. 7 vols. New York, 1963.

Miscellaneous

Adams, Charles Francis, ed. *Antinomianism in the Colony of Massachusetts Bay, 1636–1638, including The Short Story and other Documents*. Boston, 1894.

Arber, Edward, ed. *Travels and Works of Captain John Smith*. Edinburgh, 1910.

Ballard, Adolphus, ed. *British Borough Charters, 1042–1216*. Cambridge, Eng., 1913.

Bateson, Mary, ed. *Borough Customs*. 2 vols. London, 1904–6.

Bradford, William. "A Descriptive and Historical Account of New England in Verse." Massachusetts Historical Society, *Collections*, 1st ser., 3 (1794): 77–89.

———. "Governor Bradford's Letter Book." Massachusetts Historical Society, *Collections*, 1st ser., 3 (1794): 27–76.

———. *Of Plymouth Plantation, 1620–1647*. Edited by Samuel E. Morison. New York, 1967.

Brigham, Clarence S., ed. *British Royal Proclamations Relating to America, 1603–1783*. American Antiquarian Society, *Transactions*, vol. 12. Cambridge, Mass., 1911.

————. *The Early Records of Portsmouth (Rhode Island).* Providence, 1901.

Butterfield, Lyman H., ed. *Diary and Autobiography of John Adams.* 4 vols. Cambridge, Mass., 1961.

Calvin, John. *Institutes of the Christian Religion.* Edited by John T. McNeill. 2 vols. Philadelphia, 1967.

Chapin, Howard M., ed. *Documentary History of Rhode Island, Being the History of the Towns of Providence to 1649 and of the Colony to 1647.* 2 vols. Providence, 1916.

————. *The Early Records of the Town of Warwick.* Providence, 1926.

Cromwell, Oliver. *Speeches of Oliver Cromwell, 1644–1658.* Edited by Charles M. Steiner. London, 1901.

"Dale's Laws." In Peter Force, ed., *Tracts and Other Papers . . .* vol. 3. 4 vols. Washington, 1844–46.

Dexter, Franklin B., ed. *New Haven Town Records, 1649–1684.* 2 vols. New Haven, 1917–19.

Drake, Samuel G. *Annals of Witchcraft in New England.* Boston, 1869.

Forbes, Allyn B., ed. *Winthrop Papers.* 5 vols. Boston, 1929–47.

Goebel, Julius, Jr., ed. *The Law Practice of Alexander Hamilton: Documents and Commentary.* 2 vols. New York, 1964.

Kingsbury, Susan M., ed. *The Records of the Virginia Company of London.* 4 vols. Washington, 1906–35.

McNeill, John T., ed. *John Calvin on God and Political Duty.* New York, 1950.

Miller, Perry, and Johnson, Thomas H., eds. *The Puritans.* 2 vols. New York, 1963.

Pierce, Richard D., ed. *The Records of the First Church in Boston, 1630–1868.* 6 vols. Boston, 1961.

Providence Record Commission. *Early Records of the Town of Providence.* 17 vols. Providence, 1892–1904.

Sainsbury, W. Noel, ed. *Calendar of State Papers, Colonial Series, America and West Indies, 1574–1660.* London, 1860.

Spedding, J., et al., eds. *The Works of Francis Bacon.* 14 vols. London, 1857–74.

The Statistical History of the United States from Colonial Times to the Present. Stamford, Conn., 1965.

Surtees, Robert. *The History and Antiquities of the County Palatine of Durham; compiled from Original Records, Preserved in Public Repositories and Private Collections . . .* 4 vols. London, 1816–40.

Thorpe, Francis N., ed. *The Federal and State Constitutions, Colonial Charters, and Other Organic Laws of the States, Territories, and Colonies Now or Heretofore Forming the United States of America.* 7 vols. Washington, 1909.

Tyler, Lyon G., ed. *Narratives of Early Virginia, 1606–1625.* New York, 1907.

Winthrop, John. *Winthrop's Journal "History of New England," 1630–1649.* Edited by James K. Hosmer. 2 vols. New York, 1908.

Secondary Sources

Books

Andrews, Charles M. *The Colonial Period of American History.* 4 vols. New Haven, 1934.

Andrews, Matthew P. *History of Maryland: Province and State.* Garden City, N.Y., 1929.

Barnes, Thomas G. *Somerset 1625–1640: A County's Government during the "Personal Rule."* London, 1961.

Battis, Emery. *Saints and Sectaries: Anne Hutchinson and the Antinomian Controversy in the Massachusetts Bay Colony.* Chapel Hill, 1962. F67. H907

Beard, Charles A. *The Office of Justice of the Peace in England, in Its Origin and Development.* New York, 1904.

Berger, Raoul. *Impeachment: The Constitutional Problems.* Cambridge, Mass., 1973.

Booth, Sally S. *The Witches of America.* New York, 1975. BF 1573.B66

Bridenbaugh, Carl. *Vexed and Troubled Englishmen, 1590–1642.* New York, 1968.

Bruce, Philip A. *Institutional History of Virginia in the Seventeenth Century.* 2 vols. New York, 1910.

Chroust, Anton-Hermann. *The Rise of the Legal Profession in America.* 2 vols. Norman, Okla., 1965.

Cockburn, James S., ed. *Crime in England, 1550–1800.* Princeton, 1977.

———. *A History of English Assizes, 1558 to 1714.* Cambridge, Eng., 1971.

Dalzell, George W. *Benefit of Clergy in America and Related Matters.* Winston-Salem, 1955.

Dawson, J. P. *A History of Lay Judges.* Cambridge, Mass., 1960.

Erikson, Kai T. *Wayward Puritans: A Study in the Sociology of Deviance.* New York, 1966.

Flaherty, David H., ed. *Essays in the History of Early American Law.* Chapel Hill, 1969. KF 361. F27

Gleason, J. H. *The Justices of the Peace in England, 1558 to 1640.* Oxford, 1969.

Goebel, Julius, Jr., and Naughton, T. Raymond. *Law Enforcement in Colonial New York: A Study in Criminal Procedure (1664–1776).* New York, 1944. KFN6155. G6

Greene, Evarts B. *The Provincial Governor in the English Colonies of North America.* New York, 1898.

Hamilton, Alexander H. A. *Quarter Sessions from Queen Elizabeth to Queen Anne: Illustrations of Local Government and History Drawn from Original Records (Chiefly of the County of Devon).* London, 1878.

Haskins, George L. *The Growth of Representative Government.* Philadelphia, 1948.

———. *Law and Authority in Early Massachusetts: A Study in Tradition and Design.* New York, 1960.

Hearnshaw, Fossey J. C. *Leet Jurisdiction in England, Especially as Illustrated by the Records of the Court Leet of Southampton.* Southampton, 1908.

Hill, Christopher. *Society and Puritanism in Pre-Revolutionary England.* New York, 1964.

Hoffer, Peter, and Hull, N. E. H. *Murdering Mothers: Infanticide in England and New England, 1558–1803.* New York, 1981.

Holdsworth, William S. *A History of English Law.* 12 vols. London, 1937–66.

Hutchinson, Thomas. *The History of the Colony and Province of Massachusetts-Bay.* 3 vols. Cambridge, Mass., 1936.

Karraker, Cyrus H. *The Seventeenth-Century Sheriff: A Comparative Study of the Sheriff in England and the Chesapeake Colonies, 1607–1689.* Chapel Hill, 1930.

Konig, David T. *Law and Society in Puritan Massachusetts: Essex County, 1629–1692.* Chapel Hill, 1979. KFM 2999. E8 K66

Langbein, John H. *Prosecuting Crime in the Renaissance: England, Germany, France.* Cambridge, Mass., 1974.

———. *Torture and the Law of Proof: Europe and England in the Ancient Regime.* Chicago, 1977.

Lipson, Ephraim. *The Economic History of England.* 3 vols. London, 1948.

McIlwain, Charles H. *The High Court of Parliament and Its Supremacy: An Historical Essay on the Boundaries between Legislation and Adjudication in England.* New Haven, 1910.

Marchant, Ronald A. *The Church under the Law: Justice Administration and Discipline in the Diocese of York, 1560–1640.* Cambridge, Eng., 1969.

Mereness, Newton D. *Maryland as a Proprietary Province.* New York, 1901.

Morgan, Edmund S. *American Slavery, American Freedom: The Ordeal of Colonial Virginia.* New York, 1975.

———. *Roger Williams: The Church and the State.* New York, 1967.

Morison, Samuel E. *Builders of the Bay Colony.* Boston, 1958. KFM 2478. N44

Nelson, William E. *Americanization of the Common Law: The Impact of Legal Change on Massachusetts Society, 1760–1830.* Cambridge, Mass., 1975.

———. *Dispute and Conflict Resolution in Plymouth County, Massachusetts, 1725–1825.* Chapel Hill, 1981.

Oberholzer, Emil, Jr. *Delinquent Saints: Disciplinary Action in the Early Congregational Churches of Massachusetts.* New York, 1955.

Osgood, Herbert L. *The American Colonies in the Seventeenth Century.* 3 vols. New York, 1930.

Plucknett, Theodore F. T. *A Concise History of the Common Law.* Rochester, 1936.

Powers, Edwin. *Crime and Punishment in Early Massachusetts, 1620–1692.* Boston, 1966.

Semmes, Raphael. *Crime and Punishment in Early Maryland.* Baltimore, 1938.

Simms, P. Marion. *The Bible in America: Versions That Have Played Their Part in the Making of the Republic.* New York, 1936.

Smith, Joseph H., and Barnes, Thomas G. *The English Legal System: Carryover to the Colonies.* Los Angeles, 1975. KFZ11 S57

Stephen, J. F. *A History of the Criminal Law of England.* 3 vols. New York, 1883.

Taylor, John M. *The Witchcraft Delusion in Connecticut, 1647–1697.* New York, 1908.

Usher, Roland G. *The Rise and Fall of the High Commission.* Oxford, 1913.

Veall, Donald. *The Popular Movement for Law Reform, 1640–1660.* Oxford, 1970.

Wall, Robert E., Jr. *Massachusetts Bay: The Crucial Decade, 1640–1650.* New Haven, 1972.

Webb, Sydney, and Webb, Beatrice. *The Manor and the Borough: English Local Government.* 2 vols. London, 1906.

Willcox, William B. *Gloucestershire: A Study in Local Government, 1590–1640.* New Haven, 1940.

Articles and Essays

Cockburn, J. S. "The Nature and Incidence of Crime in England, 1559–1625: A Preliminary Survey." In J. S. Cockburn, ed., *Crime in England, 1550–1800,* 49–71. Princeton, 1977.

Cuddihy, William, and Hardy, B. Carmon. "A Man's House Was Not His Castle: Origins of the Fourth Amendment to the United States Constitution." *William and Mary Quarterly,* 3rd ser., 37 (1980): 371–400.

Demos, John. "Underlying Themes in the Witchcraft of Seventeenth-Century New England." *American Historical Review* 75 (1970): 1311–26.

Farrell, John T. "The Early History of Rhode Island's Court System." *Rhode Island History* 9 (1950): 65–71, 103–17; 10 (1951): 14–25.

Goebel, Julius, Jr. "King's Law and Local Custom in Seventeenth Century New England." *Columbia Law Review* 31 (1931): 416–48.

———. "The Matrix of Empire." Introduction to Joseph H. Smith, *Appeals to the Privy Council from the American Plantations.* New York, 1950.

Haskins, George L. "The Legal Heritage of Plymouth Colony." *University of Pennsylvania Law Review* 110 (1962): 847–59.

———. "Precedents in English Ecclesiastical Practices for Criminal Punishments in Early Massachusetts." In Morris D. Forkosch, ed., *Essays in Legal History in Honor of Felix Frankfurter,* 321–36. Indianapolis, 1966.

———, and Ewing, Samuel. "The Spread of Massachusetts Law in the Seventeenth Century." *University of Pennsylvania Law Review* 106 (1958): 413–18.

Hoffer, Peter C., and Hull, N. E. H. "The First American Impeachments." *William and Mary Quarterly* 3rd series, 35 (1978): 653–67.

Howe, Mark DeWolfe. "The Sources and Nature of Law in Colonial Massachusetts." In George A. Billias, ed., *Law and Authority in Colonial America,* 1–16. Barre, Mass., 1965.

Hurst, J. Willard. "Legal Elements in United States History." *Perspectives in American History* 5 (1971): 3–92.

Ingram, M. J. "Communities and Courts: Law and Disorder in Early-Seventeenth-Century Wiltshire." In James S. Cockburn, ed., *Crime in England, 1550–1800,* 110–34. Princeton, 1977.

Karinen, Arthur E. "Maryland Population: 1631–1730: Numerical and Distributional Aspects." *Maryland Historical Magazine* 54 (1959): 365–407.

Kent, Joan R. "Attitudes of Members of the House of Commons to the Regulation of 'Personal Conduct' in Late Elizabethan and Early Stuart England." *Bulletin of the Institute of Historical Research* 46 (1973): 39–71.

Kittredge, George L. "Dr. Robert Child the Remonstrant." Colonial Society of Massachusetts, *Publications* 21 (1920): 1–146.

Knafla, L. A. "Crime and Criminal Justice: A Critical Bibliography." In James S. Cockburn, ed., *Crime in England, 1550–1800*, 270–98. Princeton, 1977.

Lassiter, John C. "The Defamation of Peers: The Rise and Decline of the Action for Scandalum Magnatum, 1497–1773." *American Journal of Legal History* 22 (1978): 216–36.

Lee, Carol F. "Discretionary Justice in Early Massachusetts." *Essex Institute Historical Collections* 112 (1976): 120–39.

MacFarlane, A. D. J. "Witchcraft in Tudor and Stuart Essex." In James S. Cockburn, ed., *Crime in England, 1550–1800*, 72–89. Princeton, 1977.

Maltbie, William M. "Judicial Administration in Connecticut Colony before the Charter of 1662." *Connecticut Bar Journal* 23 (1949): 147–58, 228–47.

Morris, Richard B. "Massachusetts and the Common Law; The Declaration of 1646." *American Historical Review* 31 (1926): 443–53.

Nelson, William E. "The Larger Context of Litigation in Plymouth, 1725–1825." Introduction to David T. Konig, ed., *The Plymouth Court Records*. 11 vols. Wilmington, Del., 1978.

Prince, Walter F. "The First Criminal Code of Virginia." *Annual Report of the American Historical Association* 1 (1899): 331–63.

Prince, Walter F. "The First Criminal Code of Virginia." *Annual Report of the American Historical Association* 1 (1899): 331–63.

Roberts, Clayton. "The Law of Impeachment in Stuart England: A Reply to Raoul Berger." *Yale Law Review* 84 (1975): 1419–39.

Shapiro, Barbara. "Law Reform in Seventeenth Century England." *American Journal of Legal History* 19 (1975): 280–321.

Sharpe, J. A. "Crime and Delinquency in an Essex Parish, 1600–1640." In James S. Cockburn, ed., *Crime in England, 1550–1800*, 90–109. Princeton, 1977.

Smith, Abbot E. "The Transportation of Convicts in the American Colonies in the Seventeenth Century." *American Historical Review* 39 (1934): 232–49.

Smith, Joseph H. "The Foundations of Law in Maryland: 1634–1715." In George A. Billias, ed., *Law and Authority in Colonial America*, 92–115. Barre, Mass., 1965.

Townshend, Henry H. "Judicial Administration in New Haven Colony before the Charter of 1662." *Connecticut Bar Journal* 24 (1950): 210–34.

Veeder, Van Vechten. "The History of the Law of Defamation." In Association of American Law Schools, *Select Essays in Anglo-American Legal History*, 3: 446–73. 3 vols. Boston, 1907.

Warden, G. B. "Law Reform in England and New England, 1620–1660." *William and Mary Quarterly* 3d ser., 35 (1978): 668–90.

Yackel, Peter. "Benefit of Clergy in Maryland." *Maryland Historical Magazine* 69 (1974): 383–97.

Index